Acclaim for Meredith Small's

OUR BABIES, OURSELVES

"Meredith Small is obviously a very thoughtful, sensitive and provocative writer. I found her examples engaging and representative of a wide range of human mothering behavior to which babies can adjust. It confirms my own thesis that the human infant is remarkably resilient, competent and ready for interaction and shaping by his/her caregiver. . . . This is a valuable book." —T. Berry Brazelton, MD

"*Our Babies, Ourselves* has helped so many mothers! It validates what we already know, and gives us permission to mother the way we really want to."
—Michele Mason, Founder of Child-Friendly Initiative, Postpartum and Lactation Educator

"*Our Babies, Ourselves* is a great step forward in ending decades of backward, if well-meaning, American thinking about child rearing. This book helps me help parents feel good about feeding their baby when she is hungry, picking him up when he cries, and sleeping comfortably together. I keep several copies in my office that I lend out to new and experienced parents. I can't praise this book enough!"
—Noel Rosales, MD, Pediatrician, Syracuse, NY

"What a delight. Small brings to the intelligent reader the excitement of new findings drawn from the breadth and depth of evolution to provide options, rather than prescriptions, for caregiving in our time."
—Ronald G. Barr, MD, Professor of Pediatrics and Psychiatry, McGill University

OUR BABIES, OURSELVES

How Biology and Culture

Shape the Way We Parent

MEREDITH F. SMALL

ANCHOR BOOKS
A DIVISION OF RANDOM HOUSE, INC.
New York

First Anchor Books Trade Paperback Edition, June 1999

Copyright © 1998 by Meredith F. Small

All rights reserved under International and Pan-American Copyright Conventions. Published in the United States by Anchor Books, a division of Random House, Inc., New York, and simultaneously in Canada by Random House of Canada Limited, Toronto. Originally published in hardcover in the United States by Anchor Books in 1998.

Anchor Books and colophon are registered trademarks of Random House, Inc.

The Library of Congress has cataloged the Anchor hardcover edition of this work as follows:
Small, Meredith F.
Our babies, ourselves: how biology and culture shape the way we parent
by Meredith F. Small.
p. cm.
Includes bibliographical references and index.
I. Infants—Care—Cross-cultural studies.   2. Infants—
Development—Cross-cultural studies.   3. Parent and infant—Cross-
cultural studies.   I. Title.
RJ61.S6345   1998
649'.122—dc21   97-44348
CIP

ISBN 0-385-48362-7

Book design by Claire Vaccaro

www.anchorbooks.com

Printed in the United States of America
20 19 18 17 16 15

FOR MY TWO THAT DIDN'T MAKE IT,

AND FOR FRANCESCA,
WHO MAKES IT ALL PERFECT.

And all of it was like a boat sinking, the sea rushing in and out and everything in turmoil. Then out, and all of them yelling, and cold like the middle of space. And brightness, in the eyes—so that even though his eyes were closed the light was like needles, and they held his ankles, and slapped and slapped, and he screamed like his lungs were exploding.

And even though his eyes were closed and the room was warm, he was drifting with giants, in ice and sunlight, and sounds like thunder.

And it wouldn't be over for a long long time.

PAUL CODY
Eyes Like Mine, 1996

CONTENTS

INTRODUCTION

In the winter of 1995, in a dimly lit room in Atlanta, Georgia, I witnessed a birth. Not the birth of a baby, but of a new science. I was attending the meetings of the American Association for the Advancement of Science, and sitting in on a morning symposium on the new field of "ethnopediatrics." Although the gestation of this science had been going on for a few years, the actual delivery was relatively swift. In a series of papers introduced by anthropologist Carol Worthman of Emory University, this group of pediatricians, child development researchers, and anthropologists announced a new branch of research. Their aim, Worthman explained, was to initiate the study of parents and infants across cultures and to explore the way different caretaking styles affect the health, well-being, and survival of infants. In a time when there is an increased focus in America on family values, at a stage when the human species is moving toward a global culture, and in a world where a third of the population is under fifteen years old, this approach seemed timely, ground-breaking, and critically important.

As an anthropologist interested in the interaction of human biology and culture, I was stunned by some of the findings that were being announced. Talk after talk explained the relationship between infant and caretaker in ways that I had never thought about before. Rather than hearing descriptions of infants as dependent beings that needed food, basic care, and parental guidance and encouragement, I heard words that described the infant–parent relationship as "evolved," "adapted," and "entwined." I discovered that babies in other cultures lead lives very different from those I was used to seeing and hearing about here in the United States. Babies in some other societies, I learned, are carried in slings all day, sleep with their parents in the same bed, and are often integrated into the social fabric early on. I also heard that in other cultures, babies do not cry very often and never develop colic. This was an entirely different view of raising children than the one espoused by Dr. Spock.

The anthropologist in me was especially intrigued by the idea that human babies, and not just their adult counterparts, had evolved under particular ecological and physiological constraints millions of years ago. So far, evolutionary biology has primarily focused on adult members of species; these ethnopediatricians were asking us to step back and think about the human species from the earliest months of life. Thousands of years ago human infants were typically carried at their mothers' sides, nursing continuously. Why did this close physical relationship between mother and infant come about? And what, if anything, does that ancient behavior have to do with how we care for infants today? Suddenly a new possibility was added to the cast of characters that scientists study in looking at the evolution of the human career. At that moment I knew I had to explore and chart the findings of this new science from its birth through its early development. *Our Babies, Ourselves* is the result of that research.

The science of ethnopediatrics is a revolutionary way to think about human babies. First and foremost, it is a way of looking at infants from an evolutionarily informed perspective. By combining cross-cultural studies on the various ways in which culture influences child-care styles, we can explore the effects those varying styles have on infant biology.

More significant, these findings are not limited to academic discussion alone; this is also a proactive discipline. Ethnopediatrics has the potential to revolutionize the way people in various cultures think about parenting by presenting comparative cross-culture information, the evolutionary history of infants, and the interaction of biology and culture at the infant stage of the life cycle. For example, learning about how !Kung San mothers in Africa respond to their babies, or why the Japanese do not recognize the very concept of a "difficult" child, or the fact that Dutch kids sleep more than American kids, can only inform and expand our own parental horizons. Further, some of this information has practical and even critical value. When a researcher discovers that holding a baby for longer periods and more frequently during the day might decrease the baby's crying, or even change the baby's mood, such a study might be used to better our own parenting strategies or techniques. When we discover that the rate of Sudden Infant Death Syndrome (SIDS) is lower in countries where babies sleep with an adult, this offers the possibility of overturning cultural traditions regarding infant sleeping patterns. In a sense, enthnopediatrics combines culture and biology; with this approach it breaks through our traditional and accepted notions of child care and presents options for parental strategies that might be more in tune with evolved infant biology.

All cultures are concerned with children, not only because children are vulnerable but also because they are a society's investment in the future. It is our children who will eventually grow up to be in charge of the future. Because humans are social creatures living in complex social groups, we must all take some interest in our culture's youngest members. But underlying these societal concerns is the biology of the individual. In a biological sense, children are bits of ourselves, an individual's way to pass on genes from one generation to the next. From this evolutionary perspective, our interest in children is only natural, something that is encoded in our brains; our children are walking packets of genes that carry our DNA into future generations.[1] As a result, we are motivated to love them, care for them, nurture them, and favor them; natural selection has hard-wired this attentiveness toward children and our natural attraction to babies into our very souls. Like eating and breathing, the desire to conceive, give birth, and care for infants is one of the most elemental urges on earth. In this we are no different from a kangaroo mother who holds a joey in her pouch, or a male marmoset monkey who hauls an infant around on his back. In one of the most elegant dances that nature has ever devised, we are good parents because we must be.

But the path from producing offspring to successful parenting is not always straightforward. There are all kinds of babies, and all kinds of parents. Just because a relationship has been encouraged and selected for by natural selection does not mean it works effortlessly. As we know all too well from tabloid headlines and from watching the news, there are bad parents, incompetent parents, and babies who are mistreated. Even the most well-intended parent has days when he or she would like to throw up his or her hands in despair. And so what seems at first like a pragmatic relationship—dependent babies cared for by adults designed to respond appropriately—can, in fact, be one of the most complex and conflicted relationships on earth.

And the conflict that can arise in raising children is one that exists not only between baby and caretaker, but even more fundamentally between biology and culture. The human infant is a perfectly designed organism; it knows when to sleep, when to eat, and how to cry out and signal its needs. Although caretakers are hard-wired to respond in positive ways to a needy infant, they are also not automatons. There is, in fact, an incredible amount of slack in the "system." Every adult carries a suitcase of personal and cultural baggage that determines how he or she will parent. And every society has developed traditions that guide how adults "should" treat their offspring. Because the human child is so dependent, and so slow to mature, parents have years in which to make endless choices and decisions about how to bring up their children.

Our ideas about childrearing are an amalgam of personal experience from watching our own parents parent, thoughts about how things might be improved upon from the past, and culturally driven directives that guide acceptable behavior in a particular culture. With so many influences on parenting, it is no surprise that there are as many styles of parenting as there are parents. Moreover, every person, parent or not, feels a sense of righteousness in his or her beliefs. I remember years ago standing at a cocktail party discussing with another guest the bad behavior of some child. The hostess sidled up to our conversation with the comment, "I just love to hear people without children discuss other people's children." She was not being unkind or dismissive—she was simply interested to see how we, nonparents, saw the job of parenting. Although at the time we were not parents, we certainly had opinions about childrearing and surely felt we could have done a better job than anyone else in the room. Based on one's knowledge and value system, everyone forms opinions about parenting and its effects on the children of friends and relatives. Moreover, each of us thinks we are "right." Think of the mother and father who disagree on the proper bedtime for their daughter, or the grandmother who disapproves of a baby being held all the time, or a friend who wonders why a parent cannot control a child. Each believes he or she has the correct answer, the appropriate approach for bringing up a healthy and happy child. What no one sees is the personal and cultural influences that have brought them to their opinions.

The fact is, babies are subject to a kaleidoscope of radically different parenting styles. Although most kids grow up just fine, no one really knows how these various styles affect the long-term growth, survival, and mental health of babies. This book comes at a time when even the most confident of parents are worried about whether or not they are doing the right thing. On a larger scale, global demographic and social changes are engulfing both undeveloped nations and the modernized West, and nowhere is this change more dramatic than in the realm of child care. Most of the children in the world now come from cultures and socioeconomic classes vastly different from the industrialized West, and yet these third-world cultures are rapidly coming under pressure from the West to conform. For example, aboriginal women who once carried their babies into the field in slings are now encouraged to bottle-feed and use birth control, to abandon traditional ways and to parent like Westerners. And surely the changing role of women in many cultures is bound to have an effect, even a dramatic effect, on the development of children. More generally, peoples from third-world cultures are experiencing a shift in their economic base—nomadic cattle-herders are becoming farmers and farmers are becoming urban factory-workers. Large extended families that help each other out with child care are no longer the rule in America and many other nations, and there is a worldwide increase in the number of single-parented families. Even the cultural ambiance of developed nations is changing. In America, for example, mothers now constitute a major part of the work force; the 1950s picture of Mom at home alone caring for the kids while Dad is out at work is a scenario few American women and their kids will ever experience. In addition, high rates of immigration make most developed nations melting pots of cultures, which means they are also melting pots of parenting styles. All over the world, the family and its childrearing practices are undergoing major shifts in goals and styles. It is therefore imperative that we understand how we are molding the next generation, and how the changes coming our way will affect parenting styles and children's development.

Perhaps the most startling finding of ethnopediatrics so far is the fact that parenting styles in Western culture—those rules we hold so dear— are not necessarily best for our babies. The parental practices we follow in the West are merely cultural constructions that have little to do with what is "natural" for babies. Our cultural rules are, in fact, designed to mold a certain kind of citizen. A !Kung San woman of Botswana, for example, carries her baby at all times. She lets the baby breast-feed in a way that we in the West have unkindly, and tellingly, called "on de-mand." A San child would never be left to sleep alone. In contrast, American babies, for example, are often set in plastic seats or in strollers for long periods of time; they feed on a prescribed schedule; and the accepted rule is for each baby to have a bed, if not a private room, to itself. In general, the two styles reflect the place of person within each society. Feeding, sleeping patterns, and how a baby spends the day quickly become a lesson in expectations. San children live in a tightly knit small community, where social integration is important. In America, social independence is favored, and so babies are regulated and encouraged toward independence. The cultural milieu, then, is a powerful and barely studied force that molds how we parent.

And yet every culture is self-righteous about its parenting styles and goals and disapproving of the parenting styles of others. Kenyan Gusii mothers shown videotapes of American mothers were shocked at how slowly the American women responded to their babies' distress signals. American tourists, in turn, are often distinctly uncomfortable when they see a five-year-old African girl carrying her younger sister.[2] More important, infants can be at a disadvantage when these culturally imposed ways conflict with baby biology. Human infants are all biologically very similar in their needs; that is, they need food, sleep, and emotional attachment. However, parents and cultures can unwittingly twist those needs to their own ends. There is nothing sinister or selfish about this—all parents want the best for their children—but clearly cultures disagree about exactly what that "best" might be.

Our Babies, Ourselves utilizes the research of various ethnopediatricians, child development researchers, and anthropologists in an attempt to grasp how culture influences parenting and infant development. These researchers maintain that the human infant evolved over millions of years, long before today's culture laid a hand on who we are and what we do. Yet today culture tends to guide much of a child's growth and development. In the industrialized West, moreover, many traditions have taken on the aura of scientific credibility and thus have become ingrained. Yet until very recently, there has been no scientific documentation that raising babies one way or another is actually "correct" in a biological and psychological sense. What is needed, according to ethnopediatricians, is an evolutionary and cross-cultural view of human infancy coupled with real biological data that can be used to understand truly what is best for infants. As a result, such researchers ask the kinds of questions that are of interest to parents, doctors, and caregivers alike: Why does my baby cry so often and is there something I can do about it? Is it better to feed on schedule or continuously? Do parenting styles really mold personality and temperament from the moment of birth? What is the best way for babies to sleep? In other words—how do we parent young infants who cannot communicate their own needs?

Our Babies, Ourselves, by looking at new information across cultures, examines those decisions and choices, the path of parenting. Set against a biological and evolutionary framework, this book looks at the anthropology of babies. Although this is not a "how to" manual per se, I hope— by presenting the natural history and biology of human babyhood and by offering a global perspective on parenting practices—to be able to give some parents, and any other adults who are interested in human society, more ways to think about childrearing. This might also provide a new perspective on the reader's own history. For in *Our Babies, Ourselves* I will explore those biological, cultural, and familial influences that make us what we become as adults.

In Chapter One, I begin the tale of human infants at the beginning of our species, and look at the human infant as an evolutionary organism that evolved over generations into its modern form. We are born naked, with only a fraction of our brain complete. We cannot stand up, defend ourselves, or find food. And we grow very slowly; the human infant is the most dependent infant on earth. Why is that? For some reason, millions of years ago, our species evolved away from an ape-like ancestor and stood up. The anatomical change in the pelvic region necessary for bipedalism placed architectural constraints on the shape of the human pelvis. As brain size increased during our evolutionary history, the dictates of the bipedal pelvis required that human infants finish their neural growth outside the womb. Because human infants are so dependent, their parents must invest heavily in raising each infant; and they must form an intimate relationship with an infant who has few ways to communicate his or her needs. Nature has set up an entwined, symbiotic relationship between parents and offspring, and from this grows the infant–parent bond, a necessary feature of human biology and growth. Chapter One describes this evolutionary path of the human infant and explains the special characteristics of the youngest members of our species and their necessary relationship with adults.

Chapter Two introduces the idea that there are all kinds of ways to parent, and that these ways make societal sense. For example, African Gusii mothers rarely speak to their babies except to comfort them, while American mothers feel compelled to talk to their babies incessantly. Both approaches make sense within the cultural context of each society. The Gusii mothers disdain verbal stimulation, feeling it will encourage self-centeredness, a characteristic unwanted in a family-oriented economy where sharing and belonging are paramount. American mothers, on the other hand, are convinced that verbal stimulation is the only way to bring up a smart, successful child in a society that favors independence and self-reliance. Parenting goals, and where these goals come from, are examined in this chapter. Chapter Two also explains in more detail the concept of ethnopediatrics: the cross-cultural view of parenting behavior and infant evolutionary biology that forms the core of this book.

Chapter Three is a smorgasbord of parenting styles in other cultures. How odd to discover that !Kung San parents in Botswana never leave their babies lying on their backs, and that these parents spend extensive time encouraging babies to sit up and to walk. As a result, San infants are far more advanced than Western youngsters in their motor skills at an early age. Japanese parents tend to see their children as free spirits that need to be integrated into the family unit. And so Japanese mothers and fathers encourage dependency. American parents, in contrast, try to encourage their children to grow up self-reliant and independent, and so encourage more emotional and physical distance. The point is that culture, or the people that make up cultures, have various unstated, often unconscious goals for their kids. These goals are linked to the economy of the society, and to traditions that have been handed down through generations. But these goals are not fixed; when the economy or the political climate changes, parental goals follow suit. The way people parent, then, is both traditional and accepted, but also flexible. More significant, although every parent thinks that what he or she is doing is "correct," such confidence does not take into account the enormous variability in parenting styles across the globe.

The next three chapters in the book focus on the triumvirate of infancy—sleep, state or attitude, and feeding. These are the channels through which parental goals are translated into daily tasks and interaction. Chapter Four examines infant sleep. In the West, parents use sleep patterns as a measure of their child's development, and complain to pediatricians if a newborn doesn't sleep through the night. A wakeful baby is considered abnormal, developmentally behind. To the ethnopediatricians who study sleep patterns, wakefulness is natural and the Western pattern of sleeping alone is, at any age, contrary to human biology and evolution. Infant sleep evolved in an atmosphere of close mother–infant contact, and even today 90 percent of the babies around the globe sleep with an adult. More remarkable, new research shows there are physiological benefits when a baby sleeps with its mother. Researchers now believe that infants have evolved in an atmosphere of co-sleeping, and that they use the model of parental sleep to help them learn how to breathe during the night. Co-sleeping might even be implicated in protecting some babies from Sudden Infant Death Syndrome (SIDS).

Chapter Five deals with infant state and so it begins with crying, the state that is most dramatic and traumatic to new parents. Ethnopediatric research suggests that crying is not just a way for the baby to get food, or to get a diaper changed, and certainly not a way to annoy adults. It is an evolved adaptation, a signal by the infant that something is out of balance. Ignoring such cries only makes the situation worse. Babies in many cultures cry less frequently than babies in the West because they are held more often and because someone responds very quickly to a cry rather than allowing the infant to wail for long periods. There is also strong evidence that infant state, and an adult's reaction to infant state, can have a significant effect on infant mood. Research by psychologists on young infants suggests a biological and inherited basis for temperament—that is, the baby's mood and attitude, and especially its reaction to novelty. But when the baby is part of a mismatched, nonsymbiotic parent–infant relationship, that temperament can be significantly altered for the worse. Because the baby and the parents exist in a dyad, each influences the other. Infant state is not something that exists in a vacuum—it is partly a function of the baby's relationship with its mother and father and others in its social circle.

Nowhere is the interface of culture and biology more at odds than in the area of breast-feeding, a subject I tackle in Chapter Six. Most children in the world today are breast-fed. It is convenient and is nutritionally the best source of food for infants, providing important antibodies and other health benefits. But in the past few decades bottle-feeding has grown in acceptance, and has been promoted, until very recently, as if it were the best method for feeding infants. More interesting is the fact that bottle-feeding has taken on cultural meaning—since the 1960s it has become a sign of modernity, freedom, and sophistication in the West as well as other cultures where artificial milk is imported. Increasing numbers of mothers in underdeveloped nations, where sanitation is not adequate, have opted for bottle-feeding and the result has been high infant mortality. And so the method chosen for feeding infants has become a political hot potato and a health issue, as well as a cultural phenomenon.

Chapter Seven concludes the book by discussing how parents must navigate through all this information. Parenting decisions are not completely instinctive—conscious and unconscious choices are made every day by parents as they care for their babies. In essence, all parents weigh a series of trade-offs as they move through the day. Carry the baby and he will not cry, but he sure is heavy; bottle-feed the baby and put up with all the equipment needed or breast-feed but be tied to the baby; sleep with the baby and sleep lightly or sleep alone and worry about the baby. For every decision there is a consequence. But most important, parents might like to know that although their own culture dictates one way to parent, there are more alternative paths than any one culture provides.

Let's face it—mothers and fathers are molded by millions of years of evolution to do the right thing in raising babies. We would not have survived this long as a species if this were not so. And the fact is, babies thrive in a vast array of parenting strategies. But these strategies are not simply a matter of opinion, tradition, or fact, but a complex mixture of culture and biology, and the way we raise our children does influence our adult behavior. Ethnopediatrics aims to understand what makes us bring up our kids the way we do; and, with that understanding, to discover what is best for babies.

OUR BABIES, OURSELVES

CHAPTER ONE

THE
EVOLUTION
OF BABIES

Several years ago, The American Museum of Natural History in New York City sponsored a special exhibit of human ancestors. Their goal was to bring to the public a four-million-year record of original human fossils. These fossils are usually locked in museum vaults in Africa, Asia, and Europe, privy only to the eyes of qualified scientists. But that spring, the average person was going to have an opportunity to see their ancestors, not in the flesh but in the bone. For me, an anthropologist, this was a dream come true—to see the actual fossils that I had spent so many years studying and teaching about. I drove to New York the first weekend it opened, excited as a teenager on a first date. I had seen photographs of all of these fossils and played with plaster casts of many. And now I was going to see what Louis Leakey, Don Johanson, and others had seen when they reached down and scooped one of our ancient ancestors out of the dirt.

I walked up the main steps of the museum, passed under the banner announcing the exhibit, and entered. It was dark, and quiet, with only a few people milling about. The ambiance suited me—it echoed my own sense of anticipated reverence. Before me, the first exhibit was a tall glass case lit from above. Inside was a child's face, set high at adult eye level so that our gazes met. There was no flesh on this skull, no eyes, no mouth, just the empty face of a child with a set of battered teeth. I froze, sucked in my breath, and stared.

This was the "Taung Baby," a two-million-year-old *Australopithecus africanus*, discovered in 1925 and once thought to be the missing link between humans and apes. Long ago, when this little kid died, he or she somehow ended up in a limestone quarry where the bone tissue leaked away and was replaced by stone. Two million years later, quarry workers chucked this hunk of rock into a box of possible fossils that they routinely passed on to Raymond Dart, a British anatomist working at a South African university. Dart used his wife's knitting needles to pick away at the stone until the small face appeared. Dart was used to finding baboon fossils in his shipment, but this was no monkey—the brain was too big and the face was too flat. It was, Dart was convinced, the first evidence of the ape–human split. We know now that Taung and its relatives were a kind of human that walked upright but still had small brains, and that they were possible ancestors of our species, *Homo sapiens*. A child, then, led the way to understanding our past.

And here was that same face that Raymond Dart had looked at sixty years before. The face is gray stone, dished in from forehead to mouth, but with a flat nose. The eyes, were they in their sockets, would stare straight ahead. The right side of the inner skull is filled with a geode, sparkling crystals that give Taung a jewel-like glow. And that is appropriate. This skull, and the stone impression of this child's brain that Dart also found, are as precious as diamonds to those who are trying to figure out the human path of evolution.

Staring at that skull, I was struck by the fact that this ancient child was somebody's baby long ago. Perhaps she was sick, or maybe he was accident-prone, or perhaps this baby was some predator's dinner. Standing there, I could picture him or her long ago, smiling, laughing, and reaching out to grab a mother's breast. It was the most beautiful thing I had ever seen.

From a biological point of view, the Taung child represents a specific stage of development for Australopithecines, our ancestors that lived from four to two million years ago. Paleontologists tend to concentrate on adults of any species because adulthood is the mature end product; but fossilized babies and children also give clues to anatomy and physiology, to rates of development and growth. Children are not just miniature versions of adults. There are sound evolutionary reasons why infants and children look and behave the way they do—childhood is a specifically evolved stage in the life course. The Taung child emphasizes the fact that we are not born as adults but go through a lengthy period of growth and change. In this child, and all children, are some of the most important secrets of our anatomy and behavior. There are reasons why mice are born blind and human babies cannot hold their heads up. Natural selection has opted for fawns to stand on their own soon after birth, for human infants to smile automatically, and for baby chimpanzees to cling to their mothers' fur. And all of this makes some sort of natural biological sense. The pattern of birth, infancy, and childhood in any species follows a particular course that eventually outlines adult biology and behavior.

THE HUMAN INFANT DESIGN

In the summer of 1990, on a trip to Africa, I had the opportunity to hold a wild baby chimpanzee. Its mother, and all its relatives, had been killed by a poacher. The poacher was caught before the infant was shipped off to some European zoo, and for now he was housed at a hotel where the sympathetic manager had made it a policy to take in abandoned animals. Cradling the infant ape in my arms was uncanny— she felt just like a small child, only hairier. She squirmed a bit, looked at me with frightened brown eyes, and cooed softly, lips pouting out. After a few anxious minutes, she stretched her long arms over my shoulder toward the woman who usually cared for her, reaching for the only mother she now had.

That chimpanzee felt so much like a human child for a good reason—about 98 percent of our genetic material is identical to that of chimpanzees. We are, in fact, more closely related to chimpanzees than chimpanzees are to gorillas. I state this fact to underscore a point: Human babies, and human adults for that matter, are animals. We are primates, a kind of mammal, and our babies are animal babies. Although humans like to think of themselves as unique, we share much of our physiology and behavior with others of our kind, with other primates. For example, the shape of our head follows a continuum with other primates that shows a reduced snout and an enlarged brain case with a full forehead and forward-facing eyes. Our teeth are primate teeth, rather than dog teeth or alligator teeth. Our eyes see the way monkeys' eyes see, with color vision and good depth perception to facilitate swinging through the trees. And our flexible hands—the hands that can pick ripe fruit off a tree, type these words or tie a shoe, hold a flower or build a model plane—distinguish us, and all primates, from other mammals that have paws. Our whole upper skeleton reflects an even closer relationship to other primates, apes in particular. Using a human anatomy book, one can dissect a chimpanzee or a gorilla and find everything in the right place. We have the upper bodies of long-armed apes. The only difference, in a broad anatomical sense, is the fact that the human pelvis, legs, and feet have been adapted to upright walking. So much of our physiology is simply that of an upright-walking primate.

The point is that human babies, like all babies, are animals of a certain species, born with certain physical and mental abilities and lacking some others. As this book will show, much of the animal context of human babies and children can be understood best through the lens of biological evolution. Taking this tack, one cannot think about babies as early unformed organisms or shadows of the adults they are to become. They are instead simply what they have been designed to be.

Why the Baby Cannot Sit Up

Not all babies are the same. Human babies are rather helpless, interested mostly in food, sleeping, eating, defecating, and comfort. Compare human babies with newborn deer. When fawns are born, they immediately stand up and soon are able to run away from danger. Scientists call these two types of babies in the animal kingdom *altricial* and *precocial*. Altricial infants are born helpless, usually after a short gestation or pregnancy, and their brains tend to be not quite finished. Precocial babies usually spend more time in the womb, are more alert at birth with eyes open and a brain able to control their limbs and make them move appropriately; their central nervous systems are more advanced, compared with those of altricial infants. Altricial infants tend to be small-bodied, small-brained, and fast-breeding—such as mice. Precocial infants tend to be large-bodied, big-brained, and slow-breeding—such as gorillas.

Both are reasonable alternative paths to survival; the altricial baby tends to grow faster after birth, whereas the precocial baby has gone through more of its development while still inside the womb. The size of the brain of typical precocial babies at birth, for example, is 4.5 times bigger than the brain of typical altricial infants of the same body weight. But the difference disappears later in life. The altricial brain grows to 7.5 times its size from birth, whereas the precocial brain grows only 2.5 times; in other words, the smaller brain grows almost three times as fast once it is out of the womb.[1] This overall physical and ecological framework is necessary to put our own species into perspective. What dictates a strategy for a precocial or an altricial infant, and why did the human path lead to dependent babies? There are, of course, good biological reasons why our fetuses are born at a certain average time and at a particular size.

Most primates are relatively precocial animals. Monkeys and apes, for example, are born with their eyes open, unlike mice, and they are able to cling to their mothers' fur right away. They cannot run from predators or feed themselves, but they are able, under their own power, to seek out their mothers' nipples and suckle soon after birth, and they can explore the world with eyes and hands. Primates are also unusual among mammals in that the brain is so big, no matter the developmental stage. The brain in all primates is 12 percent of fetal weight, whereas for other mammals (except whales and dolphins, which also have relatively big brains), the fetal brain accounts for only 6 percent of body weight.[2] But if most primates—large-brained precocial animals—are able to be interactive with the world about them, why are human infants born so helpless?

Humans differ from other primates in that they are considered "secondarily altricial."[3] This means we had precocially adapted ancestors and then, for some reason, evolved some altricial traits that now overlay that basic pattern. The key to our rather new altricial status is our huge brains; human babies have been designed to adjust to this selective choice toward large brain size. We come from a large-brained order and we have been selected to take this feature further than any other primate species. For some reason, millions of years ago when we shared an ancestor with apes, one kind of ape with a bit larger brain did better—that is, survived and produced more offspring—than some other ape species; there has thus been strong selection for increased brain tissue, and so the large brain was selected. But large brain size also comes with a cost. Nature has had to figured out all sorts of solutions to adapt to this overall selection for big brains in the human species. For example, brain tissue takes more calories to maintain than any other tissue, so much of our feeding provides nutrition and warmth for brain cells. More significantly, our babies need to be born earlier than they would be otherwise, with brains that are underdeveloped. As a result, human infants lack a mature central nervous system, which explains why they cannot walk and cannot talk for a very long time; they do not have the neurological network to do so. The baby cannot sit up because its nervous system—most importantly, its brain—is unfinished. And so the primal cost of having a big brain is that our infants are born highly dependent and in constant need of care.

Obviously, babies do catch up. Our brain growth after birth is faster than that of any other mammal, and this rate continues for twelve months, after which time we switch to a more typical mammal pattern of brain growth. R. D. Martin, a primate anatomist and paleontologist, claims that humans really have a twenty-one-month gestation—nine months in utero followed by twelve months outside.[4]

But it is not brain size alone that compels human infants to be born before they are neurologically finished. Our babies are rather large, given maternal body weight, and this taxes the entire reproductive system. Most important is the placenta, which acts as the oxygen exchange system from the mother to the fetus. When the baby reaches a certain weight, the placenta just cannot do an adequate job anymore.[5] When infants are overdue, parents often think the reason the obstetrician recommends a Cesarean section is that the baby has gotten too large to fit through the mother's pelvis. Actually, physicians are more concerned that the placenta will break down and not be able to carry oxygen in to the baby and to carry waste materials out. The size of the infant in relation to the placenta is, at birth, a more critical factor in the timing of birth than is the size of the brain.

These three birthing strategies—altricial, precocial, and secondary altricial—are all related to a complex of constraints and adaptations that molds one species or another. Ecologists see these strategies as a continuum. At one end are the species that produce a large number of offspring at a rapid rate while investing little in each infant, such as insects (these are called *r-selected* species). At the other end of the continuum are species that reproduce only occasionally and invest heavily in each infant (called *K-selected* species).[6] Mice, for example, have done best by producing large litters of altricial infants that stay in a nest until they develop. For most ungulates, the horned and hoofed animals, evolution has opted for large animals with alert, fast precocial babies. And the human line is defined by big-brained babies that come out unfinished. There is no easy answer as to why one path is taken rather than another. Sometimes chance may nudge a species in a certain direction. More often, the pattern can be explained as an adaptation to a particular set of environmental circumstances that favor this or that physical change. So far, we only know that the evolutionary history of humans has moved toward favoring big brains, which in turn necessitated developmental and physiological consequences at birth and during infancy.

The Complication of Bipedalism

We might not have ended up with babies with half-finished brains if evolution hadn't introduced a complication into our infant development—bipedalism. At least four million years ago, when our human or hominid lineage split off from the common ancestor we shared with chimpanzees, our ancestors took on a new form of locomotion. Unlike apes, who hang from the trees with long arms and walk along the ground balancing their weight on the surface of their knuckles, individuals in the human line stood up on their back legs. Other primates, too, spend some time on two legs; they stand at attention when frightened, or to investigate visually their surroundings. The difference is that humans, and our ancestors, have used bipedal walking as the primary form of locomotion. That switch to bipedalism eventually brought us the pain of childbirth.

I have four pelvises on my desk. One is from a human woman who died not long ago. Another is a plaster cast of a chimpanzee. The third is that of a monkey, one of my subject animals, which died during my study and lived on in my office to instruct me about monkey skeletal anatomy. And the fourth is a cast of Lucy, an Australopithecine who died almost four million years ago. Set in a row, the affinities are clear. Lucy's miniature pelvis looks much more like the pelvis of her human sister, and the ape and the monkey are from their own similar mold. Most telling are two features. First, the blades that form the body of the pelvis, the ilium, are elongated in quadrupedal monkeys or knuckle-walking apes, whereas the blades are short and broad in hominids—in Lucy and in the human pelvis. These short wide blades are designed both to hold the body organs of a creature who is spending all its time standing up, and to leave plenty of surface area for attachment of muscles that must hold a vertical body upright and balanced during walking. Second, the pelvises are of two different shapes. Holding them together and looking down through the birth canal, one can see that the ape and monkey pelvic canals are shaped like an oval that is elongated front to back. In the two hominids, the hole is shortened from front to back and widened side to side; the oval is now sideways.[7] The difference in shape is caused by a shortening from the lower back to the hip joint in the bipeds. As a result of this wider but broader pelvis, the muscles that start on the hip blades and attach to the legs are rearranged; the butt muscle, *gluteus maximus*, is enlarged to help stabilize the leg during walking and to enable the side muscles to easily attach to the upper leg bones, while maintaining body balance as well. This in turn makes bipedal movement possible, and prevents the rotational momentum that occurs when a quadrupedal animal tries to stand up for long periods.[8] The inner space of the pelvis of the human and of Lucy are also affected. The sacrum, the lower back, is wider and thicker and it angles into the pelvic opening to help support the internal organs in a creature with a shifted center of gravity. And so, right in the middle of what should be a clear hole for infants to pass through, there is a point of the sacrum coming radically close to the pubic bones of the front of the pelvis—a detour sign for emerging babies that arose when humans stood up on two legs.

The entire architecture of the pelvis in modern humans, and in any ancestors that appeared from the point when we became bipedal, is different from that of our quadrupedal and knuckle-walking ancestors. No one knows exactly what pushed this shift to bipedalism. Various theories have been proposed, many of them discounted. The most popular is that humans stood up to carry things. Although standing up does free the hands, the resulting ability to carry objects, and maybe children, doesn't seem like much of a selection pressure. Surely there must have been a more compelling reason to push for such a dramatic rearrangement of muscle and bone. More likely, our ancestors were reacting to changes in the environment or were exploiting new resources. Bipedal locomotion might have been the most efficient way to move between scraps of diminishing forest; the ability to move out of the trees and from patch of forest to patch of forest may have been a strategy that separated our ancestors from competing apes.[9] In any case, Lucy and her fellows, and all humans since then, have walked in the woodlands and across the African savanna in a striding gait.

The Tight Fit

What did these pelvic alterations mean for the hominid fetus and for the moment of birth? Initially, not much. First of all, Australopithecines had smaller babies than we do, simply because they were smaller creatures; Lucy, for example, was only three and a half feet tall. More important, they had very small heads. Brain size of the adult *Australopithecus afarensis* was about 400 cubic centimeters, about the size of a chimpanzee brain (roughly the size of a softball). Australopithecine infants have been estimated to be about 1600 grams (3.5 pounds) in weight at birth, with a brain size of 143 cubic centimeters.[10] Passage through the pelvis was probably not particularly difficult. Infants did, however, need to compromise at one level.

Monkey and ape pelvises are long front to back, which matches infant head shape; and the sacrum, the wide bone that connects the two sides of the pelvis, does not dip into the pelvic opening as it does in the human pelvis. As a result, baby nonhuman primates usually enter the pelvic opening face up. Since the Australopithecine pelvis was squished front to back, shortened top to bottom, and had a sacrum that curved into the space where newborns should go through, these babies had to navigate a different sort of birth, one more similar to that of modern human infants.[11] They had to enter at a transverse angle and adjust their passage according to the interior inclines of the pelvic cavity, either staying transverse or rotating a bit and coming out face down.[12] They may have slipped through as easily as a monkey, but they might have had to twist and turn to do it.[13]

The real obstetrical dilemma came long after Lucy and her colleagues became extinct, when there was a sudden upsurge in brain expansion. About 1.5 million years ago, the adult hominid brain went from the Australopithecine size of 400 cubic centimeters to 750 cubic centimeters in a species called *Homo habilis*, the first member of our genus. In other words, the brain just about doubled in size. A mere million years later, the hominid brain doubled once again until it reached its present average size of 1200 cubic centimeters.[14] This is quite sudden in evolutionary terms.

What was the effect of this voluminous increase in infant brain size on the birth process? The architecture of the pelvis, once it adapted to bipedalism, remained about the same for three million years. Obviously, much larger brains were not going to slide easily through a pelvis that had been designed for efficient bipedalism and small-brained newborns. The problem is architectural—the pelvis was designed as a scaffold for bipedal musculature and is as wide as it can be while still allowing women to walk efficiently. There is no way to retrofit the pelvis to accommodate a larger-brained infant. And so compromise had to come from the infant, and it did. First, there is a biological limit placed on infant brain development. Like all primates, human infants are born with a brain that takes up about 12 percent of their body weight; although destined to be highly encephalized—that is, proportionally bigger-brained as adults than other primates—we start out with the relatively same-sized brain as any other primate.[15] Again, we make up for this by an extremely fast rate of brain growth after birth. Second, prior to birth the bones of the skull are not fused and there is thus lots of room for smashing those bones together and molding the head as it squeezes through the pelvic passage. The "soft spots" on infant skulls, more correctly called "fontanels," are the areas where various skull bones meet—often you can see the pulse of a heartbeat through the thin cranial membranes. In nonhuman primates these spots are almost totally fused, but in humans, they remain wide and flexible. The resulting "cone-head" shape of the human newborn's head is simply nature's way of squeezing a child out with little damage to brain tissue.

These two features work to accommodate head passage, but they do not compensate for the fact that human babies are also rather big relative to maternal size.[16] Usually, small-bodied animals have proportionally large infants and large animals have proportionally small infants. Oddly enough, we rather large mammals have rather large infants relative to maternal weight. And so it is not just a big head that's a problem, but the shoulders and overall body size as well. More to the point, the once rather spacious pelvic canal became, with the adaptations to bipedalism, as tight a fit as a cork in a wine bottle. And so a third accommodation had to be made, this time to the route a fetus travels to be born through such a tight space. The infant must twist and turn, bend its head to its chin, and enter the world face down. The human pelvis is not a straight tunnel as it is in other animals. Instead, the opening where the baby first enters is a transverse ovoid. The middle of the canal is elongated front to back, and the outlet is circular. Also, the sacrum is bent inward, which makes the midsection—where the fetus must pass the sacrum and the front pubic bones at the same time—a tight squeeze.[17] And so the infant enters the birth canal at a side angle, twists to accommodate the midsection, flexes the head down to bypass the squeeze at the sacrum, and ends up coming out face down. Since the outlet faces more backward than downward, the baby also has to bend a bit and thus comes out at an angle facing the mother's back. The shoulders follow a similar path, dipping and twisting; but since the head is then already out, this requires the execution of a head–body twist that would do any professional gymnast proud.[18]

The Consequences of Labor

And so we have the miracle of modern human birth—a painful, twisted journey that squeezes the infant head like Play-Doh and causes mothers unbelievable pain. And we also have all the pieces for the answer to why our infants are born so helpless. They are born with unfinished brains because the pelvis simply cannot be any wider or any bigger. If it were, women couldn't walk. Painful childbirth and helpless babies are an evolutionary compromise between selection for bipedalism, which came first, and later adult brain expansion.

Anthropologists Karen Rosenberg and Wenda Trevathan point out that the consequences are not just mechanical, they are also behavioral and social.[19] The tight fit and tortuous route for human birth causes long and difficult labor for both the mother and the child. This trauma affects how the mother feels after birth, both physically and mentally. And infants come out rather exhausted and battered from this ordeal as well. The more than difficult process might account for the difference in style between human and nonhuman primate birth. A birth in a colony of Barbary macaques that was witnessed by two researchers, Vivika Ansorge and Kurt Hammerschmidt, was described as comparatively quick but not without pain.[20] The mother, following the troop to the sleeping trees for the night, stopped several times and did stretches with her legs, a sort of dance that signaled something odd going on. She squatted, repeatedly touched her genital areas, and emitted low vocalizations which the researchers described as "moans." Eventually, she reached behind with her right arm and scooped up the baby that was coming out between her legs. She held it to her chest and it yelped. Within minutes the mother, rather dazed to be sure, moved on. There are very few descriptions of primate births because animals most often give birth at night or early in the morning. Humans, too, most often give birth in the early hours, but are hardly ever alone.[21] Rosenberg and Trevathan suggest that the idea of attending a birth is actually an evolved strategy of our species that is necessary because human mothers are less equipped than monkey mothers to help in the process. The mother is in greater pain, the birth takes longer, and the infant comes out face down. She needs someone to catch the infant and clear its air passages. She needs someone to hand her the baby and later pull on the placenta if need be. Wenda Trevathan calls this "obligate midwifery," suggesting that we need to have attendants because the evolution of bipedalism and big babies left us no choice.[22] And so our birthing is not just a biological event, but a social event as well. It relies on the help of family and friends, and emphasizes how important interpersonal interaction is to the human species, even when one of us first appears.

THE CONSEQUENCES OF DEPENDENT INFANTS

Our taxonomic order, the primates, is distinguished from other mammals by its intense sociality at all levels and especially by the necessary long-term affiliative relationship between parents and offspring. How we primates nurse, carry, and protect our infants, and the fact that we extend the parenting period longer than any other animal, is striking; intense and extensive parenting is, in fact, one of the most distinguishing features of us primates, and a major mark of the human species in particular.

The Attachment Between Parents and Babies

Natural selection demands that human parents care for their kids and that kids turn to their parents. This mutual need, then, translates into the emotional feeling called "attachment." From an evolutionary perspective, attachment makes sense. We come from a long line of social primates, animals that need each other in order to survive. Our order, the primates, is even defined by the highly interactive nature of our sociality. We are not just aggregates of monkeys or apes or people, but groups that typically spend much of the day touching, sitting, and following each other about.[23] We know each other by sight and sound and are preoccupied with each other. And as social animals for whom relationships are so important, we have an easy time defining and understanding attachment. It means wanting to be with one another, feeling comfortable in someone's presence, falling in love. And so attachment to parents, off-spring, mates, and kin is the norm for us and we expect to have all sorts of attachments throughout life.

We also assume that these bonds are somehow triggered at the moment of birth, and that the primary and most fundamental bond is that between mother and infant. It is, after all, the most familiar bond for most animal species in which parents perform even minimal care. For example, a female cat who would normally like to spend most of her life alone will attach intimately with her litter for a time, and even the most unfriendly cat will show herself to be a decent mother. Nature has selected for this mother–infant bond because it is necessary—some offspring are born self-sufficient, but most need to learn how to walk or fly and to discern what to eat. And so female animals, for the most part, have been preprogrammed to like their infants; and infants, for the most part, have been preprogrammed to attach to their mothers. Mothers and infants are set up by evolution to bond to each other so that the mother will feed and protect the infant and the infant will remain close by to be fed and protected.

Moving beyond evolutionary necessity to the emotional level, humans usually see the mother–infant bond as sacrosanct—the best, the most important, the most "natural" of bonds. There is nothing sweeter than a picture of some sort of animal mother with her infants—even hyenas and bats look cute in a mother–infant tableau. And in human society there is nothing more revered than mothers and infants. The mother–infant attachment has been taken for granted by our species for so long that few have questioned what this attachment is all about, or even if it really exists in a species supposedly so disconnected from a basic animal nature.

Bonding

A group of scientists in Europe called ethologists were the first to coin the word "bond." In 1935 animal observer Konrad Lorenz demonstrated that there was an innate connection between newly hatched goslings and a mother figure. Goslings, and other kinds of avian species such as chickens and ducks, will latch on to the first thing they see when cracking out of the shell. In Lorenz's experiment, he was the first thing they saw and so he became the mother figure; the goslings focused on him and followed him around.[24] Usually, however, the first thing young birds see is their mother. This system, called "imprinting," works well for species in which many babies hatch at once and must immediately attach to an adult figure to whom they can turn for food and protection. In imprinting, the bond is mostly established by the infant, and the infant is primarily responsible for maintaining the closeness. More significant, because imprinting occurs during a critical period during which the offspring is keyed to bond to any moving object, once that time has passed the youngster cannot be swayed to attach to anyone else.

Infant animals that are born highly precocial—that is, physically and behaviorally more independent—and thus can both see and walk are among the species most likely to imprint on their mothers. For altricial, that is more helpless, infants who are unable to see or move about by themselves, it is the mother who establishes the bond with the infant.[25] Rat females, for example, are hormonally primed to mother; certain hormones activated by pregnancy must be present for these females to act appropriately with their new pups. Researchers have demonstrated the need for hormonal triggers in rats by injecting females with prolactin, oxytocin, and other hormones, which produce mothering behavior in females that have never been pregnant; and by blocking these hormones in pregnant rats and watching the new mothers act confused at the sight of their litters.[26] Although the continued stimulus of having infants in close proximity is necessary to maintain rodents' appropriate maternal behavior over time, their mothering instincts are initially an automatic hormonal response.[27] There is also a critical period for some mothers during which this response can be triggered. Work with sheep and goats shows that mothers must be exposed to their newborns within minutes of birth so that they imprint the baby's smell and looks.[28] If these mothers are not allowed an early opportunity to connect, they will reject their infants, even when the babies are returned within hours. The bond is immediate in these animals, as would seem logical for creatures normally born in large herds where misidentification is a real possibility, or in areas where predators are prevalent and mothers must protect their infants from the moment of birth.[29] For some animal mothers, then, biology is directly involved in making them attentive to their newborns; and for many, there is a critical period when this bond is forged.

The biology of bonding for humans, and other primates, is much more difficult to substantiate. Early on, Freud believed that the roots of the mother–infant bond were purely nutritional.[30] He believed that the bond was driven by the infant as it latched on to a mother's breast for nourishment and she simply responded. Theorists after Freud believed that both hunger and relief from pain or discomfort were the mechanisms by which mothers and infants attached, and that mothers were neutral stimuli upon which infants projected their needs. In other words, they believed that the infant was responsible for initiating and maintaining the bond and that the mother, by responding and by experiencing infant needs as pleasurable, reinforced her role as provider, nurturer, and protector.

In the 1960s, psychologist Harry Harlow showed that food and relief of discomfort had little to do with the nature or intensity of the primate mother–infant bond. Harlow took newborn rhesus monkeys away from their mothers and put them in a cage with two artificial "mothers." Both artificial mothers were made of wood and wire, and both had fake monkeylike faces. One was equipped with nipples that delivered milk and the other had no milk but was covered in terry cloth. In a series of repeated tests, baby monkeys sporadically nursed from the "mother" equipped with a bottle but spent the rest of the time clinging to the cloth-covered one.[31] Harlow thus documented that whereas young primates might need to nurse, they are even more driven to find comfort. More significant, when these "motherless" rhesus infants grew up, they were socially inept and were inadequate mothers themselves; they were unable to bond because they had never bonded with their own mothers. Bonding to a nurturing mother, Harlow and others concluded, is essential to mental health and normal development in primates, and the blueprint bond from which all other attachments are modeled.

About the same time, psychologist John Bowlby was writing about the primal place of the mother–infant bond in human psychology.[32] In his first volume on attachment, Bowlby made a case for attachment between mother and infant as a long-ago-evolved system, something we share with other sexually reproducing organisms.[33] Bowlby believed the specifically human bond was also ancient, that the type of bond seen today had evolved during our hominid past in a period he christened the "environment of evolutionary adaptation."[34] The bond is elicited, he felt, by an innate urge in the mother to protect the infant, and when babies cry or fret, that response is stimulated. From Bowlby's point of view, the ethological idea of imprinting is also involved, because new mothers are highly receptive to their infants in all the sensory channels, including sight, smell, hearing, and especially touch. In other words, Bowlby felt the mother–infant bond has been selected over generations as a pattern of behavior that has helped individuals successfully produce and pass on genes by attaching to and bringing up their infants. A mother providing warmth, protection, and food, and an infant eliciting these behaviors by crying or smiling, tended ultimately to have higher reproductive success. Bowlby's views on bonding were decidedly evolutionary.

Today, psychologists and evolutionary biologists agree that it is natural, and also necessary—that is, adaptive—for mothers and their infants to be attached or bonded. The bond is demonstrated by consistent close proximity, constant interaction, and emotional attachment. It is especially strong in our species because we produce such dependent infants, who need so much care and protection and teaching. Bonding between mother and infant is part of our primate heritage, an essential component and a fundamental feature of human nature.

The Mother–Infant Bond in Human History

During most of human history and prehistory, babies have been placed immediately on their mothers' bodies after birth. In most cultures today, babies are still born this way. In fact, the idea of babies being separated from their mothers after birth is shockingly new to human thought; it applies only to the last ninety years of our at least two-million-year history as a species, and only in Western culture. Although separation of babies and mothers after birth in the hospital is now on the wane, it was standard practice until very recently; and even now infants are removed soon after birth for medical exams and then returned. It could be argued that those of us in Western culture who were born in hospitals and then taken to the nursery are an experiment in interrupting the usual contact between babies and mothers. Up until recently there was no question of bonding or not bonding, no environment in which the mother–infant relationship was ever debated. Why did the practice of separation ever begin?

In 1896, inventor Martin Cooney designed the incubator, a device developed to aid premature babies. Cooney was the first to advocate separation of infants from their mothers as a medical procedure for the health of the child. In a bizarre combination of medicine and sideshow, Cooney gathered hundreds of premature babies (they were easy to obtain because doctors assumed premature infants would die), put them into incubators, and exhibited them at various expositions and fairs in America and Europe.[35] Babies were returned when they reached five pounds. But until then, their mothers were kept away. (Cooney would not allow mothers to visit with their infants, but did give them free passes to the exposition.) A photograph of Cooney's exhibit in San Francisco in 1915 shows a brick building with the title "Infant Incubators with Living Infants" emblazoned across the facade. Inside the exhibit were rows of tiny metal cabinets looking like microwave ovens with wrapped babies inside. It looks modern for the times, hygienic and sterile, but the mothers are nowhere in sight.

Once settled on Coney Island, Cooney saved more than five thousand premature infants over the next few decades; and to offset the cost of their care, he continued to exhibit the babies up through the 1940s New York World's Fair. Cooney's technique was so successful that it was widely adapted by hospitals across the nation when they built premature infant wards. More broadly, it became standard practice even for normal babies—it was considered healthier for even these babies to be taken away and placed in incubators where they would be observed by nurses, rather than to be left with their mothers.

The issue over bonding began about the same time that hospital births became fashionable. Around the turn of the century, women in Western culture began routinely to have their babies in the hospital to curb childbirth death and infant mortality. For full-term babies, the switch from home birth to hospital birth was both a blessing and a curse. On one hand, maternal and infant mortality rapidly declined because doctors were able to control bleeding and infections. On the other hand, pregnancy and birth became part of the medical model; that is, it was now treated as an illness rather than a natural process, and as a result the medical establishment rather than mothers were given the right to dictate policy. Women were typically placed in wards with their babies in cots next to them. But in the years that followed, infection in hospital wards, especially sepsis, became rampant. As a precaution even full-term infants were separated from their mothers and placed in nurseries. Mothers were given but a glimpse of their infants at birth, if they were awake and not drugged, and then the babies were whisked off to the nursery where they lay in warmed cribs, watched over by nurses but without much physical contact. The medical establishment believed that this policy was the "safest" from the baby's point of view. Control over the birth process was maintained by the hospital and doctors with health as the guiding factor; the idea of "bonding" or what that might entail was never even considered. Part of the policy included a plan whereby babies were returned from the communal nursery to their mothers twelve hours or so after birth and then in intervals for feeding.

In the 1960s a slow revolution in birthing practices began in Western culture. As a result of the influence of John Bowlby's attachment theory and Harry Harlow's infant monkey experiments, the medical establishment realized the importance of physical proximity on the bonding process and babies were not necessarily removed to the nursery. The feminist movement in the 1970s, which helped women assert their wishes, furthered that revolution as it gave female nurses and mothers the support to demand that mother and father be integrated back into the early infant experience. In 1976 two obstetricians, Marshall Klaus and John Kennell, based on their research, theorized that there is a critical early—and limited—period for human mother–infant bonding. They noted a higher incidence of infant abuse and failure-to-thrive children among premature infants; because the infants were premature and had been sequestered in nurseries and away from their mothers, there had been, these doctors suggested, a breakdown of the normal mother–infant bond. They found that although 7 to 8 percent of live infants are born premature, 25 to 41 percent of battered infants were preemies. They surmised that a critical period of attachment had passed by the time the baby was sent home, and that the mother–infant pair consequently lacked the essential positive bond that links them together in a healthy emotional and physical way. Klaus and Kennell also evaluated the various amounts of time that different mothers spent with their newborns and found that those who had had early contact, within the first few minutes to the first two hours after birth, were more attentive in later pediatric exams and showed a few more interactive behaviors with their infants during these exams.[36] Critics pointed out that the tenor of behaviors during an exam a few months later was hardly a reasonable measure of the intensity of the maternal–infant bond.[37] Nonetheless, the Klaus and Kennell work underscored the need to have babies interact immediately with their mothers or to stay with them rather than be taken to a nursery.[38]

By 1978, even the conservative American Medical Association claimed that "bonding" is their official policy regarding mothers and infants, and that fostering the bond is an important component of the birth process.[39] Hospitals now acknowledge that "bonding" does occur early on, and that babies can be medically managed even if they stay with their mothers. As a result, "rooming-in"—where babies and mothers stay together—is now often integrated into the medical model of pregnancy and birth. The idea that mothers, and fathers, *must* bond with their newborns as soon as possible after birth is now generally accepted in our culture and sanctioned by the medical authorities. After a period of about ninety years during which that bond was ignored, dismissed, shattered, and fully re-examined "scientifically," Western culture has now returned to accepting that babies and mothers are a natural pair.

A Bond Is Not a Bond Is Not a Bond

Underlying this revolution is the solid belief that mother–infant bonding occurs early on and that it is essential for normal psychological development. What is not yet known is exactly how this bond develops or what triggers it in the first place. Yet everyone—from parents to health care professionals—has absorbed the findings of ethologists and now believes that since the bond is there and is significant, it must, as in some other animals, appear during a critically timed period. We in Western culture have moved from a "scientifically based" belief that germs will invade babies if they come in contact with their mothers (which motivated the removal of babies from their mothers) to a different "scientifically based" belief that if babies do not come in immediate contact with their mothers, they—and their mothers—will be psychologically and emotionally harmed. Is there really a biologically based critical period in humans for this bond to develop?

It has been clinically proven that rats, goats, and sheep go through hormonal changes during birth that make the mothers act like mothers. No one denies that human females also go through hormonal changes during labor and birth. Levels of circulating progesterone, the so-called hormone of pregnancy that is first produced by the ovaries and then by the placenta, is high throughout pregnancy. Estrogen levels increase during the last several weeks, and high levels of estrogen influence the release of oxytocin and prostaglandins around the time of delivery. Following birth, estrogen and progesterone levels drop dramatically, although prolactin, which is stimulated first by the drop in estrogen and subsequently by nipple contact, increases.[40] Both prolactin and oxytocin are involved in lactation, and levels of both remain high as long as a woman continues to nurse. Although this sounds like a hormonal storm, and women are obviously going through dramatic physiological changes during birth, there is no evidence that any of these changes trigger specific maternal behaviors as they do in rodents or sheep. Mothers have been poked, prodded, bled, and examined, but scientists cannot find any direct link between a particular hormone and the urge to act maternally.

Given that we are primates, rather than rodents, the lack of particular maternal hormones in humans is not so odd. Research on macaque monkeys shows that captive but well-adjusted adult females will accept—that is, care for—any infant anytime; they don't necessarily need the hormones of pregnancy and the physiological changes at birth to elicit appropriate maternal behaviors.[41] Even female monkeys who have never been pregnant, although they are a little uneasy when presented with an unfamiliar newborn, will eventually take charge. The California Primate Research Center at the University of California, Davis, has used the inherent flexibility of monkey females to the researchers' management advantage; for years they have been taking a few new infants away from their mothers in large outdoor cages and switching them with infants of the same age in nearby cages. The goal of this method, called "cross-fostering," is to hold down the level of inbreeding by moving a few infants from one group to another, as if they had already grown up and transferred. The rate of acceptance by mothers of these foster babies is high; about 85 percent of the mothers will eventually take a different infant and raise it as her own.[42] They do find, however, that there is a critical period of a few weeks during which a successful switch can occur. Once a mother has bonded and gotten to know her own infant, she is not fooled by a substitute. So although these monkey females bond to their infants, and that bond is notoriously strong, it is not necessarily instantaneous nor hormonally adapted to imprint on one specific infant.[43] Instead, a bond seems to develop over time from a multifarious set of social interactions that attach mother to infant and vice versa.

As psychologist Michael Lamb points out, it is ridiculous to think that, in a species with long-term parenting obligations such as humans or other socially complex primates, the initial attachment between mother and infant would be relegated to a few critical minutes after birth.[44] There are important hormonal changes that do affect mothers and how they feel, but none of them have proved as essential for the bond as they have in rats or sheep. Human young are so helpless that surely evolution would have selected *against* a critical period for mothers to imprint and infants to attach, and would have selected instead *for* more flexibility in the system. In no arena is human parenting narrowly defined, and so it would be unlikely that such an important attachment as that between a helpless human infant and a caring adult would be left to hormonal triggers and fixed behavioral patterns. Geese imprint on their mothers soon after birth because they have such a short time to learn what they need to know before going off on their own, and rat mothers are preprogrammed to be nurturing for the same reason—in these species, parenting is conducted over a short period of time and offspring have relatively little to learn before they are independent. But for primates, especially humans, offspring development takes years and there is much to learn before they can survive on their own. It is therefore unreasonable to insist that mothers must bond with infants right after birth or else the bond will never be established. In fact, adopted children—and fathers who closely bond with their children despite, of course, not undergoing any hormonal changes at their birth—prove the point that human bonding is not simply the result of automatic physiology. It is also clear that social and psychological factors can interrupt the bond, or prevent a connection in the first place. Anthropologist Nancy Scheper-Hughes has studied mothers in the ghettos of Brazil and discovered the startling fact that women often allow some of their infants to waste away and die.[45] When faced with abject poverty, it seems, these mothers make a conscious decision to neglect sick or weak children. If babies are perceived as not likely to make it through the struggles of life, mothers construct a series of rationalizations for withdrawing care, and they do so without grief. The bond, in other words, cannot be wasted on a child who will most likely die early; it is not a given, but something bestowed upon children who live. Cross-cultural studies also show that the idea of a monotropic bond—that is, one parent at a time connected to one baby at a time—is a limited view of human relationships. Child development researcher Edward Tronick and colleagues have shown that Efé pygmy infants are cared for by a number of adults, and this infant–adult relationship can be more communal.[46] An Efé infant will spend 50 percent of its time with some other adult than its mother during the first four months of its life, and interact with five or more adults per hour. A baby is also nursed by several women who are lactating. The baby clearly knows who its mother and father are, but it has a cadre of adults to depend upon. In a social system that values community above all else, this multifaceted bond produces a tight network of social relationships—babies are attached to several adults and adults are attached to several babies.

The parent–infant bond is the product of interaction and mutual attention. Like any human attachment, the initial biological attraction between adult and child brings them together, but it is the *process* of interacting together that builds a bond. In that sense, any time spent together is critical time.

Klaus and Kennell advocate early exposure by giving the mother some time with her baby before it is taken away, and more time when the baby is brought back for feeding. They would add a few more hours to mother–infant contact in the hospital in the first days. There are, of course, critics of Klaus and Kennell who dismiss the notion that parents and infants need a certain amount of exposure immediately after birth. And to a degree they are right—the bond is not purely physical and preprogrammed. But the critics miss the most important point: Any separation has an effect.[47] Since attachment among primates is a process, any time an infant spends away from its mother breaks the normal flow of interaction. Although there may not be a "critical period" for bonding, the time after birth is clearly sensitive to the development of a new relationship. Parents are getting to know their babies and they are primed by the excitement of the moment to see, smell, and hear everything they can about their child. In that sense, mothers are not so much hormonally or physically pushed to do this or that; rather, they are swept along by emotions that have evolved to make sure adults fall in love with their babies.

All these scientific and medical advisors, counselors, and researchers seem to miss the fact that culture, in the form of the medical establishment, has intervened in human biology. For millions of years the human female animal gave birth and held that baby to her chest. She carried the baby close and helped it find the nipple. The timing of the bond, the intensity of the attachment, and the need for hooking up physically and emotionally was never in question because the closeness was a given.[48] In all cultures except Western culture, the process is the same today.

THE INSTINCTS OF MOTHERS AND FATHERS

International census data show that 85 percent of women over forty have children; that is, 85 percent of women who have gone through childbearing age have borne children.[49] The data for men are not known because men can continue to have children into old age, but presumably at least that high a percentage of men also have children. In other words, even in these days of birth control and worry about the population explosion, most people reproduce and become parents. Although mothers are not biologically hard-wired to bond to their infants during a critical period after birth, and fathers do not go through the kind of hormonal changes that might orient them toward their offspring, it would be odd if evolution did not, in some way, ensure that parents and infants "hook up." And so I ask the question, Is there such a thing as a parental instinct, a primal urge to act a certain way toward infants, which facilitates the necessary connection between parents and offspring?

Is There a Maternal Instinct?

Not every woman wants children and not every mother is a good mother. But there is evidence that women who go through pregnancy and give birth act in similar ways toward their newborns, suggesting that there is a universal, species-specific pattern to some aspects of being a mother. For example, almost all mothers, when presented with their newborn infants, touch them in the same way—starting at the fingers, down to the palms, out to the arms and legs, and then across the trunk. All mothers orient themselves to look a newborn in the eyes.[50] The biological basis for these maternal universals is less clear. There is, for example, no consistent association between hormonal levels and attitudes toward children in pregnant women or new mothers. Being pregnant, or having a baby, does not seem to change a woman's feeling about what kind of mother she might be or what she thinks of children in general. The only difference, researchers have noted, is that pregnant women begin to attach to their babies during the second trimester, usually when they begin to feel the baby move, and this occurs even when a mother feels negative about her pregnancy.[51] Pregnant women also have an increase in their heart rate when they hear any infant cry[52]—although, in a study of pregnant women in a doctor's waiting room, they were not observed to watch babies and children any more than nonpregnant women did.[53]

There is a possibility that cortisol, a volatile hormone that rises in response to stress, might heighten a mother's awareness and help attune her to the new infant. Cortisol is important in the flight-or-fight response—it makes the body more aware of external stimuli and readies the body to respond. In that sense mothers under stress after a difficult birth, with its correspondingly high cortisol levels, might be primed to smell, feel, touch, and take in everything about a new infant and to respond to those cues in one way or another. One study, for example, found that mothers with high cortisol levels spent more time talking to their infants than did other mothers; however, no one knows if this is simply a difference in the way some women make it through the birth process, or a personality difference, or a meaningless artifact.[54]

In other animals, especially rodents, oxytocin is important for all sorts of social attachments, including maternal behavior.[55] Although new human mothers are awash with oxytocin, no one has seen a direct connection between levels of oxytocin and human mothering skills. But there might be some interaction between the mechanics of nursing, which involves oxytocin and prolactin, and mothering. These hormones, especially prolactin, are involved in the production of maternal β-endorphins, those chemicals that bring about a sense of peace and suppress hostility, anxiety, and irritability, while increasing affectionate behavior. More significantly, β-endorphins are addictive in the sense that they reinforce pleasurable feelings.[56] It is possible that nursing somehow increases the release of β-endorphins, but the data on this interaction is still unreliable.

Evidence that there is some sort of heightened awareness by mothers, caused either by biology or emotions, is seen in a mother's ability soon after birth to recognize her infant by smell and voice alone. In several studies, mothers who had spent only a few hours with their newborns were able to smell out their babies when comparing their shirts with the shirts worn by other babies.[57] Mothers are also pretty good at hearing their infants. Women with new infants in wards usually sleep through the cries of other infants but wake up immediately upon hearing their own babies' cries. New mothers are also good at picking out the recorded cries of their own infants, sounds that are spectrographically as individualized as fingerprints.[58] They can also correctly identify the type of cry, be it hunger or wet diapers, when recorded under varying circumstances and played back.[59]

Although this evidence points to an innate maternal instinct for identifying and interacting with infants, it is not a fixed interaction. In fact, all these studies show that with time, mothers get better at smelling and hearing their infants, and that mothers with previous children are better at it than first-time mothers. Although women might come equipped with some of these abilities, their accuracy and skill at using them is improved with experience and learning; this would be expected in a species such as ours, in which learning plays such a major role in behavioral patterns. Even maternal attitude—a positive attitude toward children and one's own baby, which should be the most innate maternal response—changes with experience. In one study, 68 women were interviewed three times: when they were pregnant, three days after birth, and when their children were over a year old. These mothers expressed a definite increase in positive attitude toward their babies—with time, they became more and more attached.[60]

It is no surprise that mothers need to see their offspring, spend time with them, and get to know them as individuals, in order to form a deep bond. We are complex emotional organisms, and to take on another ego, even if it shares half our genes, takes some negotiation. So there is nothing necessarily automatic about maternal behavior, even if there is an instinct to be open to the attachment. Clearly the mother–infant bond, while primed to occur, needs interaction over time to be truly strong.

Is There a Paternal Instinct?

Since males do not give birth, their attachment to children is expected to be less strong than that experienced by mothers. For most animals this is true. Mammalian males, for example, are not often interactive fathers; lactation by females usually makes it impossible for males to contribute much. Biparental care—that is, care in which fathers help out—is found in less than 5 percent of mammalian species.[61] And so no one really expects male mammals to have much of an instinct for infant care, and when they do, special explanations are invoked.[62] But whenever infant care is demanding, and when males can help with that care, they too are sometimes pushed by evolutionary forces to contribute to parenting. Many male birds, for example, sit on eggs and bring food to hatchlings. Some fish males brood fertilized eggs by holding them in their mouths or by guarding clumps of eggs set in safe places in stream beds. In humans, infants are so dependent that we can assume paternal care is part of our basic evolutionary parenting system. In fact, the need for male care is considered by some anthropologists to be a major selective force in the evolution of the current human mating pattern, the pair-bond.[63] Yet most people tend to have a greater belief in a maternal instinct than in the possibility that males might also have an instinctual paternal drive. But if anthropologists are right, and the need for paternal care is a driving force in our evolutionary history, then we should find that human males are pushed almost as much as human females to attend to infants.

There are all sorts of ways fathers can contribute to care. True, they cannot lactate very well, but this is only one parental venue among many that keeps a child alive and healthy. In other animals, males protect territory; and if that territory contains food, which is the major reason why territories are usually defended, the male is often sequestering food for infants and lactating mothers. Among gibbons, which live in pairs of one adult male and one adult female, males do not carry infants nor do they protect them. Male gibbons do, however, assist females in protecting a territory that is essential for their fruit and vegetable diet.[64] Among marmosets, tiny monkeys from South America, males carry infants almost from the moment of birth, and the only care that a mother provides is nursing the infant when it is passed back to her.[65] Other nonhuman primate males vary in how much they interact with infants. Some, like gorillas, are tolerant of infants but pay little attention to them; whereas others, like male baboons, carry and play with infants frequently. In one twist on the nurturing relationship, Barbary macaque males use infants as social pawns in male–male status games, but they are also very caring.[66] Clearly, male mammals, including some primate males, are able to provide everything females provide—except milk.

In all human cultures there is some sort of father in the typical family, either the biological father or a male maternal relative, who acts in ways that all societies would agree are paternal.[67] Anthropologists suggest that biological fathers in particular have an important parenting role in societies where family life is strong, women contribute to subsistence, the family is an integrated unit of parents and offspring working for the same goal, and men are not preoccupied with being warriors.[68] These fathers must be assured of true paternity if they are going to invest in children; thus all societies have many mechanisms, such as legally sanctioned monogamous marriage and heavy punishment for adulterous wives, to reassure fathers that the children of the household are theirs. Although the degree of fathering across cultures varies, the potential for human males to contribute to infant care is great. They can provide food, shelter, protection, and daily care, and they usually do. There is also evidence that males can be intimately connected to their children, and that they have been selected by evolution to be good fathers.

In some traditional societies, for example, fathers are so intimately connected with their babies that they exhibit all the signs of pregnancy and birth. This phenomenon has been termed *couvade*, which comes from a Basque word for "brood" or "hatch."[69] Males in these societies have morning sickness and must lounge in the village to keep up their strength. During labor, couvade males take to their beds, scream, and receive attention from the community while the woman is giving birth somewhere else. And this is not some bizarre aberration of more "primitive" societies. A 1982 report in the *Annals of Internal Medicine* shows that couvade is alive and well in our own society. In a study of 257 pregnant women with partners, 22.5 percent of the fathers reported at least one unexplainable symptom to their health care professional, symptoms that were new to these men and strikingly like those reported by their pregnant wives—nausea, bloating, and such.[70] The expectant fathers also visited the doctor twice as often as before their wives' pregnancies, and filled twice as many prescriptions as usual. Oddly enough, the charts of these men did not note that they were expectant fathers. In another study, 65 percent of expectant fathers complained of uncomfortable physical symptoms and made dietary changes or stopped smoking because of the pregnancy.[71]

After the birth of the baby, new fathers report the exact kinds of emotions as mothers when first viewing the baby; and when given a chance, fathers explore a newborn's body in the same pattern as mothers—fingers first, then palms, arms, and legs, then trunk. When talking to a baby, fathers alter their speech to a higher pitch, as mothers do, and they use shorter phrases and repetition of phrases just like mothers.[72] When asked, 90 percent of fathers say they are confident they can pick out their own child based on looks alone, although they are usually unable to identify their baby's cry or understand what the cry is about.[73] In controlled laboratory experiments where father, mother, and baby were videotaped during playful interactions, fathers gave the same responses to infant movement and were just as sensitive to infant cries as mothers were.[74] In one study, mothers and fathers were wired to chart their heart rate, blood pressure, and skin conductance, and were then shown photographs of babies in various states of emotion—smiling and crying. When asked to fill out a questionnaire about their reactions to the pictures, women were much more extreme in their descriptions. But physiological measurements showed that the two parents actually reacted the same, supporting the notion that whereas mothers and fathers have the same biological reactions to their babies, women are by and large more verbal and expressive in their physical reactions.[75] Fathers even share with mothers a sense of postpartum depression after the initial exhilaration. Sixty-two percent of fathers interviewed report sadness and disappointment at about the same time that mothers are feeling blue.[76]

Babies, too, seem to experience little difference in their reactions to their mothers and their fathers. In experiments where infants were monitored for reactions to a mother, a father, and a stranger, babies clearly distinguished the stranger from the parent, and showed that distinction with certain happy or unhappy facial expressions and by either focusing or turning away; but they made little distinction between mother and father. Babies did, when under stress, connect more with mothers; but if everything was calm, they were just as happy to see the father.[77]

There are differences in the way fathers and mothers interact with their infants. Across cultures, fathers tend to play more with infants than mothers do, and to engage in more risky behaviors, such as throwing babies up in the air.[78] Fathers also think their babies need more active stimulation than mothers do, which probably explains the difference in play.

Although close connections are fostered over years of consistent interaction between father and infant, being there for the moment of birth clearly makes a difference. Fathers who were present in the delivery room are more confident about knowing their babies than are fathers who were not in the delivery room, and they comment repeatedly about this instantaneous connection.[79] In fact, this moment might prove to have evolutionary significance. Since conception is concealed from fathers, and human males are expected to invest heavily in their offspring, it would make sense for anything that promotes a connection between father and baby to be selected by evolution. In an intriguing study of how family members see a newborn, evolutionary psychologists Martin Daly and Margo Wilson asked people who they thought the newborn in their families most resembled. Overwhelmingly, mothers responded that the baby looked like the father.[80] And the mother did this repeatedly when the father was close at hand—commenting on how much the baby resembled him even when the father protested. It has been observed that mothers and fathers, and even families, appear to unconsciously conspire to make the father believe the baby is his, no matter what. Perhaps for good reason: A few studies using blood work to establish true paternity have shown that at least 10 percent of the men named as the father on the birth certificate could not possibly be the biological father.[81]

Psychologist John Bowlby felt that the infant–parent bond was monotropic—that parents are designed to attach to one baby at a time, and infants are capable of fixing on only one parent, usually the mother. But new research has shown that this is not true. Babies clearly know parents better than others, even when fathers are gone much of the time, or even when mothers are gone, and babies are attached to both.[82] It is also clear that the more fathers interact with their babies, the more the father and baby are mutually attached. Fathers report having the exact emotions that mothers do upon seeing their newborns; given the opportunity, they follow the same sequence of touching the new baby from fingers and toes inward; fathers, like mothers, also alter their speech to slower and shorter cadences in order to engage the infant.[83] And it makes sense for human males to be primed as fathers. No one denies that mothers have a special connection to infants; women conceive and gestate. But those nine months are only a short period compared with the many years of childhood and adolescence during which kids need help. If the human species has been molded to produce and then care for dependent young—and we are the only species in which offspring are still fed by their parents even during the juvenile stage—then fathers, like mothers, must have been selected to bond with their babies.

THE ENTWINED RELATIONSHIP

Infant sleep researcher James McKenna (see Chapter Five) often begins his articles and talks on infant–mother sleep patterns with the following saying by pediatrician D. W. Winnicott: "There is no such thing as a baby; there is a baby and someone." This statement so aptly sums up what scientists like McKenna have been discovering about human infants: that their biology is not so much an entity in itself but is intimately connected to the biology of the adults who are responsible for their care. The word "entrained" is often used to explain this relationship. Entrainment is a kind of biological feedback system across two organisms, in which the movement and patterns of one influence the other. Entrainment, in this context, means that the physiology of the two individuals is so entwined that, in a biological sense, where one goes, the other follows, and vice versa.

For babies and parents, the entrainment starts early. It is first and foremost a physical relationship. Nonhuman primates have been used extensively in studies of mother–infant separation and the effect of that separation on infant physiology. In one experiment, for example, they removed three- and four-month-old infant rhesus and squirrel monkeys from their mothers for thirty minutes and then returned the mothers to the cage. Once separated, the infant monkeys immediately began calling in distress and as they became agitated their hormonal profiles changed; the level of cortisol, the hormone of stress, shot up. More surprising, even after undergoing this separation experiment twenty times and learning that their mothers would eventually come back, the babies never adjusted; separation the twentieth time was just as physiologically traumatic as separation the first time.[84] Studies of premature babies, and how to best care for them, have demonstrated that physical proximity and skin contact are essential for healthy infant development. In one experiment, premature babies were stroked and massaged on their bodies and heads for fifteen minutes four times a day. The babies became calm, showed healthy skin color changes, and enjoyed quieter sleep than did a control group of other premature babies. And at four months of age, the stroked babies had also made greater strides in their neurological development, mental development, and reflexes than the others.[85] In another study with a similar protocol, physically stimulated premature babies took in more formula and gained more weight than did those under standard nursing care.[86]

The connection is also visual and auditory. A newborn recognizes its mother's voice, and prefers it, over the sounds of other adults.[87] In one study, infants less than a day old were placed in plastic seats, and each was given a fake nipple that was wired to a tape recorder, and a pair of headphones was set on each baby's ears. If the baby sucked on the nipple for a certain length of time, the voice of the baby's mother reading a Dr. Seuss story came through the headphones; but if the baby sucked for only a short period, another woman read the story. Babies quickly learned how the system worked and they chose to call up their mothers' voices over those of the other females, and to listen to those particular voices for longer periods. This was true despite the fact that these newborns were nursery babies and had so far spent very little time with their mothers.[88] Universally, researchers have found, parents raise and lower their voices in similar ways as they denote approval, attention, comfort, and the like when talking to babies.[89] And from the first day of life, infants move their bodies in synchrony with adult speech; babies apparently coordinate their arms and legs and move them at the speed and rhythm of whatever they hear.[90] Even without looking at the adult, babies will synchronize their body movements as soon as someone begins to talk—a game that parents play without even knowing it as they modulate their speech into a high-pitched singsong.[91] Presumably, both the way parents talk to babies, and babies' corresponding alertness and reaction to human speech, are adaptations that serve the acquisition of language later on. Babies, and then children, are clearly hard-wired to absorb the cadences of speech and the general nature of language; newborn body movements that mimic adult speech are simply a sign that the baby is naturally primed, that is adapted, to pay attention.[92] But more significantly, this linguistic tango is a clear sign of entrainment. No matter the language, no matter the culture, "baby talk" is the same the world over because all human parents are adapted to engage their babies vocally in a similar way, and all babies are ready to hear what their parents have to say.

Although human infants are born with their eyes open, they do not focus well, and the practice in hospitals in the West of putting silver nitrate drops in their eyes at birth further obscures sight for some time. Still, babies quickly recognize the arrangement of a human face with two eyes, a nose, and a mouth all in the right place, over other more Picasso-like rearrangements. On the delivery table, a newborn's attention can be caught with a schematic black and white drawing of a face, but when the image is garbled the baby is only briefly interested.[93] As early as three weeks of age, infants can tell the difference between an object and a person, and they are more interested in people.[94] Parents encourage this difference as they exaggerate their features and alter their voices to keep a baby's attention.

But there is more to the interaction than a matter of adults putting on a show. When babies and adults interact, they are partners in an interactive social dance in which they jointly regulate each other, and this dance is essential for the baby's social and psychological development.[95] Renowned pediatrician T. Berry Brazelton noticed in his practice that babies and mothers seem to follow a typical pattern of play, a synchronized score that moves from attention to nonattention with both partners cueing in on each other's signals. In the lab, babies were offered a fuzzy monkey on a string; and later, when the monkey was removed, mothers were asked to play with their babies. The babies played with the stuffed monkey in a different way than they did with their mothers. With the monkey, they focused on it and reached for it, but soon became bored and turned away, never looking at it again. With the mother, the baby engaged with her face, became attentive and excited, and then slowly showed signs of inattention. The mothers all seemed to be highly sensitive to the cycle of attention/nonattention and responded to the "down time" by letting the baby be; and then the cycle started all over again. In experiments where a mother was instructed to act unresponsive to baby movement, the baby repeatedly tried to engage the mother by flapping around and looking at her. When she did not respond, did not take up the baby's initiative toward interaction—looking at each other and paying attention to each other—the baby gave up, looked hopeless, and began self-comforting movements such as sucking on its fingers (see also Chapter Five).[96] As Brazelton points out, with objects the goal is to explore and discover but with people the goal is to engage. And babies happily engage in social play not with some specific goal in mind but simply to establish joint regulation with another human. This is just what one might expect from a human baby, a creature that is adapted to be both an object manipulator, or tool user, and a highly social animal. Child development expert Edward Tronick has pointed out that our most central human adaptation is our communicative competence, and one of a baby's most powerful, most highly adapted, most necessary skills is the ability to exchange on a social level with adults.[97]

More remarkable, lab research has also shown that the connection between babies and parents is deeply physiological. In one study of infant reaction to mothers, fathers, and strangers, an infant girl was brought into a lab and set in a plastic seat that was curtained off from distractions. The baby was then approached by her mother, then her father, and then a stranger. Chest monitors on the baby and the adults showed that the baby synchronized her heart rate to that of the mother or father when they approached, but she did not synchronize her heart rate to the stranger's.[98] These data suggest that babies and their caretakers are entwined in a homeostatic relationship, with the baby clicking in with the parents to achieve some sort of balance.

In essence, there is a synchronous nature to the interaction between babies and their caretakers. After decades of watching babies and their parents, Brazelton is adamant about how important this synchrony is to infant development: "We are convinced that in a 'good' interaction, mother and baby synchronize with each other from the beginning, and that the pathways may be set up in intrauterine life ready to be entrained, especially by the mothers, immediately after birth."[99] This synchrony, Brazelton believes, is vital. He suggests that, in many cases of failure-to-thrive infants, these interactive patterns simply never click in, and that as a result, mother and baby are out of sync, not entrained. For the baby, the lack of synchronicity is a "violation of an expectation," as Brazelton calls it, and the necessary rules of engagement have not worked. Such lack of synchrony can occur because, although the adaptation to synchronize is present for both partners, patterns of interaction are also not fixed, not completely hard-wired, and so there is extensive variation in how parents play with and respond to infants. Sometimes it just does not work. Also, humans being sentient and emotionally complex, some parents consciously choose to not engage much at all—they refuse to synchronize or they simply ignore the signals given by their babies. On the bright side, slack in the system also allows nonbiological parents—such as adoptive mothers, adoptive fathers, and men who didn't give birth—to take on the parent–baby engagement because they want to.[100] In other words, synchronicity, or attending to babies, can be taught or learned or can appear spontaneously in those who are naturally attuned to infants or consciously want to be.

No matter its source, whether a conscious choice or a spontaneous urge, there does seem to be some sort of synchronicity, some sort of "knowing" each other, that both baby and caretaker attend to. From an evolutionary view, a system that entrains baby and parents is expected. The baby is so dependent, and the mother, as the usual caretaker, so much wants the baby to thrive, that they are both adapted to be in sync. Fathers too participate in this entrainment, and babies are keyed in their role as well.

Entrainment then explains why infants left alone will cry. They are dealing with the unexpected—they are alone. Being tiny primates, they are adapted to expect an entrainment, a physical and emotional attachment, a connection with a more mature version of their kind. They cry out of surprise, out of confusion, out of an unconscious "knowing" that something is wrong. Brazelton believes that babies come equipped to respond in predictive ways to positive and appropriate moves by parents—when the baby is picked up, he stops crying; when she is fed, she stops crying. In the same way, the baby is equipped to respond in negative ways when the stimulus is negative or inappropriate or overloading.[101] Regulating its world by sleeping, crying, or staying quietly alert is the most powerful thing a baby can do, says Brazelton, and we should respect this ability and attend to it.

From all we know, every primate baby is designed to be physically attached to someone who will feed, protect, and care for it, and teach it about being human—they have been adapted over millions of years to expect nothing less.

Parents and babies are normally entwined in a mutual relationship that has evolved to serve them both. Babies need parents in order to grow and survive, and parents need babies, in the most literal sense, as the bearers of their genes. And yet many cultural practices seem designed to disengage or disrupt this connection. For example, breast-feeding mothers report that they want to interact with their babies and that they are more responsive to their babies than women who feed with a bottle,[102] and yet bottle-feeding is encouraged both in Western culture and across the world. Fathers who participate in the birth repeatedly comment on their close connection with the new infant,[103] and yet most fathers in Western culture continue to be left out of both the birth and the childrearing. Parents are clearly attuned to their babies' movements, and right after birth a kind of entrainment is established that probably sets up behavioral patterns and language—and yet women are still medicated during the birth process, leaving them incapable of responding to the cues of their newborns, while babies are left in rooms to cry for the expected touch of parental skin. Why are cultures so intrusive? Why do we not follow what should be a very natural path of parental care? In the next chapter, I attempt to explain how and why cultures mediate one of the most basic attachments among individuals—the connection between parents and children. The simple answer is that we treat our babies as we treat ourselves, and so our ideas about parenting and infant care are as culturally constructed as what we wear, what we eat, or how we dance.

CHAPTER TWO

THE ANTHROPOLOGY OF PARENTING

As any new mother or father knows, nothing so invites advice as a new baby in the house. Other parents, Grandma, the lady next door, a stranger on the street, the family physician, and stacks and stacks of child-care books are happy to give directions about the "correct" way to care for an infant. What most parents do not know is that these various tidbits of advice, and even the consensus "rules" of parenting that have such an aura of credibility, are, for the most part, based on a mix of tradition, fad, and folk wisdom with a modicum of science. In fact, few have ever studied whether or not the rules of one society work better than the traditions of another society in producing functional, happy adults. If a parent talks to his baby, will it learn to speak earlier? No one knows. If you sleep with your baby, will it become emotionally dependent? Who knows. Yet societies establish these "rules" about various parenting techniques that imply there is a right and a wrong way to go about parenting. And the advice is usually offered in such ominous tones—make a mistake and your child may turn out socially inept, not very bright, maladjusted, or worse—that parents often follow these rules, or accept the advice, without considering that there might be alternative ways that also make sense. In addition, even the hard-and-fast parenting rules slip and slide, evolve and change, as societies change.

THEORIES OF PARENTAL BEHAVIOR

Scholars and scientists have been trying for years to figure out just how the parent–offspring relationship really works. And so far, they aren't really sure. They know that parenting advice has a social, cultural, and scientific context just like everything else that people do and say. And parenting specialists agree that parenting does have an effect on a child's physical and psychological development. As yet, however, no one is absolutely clear on exactly how the effect occurs. Human children are psychological and intellectual sponges—they watch and listen and grow with what they learn. But why does one event or interaction affect them more than another? And to what degree do the various threads of parents, family, and culture influence the way a person turns out? Is Mom most responsible? Siblings? Dad? TV? The entire culture? Or do none of these forces really matter, because much of personality is hard-wired and genetic?

Culture and Personality

At the turn of the century, Western scholars assumed that people the world over act basically the same. They felt that all individuals were unified in thought and action, in desires and motivations, simply because we humans are one species framed by similar psychological mechanisms.[1] Much of this work was, of course, based on the psychological theories of Sigmund Freud, who saw broad patterns of psychological thought in his patients. Anthropologists were the first scholars to turn toward non-Western cultures to support this paradigm. They assumed that by watching people in their everyday tasks, and by questioning informants about "normal" behavior in their culture, they could place behavior and thought in some sort of coherent psychological package, a package that would resonate with the psychological makeup of the Western mind. Therefore, according to this early work, culture would have only a superficial effect on the deep motivations of people; the belief was that underneath the skin, we humans are all pretty much the same.

It wasn't until the 1920s, and a flowering of anthropological field research across the globe in various non-Western cultures, that researchers began to realize the enormous impact of culture on the human mind and heart.[2] From that point on, scientists realized that all people were not necessarily alike, not necessarily driven by the same psychological urges, and that wildly different cultures could produce wildly different people. This view also suggested that all cultures were of equal merit—a village of hunters and gatherers was finally considered just as interesting and complex and sophisticated as an industrial city.[3] More important, anthropologists during those formative years of the discipline were instrumental in furthering the notion that culture, no matter what kind, is not a passive instrument but a heavy cloak that muffles what nature intended.[4] This cultural mantle, the social scientists of the time believed, is what separates us from other animals; humans are marked as different from other animals because we have human-made culture as an interface with the natural world.[5] And it was in this atmosphere—this acceptance of cultural shaping of the human condition—that the first studies of children and parents in various cultures were initiated.

Anthropologists Margaret Mead and Ruth Benedict in the 1920s were instrumental in guiding anthropology away from individual psychology and toward a focus on the role of culture in shaping personality. They founded the "Culture and Personality" school of thought, a perspective that was, and still is, extremely relevant to studies of parenting across cultures. The framework of Mead and Benedict seems obvious now, but in their day the idea that culture might shape personality was quite radical. Mead was a pioneer field worker, and although some criticize her work today, especially her methodology, there is no denying that she bravely sailed to foreign ports and attempted to gather information first-hand from the way people in other lands lived. It may be that her informants in Samoa were pulling her leg when they described the loose sexuality of adolescent girls, and one can argue that she didn't live long enough in Manus, New Guinea, to really gain a clear picture of childhood there; but in the end, it was Margaret Mead who announced to the West that there were other, equally valid ways to grow up, and that these differing ways had a dramatic effect on molding adult personality.

Once the data from other cultures began to roll in, it was clear that people in different geographical regions not only behaved differently, they also thought differently. Ruth Benedict was famous, or perhaps infamous, for describing cultures in sweeping generalizations of differing personality types, a framework that today would be considered too stereotypical, even "racist." Nonetheless, both of these women were the first to point out that culture affects the individual, and that this effect occurs from the moment of birth, as parents make culturally approved decisions about how they raise their children.

Mead, in particular, was the first to show with detailed ethnography on several "foreign" societies that the general structure of any culture can be understood at a fundamental level by following the treatment of children.[6] What parents do on a daily basis, Mead proposed, is merely a reflection of what the culture dictates. And so the way parents go about parenting has a dramatic effect on how their children behave as adults. More important for the times, these scientists believed that whole societies could be changed by altering the way children were raised, an optimistic view that was certainly needed during the years between World War I and World War II.[7] For example, they assumed that aggression and competition could be filtered out and cooperation fostered, and that more "correct" parental management systems could be substituted for less correct ones.[8]

But Mead and Benedict's greatest contribution to parenting studies was the notion that the way parents act toward their children reinforces various cultural rules; that the construction of culture is essentially passed on to the next generation through these parental styles.[9] Inherent in this model is the idea that humans are behaviorally plastic; culture and parents can influence who we are and what we become only because humans are flexible beings able to learn and change, able to be influenced by others.[10] The Culture and Personality school, with Mead and Benedict as the founders, was not interested so much in how cultures differ from each other, but how in *every* culture parents unconsciously transmit the rules, the structure, and the goals of that society to their children. Each one of us, as a result, is a product of our culture, and parents are the channelers through which we receive the cultural and social message.[11]

The Culture and Personality school appeared at a time when psychologists were testing in the lab to document what babies can do and what they know. There were tests on babies' eyesight, motor skills, cognition, reactions, and just about everything anyone could imagine a baby able to do. Unfortunately, only the babies of middle-class white American parents were used as subjects, and they were tested for white middle-class cognitive and emotional skills. As anthropologist Robert LeVine has pointed out, the structure of the experiments during those times simply reflected Western assumptions about child development, and the belief that babies should act in certain ways and be treated in certain ways to reach these goals, and no one questioned the universal nature of their abilities.[12] The work did underscore, however, that babies were highly capable and adaptable organisms. They could communicate, think, and absorb knowledge; instead of seeing babies as inert lumps, people now marveled at what babies could do. This shift in attitude appeared during a time when Western culture was also shifting away from strictness in upbringing, beginning to favor a style in which the emotional health of the baby was of central concern. Western society, in a sense, became more baby-conscious.

In the 1950s, the Culture and Personality approach was used to launch one of the most ambitious and exciting projects in cultural anthropology. A group of social scientists from Harvard, Yale, and Cornell, and led by John and Beatrice Whiting, collaborated on a plan to send out teams of anthropologists to study childrearing in six different cultures. The hypotheses would be the same and the methodology would be tightly controlled, they proposed, so that data could be compared more easily. The teams would be composed of couples so that both men and women in the various cultures could be observed easily. They chose a broad range of cultures and subsistence styles in order to test hypotheses about the universality of some behaviors and to provide contrast. For example, subjects included both rural horticultural Gusii of East Africa as well as middle-class whites from the Boston area. The project was based at a central laboratory run by Beatrice Whiting to which data were sent from the field. The idea was to gather highly comparable data that had been taken with the same framework in mind and gathered at the same time by similar methods.[13] This project moved beyond the idea of individual ethnographers sailing off to foreign lands seeking a romantic vision of non-Western life, and into an era of rigorous scientific comparative research.

The "Six Cultures" theoretical approach to social structure was ecological and economic. The scientists presumed, as any ecologist would when approaching any animal group, that people are distributed across the landscape relative to resources. In this view, household composition is a result of how homes, villages, and communities are situated to best take advantage of those resources, given a particular subsistence pattern. Then these ecologically based layers of social structure in turn set the parameters for childrearing; subsistence determines the makeup of the household, which shapes parental styles, which in turn mold personality.[14] Given this framework, the proposed studies focusing on children would be windows to the world of different cultures (see Chapter Four). The Whitings and their colleagues believed that any social and political structure molds parents, and that parents in turn shape children to fit into a society by promoting culture-specific patterns of personality. Even the more elaborate displays of culture, such as ceremonies, rituals, and the arts, presumably can be traced back to individual motivation, parenting styles, and the underlying cultural framework. In other words, no matter the act, no matter the behavior, no matter the culture, everything fits together and makes sense.

This approach to other cultures, and to our own, is still used today to analyze the way parents raise children. For example, anthropologists have used subsistence patterns—that is, the ways people obtain food—to explain features of personality. The stretch from food to personality might seem like a long one, but if people are in any sense molded by their culture, then there should be links from how we go about surviving at the most fundamental level to who we are at the most esoteric level. To be a hunter and gatherer, for example, requires initiative and persistence, and so it might be expected that in such a system parents would foster self-reliance. And in a society of pastoralists, where obtaining and holding on to cattle is the measure of success, parents might be inclined to push for responsibility rather than creativity.[15] And as societies move from one kind of economy to another—as the !Kung San of Botswana have moved from a hunter-gatherer life to settlements, or as agriculturalists become urbanized—parents should foster new and more appropriate cultural traits. Research on several communities in transition shows that parenting styles do echo changes in the economic base; for in communities in transition, parents do shift to a pattern of care that fosters different values required for the new lifestyle.[16]

Implicit in this approach is the notion that what parents do and how they act toward their children has an effect on children's personality and, eventually, adult personality. Today, this seems obvious. Most of us in Western culture have been so steeped in psychological theory—both intellectually in school and socially in the popular culture, with the growth of the therapy industry—that we "naturally" assume a parental effect on a child's developing personality. We even blame our own parents for our behavior and spend hours trying to trace our mental selves back to something that occurred in childhood. But this is a rather modern, and decidedly Western, approach to personality. Others, for example, believe that personality is innate, not formed, or that other spiritual or ancestral forces are responsible for how people turn out. But contemporary anthropologists, who are mostly trained in a Western tradition, have picked up on the developmental psychology approach and incorporated it into their model of parents and society.

Cross-cultural studies, those conducted today as well as the work initiated by the Whitings in the 1950s, approach the study of parenting in a similar way. All agree that parenting is part of a larger integrated system of behavior that is mediated by culture as well as individual personality; in other words, that parenting is connected to everything else.[17] Parents, they propose, also have general themes that run through their activities with children. That is, parents have a conscious or unconscious philosophy about parenting. By closely watching parents and children over time, therefore, a researcher can pick up on these themes.[18]

There is no evil mastermind at work here, no Big Brother pushing parents to indoctrinate their kids a certain way. The "cultural ethos" and the values that societies adopt are passed on because they work—at some level, people unconsciously agree to a particular set of values and pass them along because they serve the society economically and serve individuals both personally and spiritually.[19] More important, this cultural ethos becomes almost invisible; it is difficult to define or tease out because it is so ingrained, generation after generation, that it appears "natural" or "right," and part of one's identity. Culture is seen not as some overlying mist that cloyingly wraps around people and families, but as a lacy film that ingratiates itself into every crevice of behavior, silently but powerfully influencing what people do and how adults treat their children.[20]

A New Niche

Recently, the term "developmental niche" has been attached to the parent–infant framework by scientists to emphasize the holistic, almost ecological lens through which parenting should be studied.[21] The developmental niche is more accurately defined by child development researchers Sara Harkness and Charles Super as that which includes the physical and social setting of a child's life, the cultural customs that every child is brought up with, and the psychology of the caretaker, which, of course, is the funnel through which all dependent human children are given a glimpse of the world.[22] "Developmental niche" describes in two words a child's world with its layers of family, culture, socioeconomic status, ethnicity, and personality.

This world is best understood by looking in the mirror; the developmental niche appears most clearly when it begins to crack up. I remember the first time I realized that other families were not like mine, that my "developmental niche" was not the family environment of all my friends. We shared the same middle-class socioeconomic level, practiced the same religion, and were basically of the same ethnicity. But in other households, they followed unfamiliar rules. To my mind they ate odd things for dinner, and their mothers did not work, which I thought was so strange. We are a chatty family and have always spent many hours talking about the day. And we had household chores to do in the evening and on weekends; everyone was expected to pull his or her weight. But no chores ever got in the way of a better invitation to the beach or a movie. My parents were also very social and there were parties all the time. But the houses of my friends were much less lively. Their mothers were home after school, but there were never groups of adults in the house joking and laughing. Those kids did not have household chores, but they also never went out to the movies with their parents. A comparison with my friends was an early lesson in "developmental niche" differences—and it bespoke different attitudes toward parenting as well. We all had the same culture, but our micro-environments were entirely different, so different that they produced, or influenced, differences in our individual personalities. My house was loud with talking while my girlfriend's house was calm and quiet. I had chores and household duties each week while she had none. Our worlds, at least away from school, were vastly different and as a result we reacted quite differently to situations outside our individual homes, and today we are quite different adults. Different developmental niches also crash head-on when two people move in together and try to negotiate around different ways of living and thinking, when each believes his or her ways are only natural and right—and everyone else's seem comical, odd, even stupid.

The differences in personal niche come into even greater focus during travel, when customs and beliefs are so disparate in color, texture, and action that no one can fail to see how wildly different other ways of living, working, and socializing can be. There are so many more options in living and behaving than most of us realize. In recent years I have focused particularly on how people in other cultures interact with children. In the United States, babies are watched primarily by one person, usually the mother, whereas in Bali, babies are part of a larger household and everyone has to keep an eye on a crawling youngster. I've noticed that babies do not cry in Africa, that children run up and down the streets of Bali chasing chickens without any supervision, that Japanese kids spend much of their time in school dressed in uniform outfits—all around us are examples of the very different ways that people and cultures mold their own. But we often fail to see that each person has developed within a particular niche that has a history, a culture, and a reason for being as it is, and that all of this plays a major part in our very makeup.[23]

Parental Goals

Parents today, in the more modern anthropological view, are seen not as passive translators of culture but as active participants, making choices about this or that pattern in bringing up a particular kind of adult citizen. These themes are often referred to by child development scholars as "parental goals," wherein parents have conscious or unconscious objectives that influence every action with their offspring.[24] Parents implement these goals in layers of ways as they go through the day. The goals are usually unconscious, although at times parents are very clear about what they are doing. I remember years ago my sister telling me that she never wanted anyone to say "no" to her children. Her well-articulated parental goal was to raise children who would think anything in life was possible. My sister believed that saying no might discourage them from a task, and she wanted them never to be discouraged. Other parents, when asked, also have agendas. My good friend Ann wants very much for her sons to be in tune with their emotions, something that she feels our American culture doesn't really allow for males. She believes that part of her parenting task is to fight the culture on this issue. As a result she talks about emotions and feelings all the time with her boys, and she takes their crying and worrying seriously. She hopes that this parental goal will eventually be realized and that they will see emotional issues as a "natural" part of being male, even in a culture where male emotions are traditionally repressed.

On a broader scale, American culture as a whole clearly fosters "independence" as a major goal. This collective goal has been documented in several studies of white middle-class parents; independence is mentioned repeatedly in interviews as something that "all" parents want for their children. Interestingly, parents in other cultures never bring up the subject. What parents want even influences the very ways they label children. Sara Harkness and Charles Super found that when parents in three cultures were asked about intelligence, their views of what constitutes a smart child differed.[25] In America, an "intelligent" child is one who is aggressive and competitive; in Holland, the intelligent child is one who is persistent, strong-willed, and demonstrates a clarity of purpose; for the Kipsigis Africans, the most intelligent child is the responsible one who does his or her chores.[26] Each household tries to provide a setting that is believed to foster the culture's particular brand of intelligence. Americans use all kinds of visual and verbal stimuli to catch the baby's attention and encourage it to interact. We line the crib with black-and-white signs to stimulate vision; we converse for hours in one-on-one lessons, convinced that this verbal interaction will improve cognitive abilities. Americans try to instill self-esteem in their children; self-esteem is a word not easily translated into other languages because the trait is not part of the cultural milieu of other groups—it is of import only in a competitive self-achieving society.[27] The Dutch, in contrast, believe that regularity, rest, and cleanliness promote intelligent development, so much so that when children throw tantrums, as they do all over the world, parents assume there has been a break in the child's routine that has caused the episode. And Kipsigis parents load their children with chores. Beginning at two years old, an age at which Americans would call them toddlers, Kipsigis children are given household tasks. By the time they are six years old, these kids typically spend half of their time working for the family.[28] People from each culture would be incapable of raising their children any other way. Imagine an American child doing household chores at two, with little playtime. We would mourn the loss of "childhood," that carefree time of exploration and development. In the same way, a Kipsigis mother would be horrified to see irresponsible, lazy American children with nothing to do but play games. How could that child, she might comment, grow up with any brains at all? The point is that we all agree in a general sense on what intelligence is, and we all agree that to be intelligent is better than being stupid, but each culture emphasizes and appreciates different aspects of intelligence.

Parental goals are translated or transcribed into daily routines, slipped into trivial interactions; they are insidiously unconscious reinforcers that make us who we are. In the way parents talk to their children, in methods of discipline, in how they go about parenting, their actions relate in a systematic way to how they see the role of parent. It might be as simple as choosing between various alternatives when a child is doing something wrong. One mother might ignore the child, another might emphatically say "no," and another might try to distract the child. Each strategy carries a different kind of implicit message, either passive or interactive. Anthropologist Robert LeVine feels these goals have little to do with the immediate situation of the child, but more to do with the entire social system and its institutional goals—especially in the areas of interpersonal relationships, the level of personal achievements expected, and the degree and manner of social solidarity that is favored in that particular society.[29] LeVine divides current cultures into two types, agrarian and urban-industrial. In both kinds of societies, parents want various things *from* their children, and other things *for* their children. In agrarian societies, those groups still living off the land or herding animals, parents need children as unskilled labor to help with family economics by working in the fields or with livestock, and to support the parents in their old age; parents want things *for* their children but also expect many things *from* them. In more urban-industrial societies, LeVine suggests, parents don't need much *from* their children because the economic system is constructed so that children are peripheral, but they want many things *for* them.[30] And like dominoes stacked up and then set off in two different directions, these systems fall into two distinct patterns of parenting. In the agrarian societies, children do not cost much because there is nothing much to give them, but parents deal with high infant mortality because the economic base is so low compared to developed societies. Early parenting is, for these cultures, a matter of dealing with risk. Infant mortality is quite high in these cultures, as much as 50 percent during the first years. And so parents focus on keeping a child from harm, carrying it at all times and feeding it at will. There is little concern, at that time, about the future individual achievement of that child. Once the child has outlived the danger zone of infant mortality, its role is to contribute to family subsistence. In the urban-industrial society, where medical care and sanitation make the probability of infant survival more realistic, parental goals focus on the child's future, and much parental energy is put into what the child will become. The issue is not so much survival as it is the encouragement of mental and social stimulation, which will, parents believe, make or break the child's future success as an adult.

In many ways, detailed records of patterns of parental styles fit these two general trajectories. For example, a study of Mayan mothers in the Yucatán found that infants were kept in hammocks in the dark recesses of the house. There were no toys, no special equipment for the baby.[31] The Mayan mothers did not see themselves as responsible for developing or shaping the baby's personality or mental abilities, but rather they were charged with keeping the baby quiet and comforted, away from harm. Mayan mothers are quite shocked to learn that American mothers put their babies in their own rooms to sleep alone.[32] As these Mayan women see it, their role is to protect and nurture their children, not to teach them anything. Contrast this parenting scenario with that of American mothers, who by and large cannot imagine going through the day without talking to or playing with their six-month-olds for fear of abrogating motherly responsibilities. These mothers are less concerned about keeping a child from harm than they are about directing their energies toward shaping the child's development. As linguist Steven Pinker puts it, "In contemporary middle-class American culture, parenting is seen as an awesome responsibility, an unforgiving vigil to keep the helpless infant from falling behind in the great race of life."[33] And that race goes to the smartest, the most competitive, the most independent. In both cultures, the parents are simply responding to long-term goals that are presumably appropriate for the situation.

The point is that all parents are guided by what researchers now call "parental ethnotheories,"[34] parental belief systems that have complex cultural, psychological, and personal histories. These parental ethnohistories are handed down from one generation to the next, not untouched like photographs of the ancestors or articles of clothing, but in the way all belief systems are passed through the ages—with each generation adding bits and every parent altering interpretations this way and that way. The changes reflect both personal tastes and family traditions, as well as dramatic demographic or economic social changes. The belief system remains, on the whole, intact but it is colored by the very people who mutually agree to pass it along. As many of my friends lament, they now are treating their children just like they were treated by their parents. Yet what else would we expect? We learn how to parent by being a child. It is all we know, and despite our conscious efforts to be different, those old parental ethnotheories creep in.

Today we have a rather sophisticated view of parenting that takes into account culture, individual psychology, the micro-environment of home life, and a child's individual temperament. It is almost an organic model, with each part interacting with and impinging on the others. Researchers move among these levels, trying to tie the layers together with a common thread that explains why parents do what they do and how their actions affect a child's personality, growth, and health. It is a mix of cultural anthropology and developmental psychology, with a soupçon of evolutionary biology thrown in; and as of the mid-1990s, this field also has a new name.

ETHNOPEDIATRICS

Up until recently, parenting behavior was studied and analyzed in an attempt to understand the effects of various parenting styles on the development of individuals as they become adults. Social scientists, including anthropologists and developmental psychologists, were most interested in personality. Anthropologists did incorporate culture as a factor in their analyses, but the major focus was on how adult personality is formed and behavior is expressed. But today a revolution in parent–infant studies is afoot. A group of anthropologists, developmental psychologists, and pediatricians have banded together to create a new discipline. Called "ethnopediatrics," this new field calls for a more holistic, and more realistic, look at parental care.[35] The name of the field easily explains its goal—*ethno* for culture and *pediatrics* for child health. Based on the earlier cross-cultural work described above, we know that children grow up differently in different cultures. More significant, many of the cultural differences translate into differences in health and survival. Parenting in various ways, then, has a direct effect not just on personality, but on the bare essentials—growing up healthy and staying alive.

The human infant, as I showed in Chapter One, evolved over millions of years, since long before culture overlaid who we are and what we do today. Clearly, babies are biologically designed to take in all sorts of social and mental stimuli, and from the moment of birth, perhaps even in the womb, they soak up whatever information they can about the world around them; babies were evolutionarily designed that way. Long ago, parents presumably acted in rational ways that responded to environmental contingencies—after all, we are all here, so those parental ancestors must have done something right. We can assume that parenting styles made biological sense at that time and so they were assimilated into cultural tradition, as humans invented the various faces of culture. The problem is that the cultural environment has evolved, especially technologically, and the parenting structure has changed accordingly, but the human baby has been biologically designed for a whole different set of contingencies.[36] The biology of the baby has remained the same, while culture has sped past with its playpens, car seats, and bottle formula. Modern culture, with its particular set of parenting goals and rules, now seems to dominate the development of this baby organism that was evolutionarily designed with a very different set of environmental and social pressures in mind. Ethnopediatricians are trying to understand how parents, who are molded by culture, practice patterns of care that affect—sometimes negatively—the growth, health, and happiness of their babies. These scientists want to uncover whether mismatches might exist between the biology of the baby and the cultural styles of the parents, with an eye toward realigning parents and babies into a smoother, better-adjusted biological and psychological relationship.

Imbedded in this approach is the notion that for all societies, the whims of culture often take on scientific credibility. As a result, parents feel they must listen to authorities or follow traditions handed down from their parents and their parents' parents. But until very recently there has been no scientific documentation that one parenting style is more "correct" in the biological and psychological sense than other parenting styles. What is needed, ethnopediatricians now suggest, is an evolutionary and cross-cultural view of human infancy coupled with real biological data that can be used to understand what is best for infants. The results of this compelling new work not only highlight the role of culture in upbringing, as early cross-cultural anthropological work has done; they also have the potential to revolutionize the way we, especially those of us living in highly industrialized and mechanized Western culture, bring up our children.

The ethnopediatric approach to parent–infant studies grows from cross-cultural work over the past few decades and from a significant shift in the sciences. This shift began long ago but is just recently in vogue— the move toward incorporating the influences and interactions of both biology and culture when viewing how people function.

Nature and Nurture

Last fall, ornithologist Stephen Emlen and I taught a class on the evolution of human behavior. We wanted to ask if there was any evidence that patterns of human behavior have been encoded in our genes and passed down through generations. We know that human physiology—that is, the size and shape and workings of our bodies—is molded by evolution, but we wanted to explore the possibility that human *behavior* might be designed by evolution as well. The class was a mix of biology students working on insects and birds as well as several undergraduate students in anthropology. We planned to explore such topics as mate choice, altruism, and morality; we expected confusion—and we got it. About halfway through the course, we realized that all of us, professors and students alike, were unclear about the very terms we were tossing about the room each week. Most confusing of all was the word "culture." There we were discussing how culture interacts with or impinges on biology, and we hadn't really defined what we meant by culture. The biology students asked the anthropology students to tell them, one by one, what they meant by "culture." We went around the room and although there were many agreements, the most striking feature of the various definitions of culture was that everybody had his or her own translation. Most included things like "belief systems," "symbolic behavior," and "mutually agreed-upon traditions" to define culture, but clearly we were dealing with an amorphous mess. The biology students were feeling rather smug, thinking they at least had a cleanly defined and objective scientific framework to guide their studies—until the anthropologists pointed out that biology was not exactly free of distortion either. The biological framework, they explained, is merely another culturally constructed lens through which some choose to view the world. Biologists might think the scientific method results in some sort of "truth," but that truth, the anthropology students explained, is warped by the people who ask the questions, people molded by their very own cultural traditions to be interested in certain subjects and seek certain answers. We were back where we started.

This class echoes what scientists and philosophers have been arguing about since time immemorial, the importance of biology versus culture to human behavior—what has been dubbed the "nature–nurture debate." What part of human behavior is driven by biology and what is culturally molded? Is biology—that is, genes and hormones and muscle action and the way the brain fires neurons—the driving force behind what we do? Or are we free enough of those physiological constraints to be able to merely "think" our way through life? This debate has plagued the humanistic sciences for decades, and as our seminar last fall showed, the debate is still raging.

What Makes Us Behave This Way?

In the 1600s, Descartes believed that everything we or other animals do is a reflex, a reaction to a stimulus that is absorbed through the senses, translated by the chemistry of the brain, and then passed on to the rest of the body for reaction. To Descartes, humans were different from other animals only in that humans had a soul to mediate such reflexes. And so between the stimulus and the response, there was a human filter that might alter human behavior and distinguish it from that of a dog or a fly.[37] Eventually, behavioral theorists of the nineteenth and early twentieth centuries expanded on the Descartian view by focusing on learning and how behavioral patterns could be altered and become more flexible. For example, Pavlov demonstrated—with a few dogs, dishes of food, and a bell—that even automatic responses like salivating in hunger could be turned into conditioned reflexes with the use of an intervening symbol. This mechanistic approach to understanding the thought processes behind behavior culminated in B. F. Skinner's experimental box in which pigeons and other animals demonstrated that, with a little reinforcement, any animal can learn just about anything. To other behavioral theorists working at the same time, the roots of all behavior could be sought in cognitive processes, not in bells, whistles, and levers. For example, German psychologist Wolfgang Köhler watched captive chimpanzees use sticks to rake in bananas that were just out of reach, and pile boxes on top of one another to climb to dangling fruit. To Köhler, the chimpanzees were not acting by the rules of mere stimulus/response, but utilizing thoughtful insight, a more complex cognitive maze that reflected an adaptable mind. Köhler felt that this kind of puzzle-solving was a sign of intelligence, and that intelligence was a property that varied among animal species, with humans the smartest animals of all. These experiments suggested to psychologists that there were universal paths of learning, and that any mind could be dissected into easily understandable parts of motivation and action. They believed that humans were no different from other animals, that we could also be programmed and pushed to behave in certain ways, and that we were products of nature overlaid by a bit of nurture that made us slightly different from other animals.

In sharp contrast, cultural anthropologists took a more *tabula rasa* view of human behavior. Influenced by Mead and Benedict's culture and personality school, ethnographers assumed then, and many take this same line today, that biology has little or nothing to do with behavior—only culture counts. Under this scheme, people sometimes act the same not because there are any human universals that have evolved and are encoded on genes, but because cultures drive people down similar roads. Most cultural anthropologists were horrified by the rise in the 1970s of sociobiology, in which evolutionary biologists were suggesting that human behavior was as subject to the rule of natural selection as was ant behavior. The cultural anthropologists claim that biology—that is, genes and hormones and physiology—is only peripheral to what people do or think.

These various schools of human behavior all exist today. Some claim that humans are primarily cultural beings and that culture directs almost everything a person does and how a society functions. Others claim that humans are not exempt from the rules of natural selection, and that what we think and how we behave are a result of evolved strategies that formed along with our species.[38] And still others take a middle-of-the-road approach. In our class on human behavior, we had agreed that human behavior resulted from a mix of biology and culture, but there was no way we could tease the two apart, no way we could examine the influence of one without bringing up the other, and I count myself among the fence-sitters. Human behavior does not appear in a biological or evolutionary vacuum; we act like humans because we are humans. Culture, I believe, is part of our environment, even if it is a product of our own design; it does indeed mold who we are, but only because our biological brain and our biological intellect allow this to happen. Culture, then, is simply part of our world, like a forest is to a monkey or an ocean is to the whale. So what if humans make the building? The monkey breaks a tree and the whale spits in the ocean. All these environments are part of a feedback system that each organism deals with from day to day. And so this perspective is an integrative one—culture and biology are not necessarily distinct layers, but part of a whole.

The Birth of Ethnopediatrics

Most social scientists today realize that no organism stands alone as either a biological entity or a cultural entity. Even a slug is influenced by its environment. Ethnopediatrics, more than any other science today, embraces this view, and this is one reason the field is so remarkable.

Oddly enough, ethnopediatrics owes this line of reasoning not so much to the nature/nurture debate or the rift between cultural anthropologists and biologists, but to an obscure Russian psychologist named Lev Semyonovich Vygotsky.[39]

Working in the 1930s, Vygotsky proposed a new way to look at children. He disagreed with Piaget's system of child development, a system which assumed that all "normal" children go through universal developmental steps one at a time in a set sequence. Piaget had outlined these steps while watching babies and children in a laboratory setting, and Vygotsky disagreed with the lab context. In contrast, Vygotsky felt that child development was inseparable from society and culture and so the lab was just another "institutional" setting in which society's needs were played out.[40] He believed that the institutions—meaning schools—along with the political system and society all pushed the developing child in certain directions, and that paths of cognition could be directed by such simple things as what the culture values as important. For example, in modern cultures with grocery stores, food is arranged in lines on shelves, by category of food, and in alphabetical order. This sends a message to children of that culture that this type of system is important. To assume that all children in all cultures will absorb this linear and alphabetical system is absurd.[41] For hunters and gatherers there is no value to alphabetizing and so this step in cognition is meaningless. If !Kung San children are dragged into the lab and tested for linear categorization skills and alphabetizing acumen, they might fail miserably; but this does not mean they are cognitively inferior. They are just cognitively mapped by a different scheme. Development, considered by Piaget to be a fixed biological process, could under the Vygotsky scheme be speeded up or slowed down by the culture and society.

Ethnopediatricians take Vygotsky's view; there is no debate about culture and biology for them, no wondering about the impact of environment on human behavior. Those working in ethnopediatrics take as their fundamental philosophy that children, and the way they develop, think, and behave, are products of both.

The word "ethnopediatrics" was first coined in 1963 by Carton Gajdusik. Gajdusik's paper, published in the *American Journal of Diseases of Children*, was a call for cross-cultural studies of children; he saw various cultures as ongoing laboratories in which scientists could take notes on how various cultural practices influence child health and development, and he saw those children as windows into a larger world. He wrote, "They [children] present different experiments in cultures, each programming uniquely the human nervous system from birth to maturity. Each is a different experiment in communication and language, and each produces a different pattern in the style of symbolism and thought and in the structure of logic in the use of the brain. Study of thought and behavior of children in these primitive [sic] cultures often reveals possibilities and potentialities of the human condition that could or would otherwise never be expected or considered possible by civilized man."[42] Gajdusik was a physician and interested in how culture alters the nervous system and influences disease, development, and growth. He advocated a multifaceted approach to child development, one that took into account the influence of culture; he felt that by comparing cultures we could better understand the full child development milieu.

Thirty years later, the word *ethnopediatrics* was used again by Carol Worthman, an anthropologist at Emory University, to announce the birth of a new science.[43] A workshop funded by the Social Science Research Council in 1994, a symposium at the annual meeting of the American Association for the Advancement of Science in the winter of 1995, and a symposium at the Society for Behavioral Pediatrics in the fall of 1995 galvanized this new approach. Worthman gathered researchers from anthropology, child development, and pediatrics, and proposed a new way to look at children.

Worthman's call to ethnopediatrics was, in part, motivated by the world crisis in childhood health. We may not recognize it in developed Western countries because our birthrate is so low, but one-third of the world's population is now under fifteen years of age. More striking, most of these children are at risk. Differences in life expectancy, which are dramatic when comparing developed and less developed countries, are primarily the result of differences in infant and child mortality.[44] In many countries, this figure reaches 50 percent; that is, every child born has only a 50 percent chance of surviving past the age of two or three. As Worthman has pointed out, concern about this issue has so far focused on health and hygiene, and for good reason. Diarrhea, which is caused by tainted food and drink, kills five million children a year (that is, one every six seconds); malnutrition and contagious diseases are implicated in most other infant deaths. Most often, the medical approach has been to treat sick children as they would be treated in a highly industrialized Western culture, with no clue as to how that treatment is viewed by the patient or the parents. Culture is clearly influencing not only the spread of diseases but also the routes through which a disease could be cured or eliminated.

And it is not just culture that affects biology—it also works the other way around. People's notions of health influence how they operate within a culture.[45] For example, women in the slums of Brazil withdraw care from their infants based on developmental signs that they believe indicate a baby is not going to survive anyway.[46] All over the world, higher male mortality often leads to a parental system whereby baby boys are given more care and more food while females are neglected. And all parents make noises about the inborn "temperament" of their children, and bad-tempered babies are treated quite differently from happy-tempered babies.

Worthman and other ethnopediatricians now suggest that death rates and other health or social issues can be better and more easily altered by understanding children's developmental niches and then working within various cultural contexts. It is medically obvious that emphasizing cleanliness to combat bacteria and viruses, and encouraging a return to breastfeeding for hygienic and immunological reasons, and promoting the need for hydration during bouts of diarrhea, are the logical ways to end much of child mortality. But these changes must be implemented with the ethnotheories of other cultures in mind. What are their concepts of "health" and "sickness"? Might they have different ideas about the stages of child development? And surely they have starkly different parental goals.

A case in point is UNICEF's highly successful campaign to teach mothers in less developed countries to use a solution of salt, sugar, and water for rehydration during infant diarrhea. Integral to UNICEF's campaign was refashioning the cultural beliefs about the causes and process of diarrhea and the very idea of illness.[47] Using these cultures' own already existing concepts of disease, UNICEF workers taught women that diarrhea is a "hot" disease that needs the cooling of water. In other words, they were wise enough not just to treat the illness but also to recognize that cultural beliefs played a major role in the high mortality rate in these places. To save children you have to understand and work within foreign parental ethnotheories.

More often, as Carol Worthman points out, the medical or physical model seems to operate under the false notion that child mortality occurs in a vacuum. But all children are born into and grow up in a cultural milieu that influences their progress. Mortality, then, is not simply a product of pathogens, but a product of a child being situated in a complex of culture and biology that determines its fate. At some level, we know this. We expect infant mortality to be high in the third world. We know that the health care in poor countries is nothing like what we have in industrial nations; that the nutritional content and abundance of foods we have here are just not available to people in slower economies; that it must be hard to keep a baby away from bacteria when living in a mud hut. But so far, the approach has been to emphasize the path of the pathogens rather than to investigate how cultural traditions form the roads down which those pathogens can so easily travel. And this is what ethnopediatricians intend to do.

From a global perspective, the new discipline has appeared at just the right time. As the pop pundits keep reminding us, we are becoming a global culture. We share the same TV shows and movies, drink the same Coca-Cola, and shoot the same Kodak film. But this "global culture" is highly superficial—it is only the gloss of popular culture, apparent only in what people over the world would like to buy. I am guessing that those boasting of an electronic superhighway where "anybody" can be connected to "anybody" have not traveled much in the third world; they are blinded by the affluent economy of their own culture into thinking they share much of anything with a Malaysian forester or Sudanese refugee. More illustrative is the fact that one out of every five women on the planet is Chinese, and that most of the people in the world have never spoken on a telephone. We do not share the same culture or the same economy, and it will be a long time before we do, if ever.

But the pundits are correct at one level—the cultures are coming in contact with each other more often because human groups are on the move and running into each other.[48] One out of every three people in Africa is a refugee; Berlin ranks only second to Istanbul as a home to Turkish people; and people of color will hold the majority vote in America in the next decade. But this does not make us "one." We are not yet a unified global culture, but we certainly are becoming an ongoing turmoil of clashing cultures. More important for the science of ethnopediatrics, people do not throw off all vestiges of their own cultures or ethnicities when immigrating into a new area. They hold on to their history and their values and continue to pass them along to their children.[49] In one very telling study of Lebanese mothers transplanted to Australia, for example, the clash of cultures was clearly illustrated by how the women approached parenting. The Australian mothers expected their preschoolers to be highly verbal and to be prepared for the rigors of school. The Australian mothers also felt that certain developmental tasks have only a small window of opportunity during which a child can acquire those skills, and that if kids are not poked and prodded they will fall behind and be losers. The Lebanese mothers, in contrast, felt no urge to teach their children any particular skills before they went to school and felt the kids would learn skills as they needed them; there was no sense of "it's too late." In addition, the Lebanese mothers were much more concerned about their children's welfare at school. As a result,

Australian teachers labeled the Lebanese kids as unprepared for school and overprotected, but the Lebanese mothers felt they were doing what was expected of any mother.[50] In this and other studies of mothers-out-of-their-primary-culture, it is not socioeconomic status or religion or parental education that makes for a clash; it is ethnicity.[51] And this is why ethnopediatric studies are so critical right now. Imagine the Cambodian woman new to America who is told by her physician to make sure the baby sleeps in his own bed. Or imagine the Guatemalan woman who is confused by all the toys that her new culture says she must buy for her baby's happiness. Or what about the British woman who looks in disdain at the Nigerian woman breast-feeding in public. Now, more than ever, we need to understand how culture molds what we do and what others do. By comparing ourselves with others, and comparing each group with yet another, we also obliterate any notions of "normal."[52]

Worthman's call to arms for a new discipline of ethnopediatrics has received an enthusiastic response. She was able to gather a cadre of researchers from various fields and it was easy to get them to agree on a purpose—to use a cross-cultural approach to understanding the influence of culture on parental strategies. But Worthman was also smart enough to see that this subject—child health and development—went beyond anthropologists. The welfare of children is just too precious to be left up to the academics; these may be cultural issues but they are life-and-death issues as well. And so she sought to reach and include a larger audience, especially those who actually deal with kids from day to day, the pediatricians. Thus the health practitioners and the academics could put their heads together for the same purpose—to understand how parents and cultures influence the younger and smaller members of our species. Maybe it was the subject matter—kids—or maybe it was the timing—at just the moment when the interface of culture and biology was beginning to be the sharpest cutting edge in the sciences—that made this an easy coalition among various disciplines. Their backgrounds are diverse, their methods of study often unrelated, but ethnopediatricians all share a paradigm: that culture molds parenting styles and goals, which in turn directly affect the health, development, and survival of children. Now they just had to explain how.

From the beginning, parenting styles and child care have been important subjects of study for anthropologists. In fact, watching how different societies handle their children has, in many cases, been the key to understanding the very foundations of culture. And now ethnopediatricians are turning the tables and claiming that parenting styles, scripts that are drafted by cultural traditions and parental goals, also determine child health, survival, and development. How do they know? They know from studies of children in various cultures, various economic subsistence patterns, and various cultural traditions. And these cross-cultural studies are currently the essential ingredients of ethnopediatrics.

CHAPTER THREE

OTHER PARENTS, OTHER WAYS

In the spring of 1996, the *New York Times* printed a story about the clash of cultures in Brooklyn, New York. This might not seem like big news—every American city is a hotbed of culture clash—but what makes this story interesting is that it deals not so much with culture per se but with the collision of different parenting styles. As reported by journalist Celia Dugger, parents and grandparents from other countries are having trouble managing their kids because they operate by other rules.[1] In the story, some Brooklyn parents claimed that when they hit or spanked their children they were only following the parenting behaviors of their home country, be it Nigeria or in the steppes of Russia or in the Caribbean. No one really knows if this defense is culturally credible. Children of such immigrants, however, frequently demand the right to be treated by the rules of American custom, and they have discovered that they can get physical protection from the state by calling in the cops. Caseworkers often ignore reports of corporeal punishment because they accept it as a cultural difference, or because they themselves are products of the same subculture and accept the usefulness of a good spanking. The court system, caught in the middle of this, is supposed to navigate between what it believes to be in the best interest of the child, and its respect for parental traditions. In the end, parents are baffled by a state that can come between them and their children; the social agencies are confused about what is right; and children are caught in the cultural cross-fire.

Who is right in this situation? Nobody and everybody. The problem is that each group believes that its traditional parental goals and styles are correct, regardless of the culture where they currently reside. The best defense against such confusion is education about other ways of parenting and of living.

PARENTING CULTURES

Culture. We all have it, are steeped in it, but find it almost impossible to define. Many people think of culture as simply the arts—such as literature, painting, architecture, and music—but the academic definition encompasses so much more. Culture is the shared and learned ideas and products of a society.[2] It is, in other words, the shared way of life of a people, including their beliefs, their technology, their values and norms, all of which are transmitted down through the generations by learning and observation. Most often, we use the material expression of certain acts to describe a culture—one group makes this kind of poetry while another group practices that kind of dance. But each group also has a particular ideology and political structure, a particular subsistence pattern and history.

As anthropologists Sara Harkness and Charles Super point out, we are all cultural creatures, products of shared ideas, practices, and institutions that shape everything we do.[3] Humans are by nature cultural creatures; we are social animals living in population groups, and each group reaches a consensus about how to act in ways that promote a sense of community and belonging. This is not to say that other animal species don't have culture as well. Other animals have rituals and lifestyles, and all kinds of animals, from birds to otters, use tools. Recent work with chimpanzees has shown that they act in ways that we would certainly call cultural if the behavior had been recorded for people rather than apes. Studies of various populations of chimpanzees shows that they are even multicultural. For example, some chimp groups crack nuts while others do not, and they have different vocal dialects and behaviors that can only be explained as cultural differences between groups of the same species.[4] But the roots of human culture run deep, and at this point in our evolutionary history it is frequently impossible to separate biological human behavior and traits from those that are cultural, because they often are one and the same. Our culture does not just interact with our biology, it is *part* of our biology, part of the way we adapt to changes and deal with life, part of our past and our future.

Although culture and its integration in humanness is a universal, it is also a major factor in our variation. Because culture can take on so many guises, it refracts human action in myriad ways. And it is this warping that is of so much interest to the study of human behavior. We can be assured that culture will have an effect on behavior—this is a human universal—but more intriguing is the direction that effect takes, and where it leads. We have the easiest time defining other people's cultures, and a harder time seeing and understanding the effect of culture on our own society. In a sense, we pretend that culture is something we see in others but not in ourselves. No one has trouble designating Balinese dance as part of Balinese culture, or seeing African beadwork as part of Maasi culture, but it is more difficult to see our own ways of dressing, acting, and thinking as part of some coherent whole.

In this chapter I intend to offer a sample of studies of parenting in several cultures, short vignettes of how people parent and how children grow in different cultures. The examples here are by no means exhaustive, and they are not meant to be. The intention here is to give a broad range of examples, present a broad range of societies and parenting styles. But the choice of cultures presented is not random. I have chosen those societies for which there is long-term and extensive information on parenting. The very method by which I chose these cultures, of course, reveals a bias in my sample, to be sure; but this sample will nonetheless provide a rich and well-documented array of parenting styles. I also wanted a sample that would be true of parenting styles today, not something dusted off from the files of ethnographic history. And so I chose cultures that are intact today, still under study, still functioning. I also chose cultures of various subsistence types and from various geographical locations in order to give readers some familiarity with a full spectrum of other cultures, and a chance to compare these cultures, at least superficially, in the domain of parenting.

"TRADITIONAL" AND "INDUSTRIALIZED" SOCIETIES

Perhaps the greatest gift anthropology has given those of us in North America and Western Europe, the industrialized West, is the concept of cultural relativism. Before we had a clear picture of how other societies worked, it used to be thought that technologically sophisticated societies were the "best" and that other civilizations and societies had little to offer. Early social thinkers even delineated stages of cultural evolution from "savagery" to "civilization," with white Western industrialized nations, of course, at the pinnacle of social and cultural evolution. People were blinded by the shine and flash of industrialization into thinking that a multiplicity of goods equaled cultural sophistication. We now know that every human group exists in its own cultural complexity—the life of a Tiwi from Australia living in the bush and catching small animals in a snare is just as complex and rich as that of a stockbroker in Manhattan who shops at the corner grocery and logs into the Net (perhaps more so!). Each member of a group lives by a set of social rules, operates within a particular spiritual belief system, and adheres to an ideology that helps the society run smoothly. Each group can be described relative to the subsistence pattern, the production of goods and their distribution, the interpersonal interactions and social rules, and the history of its society. Most important, each helps us to understand how human groups adapt and live.

There have been two epochal changes in human history that transformed human societies in a general way. The first, about ten thousand years ago, was the agricultural revolution. Before people started growing crops on a large scale, most human groups were not sedentary—they earned their food by hunting and gathering. Such societies were rather small due to the dictates of food; large-bodied animals have to travel widely in relatively small groups to be able to find enough food. With the establishment of agriculture, people for the first time settled down for long periods of time and were able to claim ownership of land and to produce generous amounts of food in a predictable way; this in turn allowed for population expansion. Agricultural settlements opened the way for all sorts of human social patterns. Although people certainly had complex ways of dealing with each other before they became settled and relatively sedentary, close contact on a daily basis and urbanization into areas of higher population density resulted in both increased opportunities and restrictions. Civilization as a whole shifted from small nomadic bands to large, settled, multilayered communities.

The second major shift in human history came more recently, several hundred years ago, with the industrial revolution.[5] Today most people in industrialized countries have little to do with the production of most of the goods they consume, especially food. Life is no longer directly connected to the production or acquisition of food, but rather to the acquisition of other goods that pay for a lifestyle, and food is only a small part of that lifestyle.

As a result of the industrial revolution in some parts of the world, today we have a vast array of cultural types and subsistence patterns. Although we assume that early humans were hunters and gatherers up to about ten thousand years ago, since then human groups have fanned out into all sort of niches. Some groups remain hunters and gatherers, although these societies are few and far between. Others make their living directly from the land, and anthropologists call them "traditional" or "aboriginal" societies because they have not yet become as disconnected from growing or finding their own food and other products. Even among these groups, it is impossible to find many commonalities by which they might easily be collectively defined. Mostly, these groups are distinguished by their lack of industrialization. Some Amazonian Indians are considered traditional because they still live in the forest, hunt forest animals, and practice ancient belief systems. But such tribes might also wear Western dress and trade with more westernized tribes for goods. They might even have adopted Christianity and might attend a missionary school. And so the lines that separate "traditional" from "Western" societies are not all that clear. But have they ever been clear? Some of those in more affluent societies idealize the more traditional societies, giving them a gloss of exoticism and believing them to be more natural and real, ignoring the fact that all human groups have been subject to influence and change over time. More significant, few societies have ever been truly isolated—human groups are characterized by their urge to migrate, their need to interact with one another and learn skills from other groups. Genetic studies reveal that the human species has been mixing, matching, and marrying ever since our human ancestors first migrated out of Africa about 200,000 years ago.[6] And so culture, and the human groups that adhere to this or that culture, must be viewed as dynamic interacting systems, not as isolates that have been or should ever be frozen at some point in time, and preserved.

I have divided the examples below into "traditional" and "industrial" societies. These labels are efficient, but they are really smoke and mirrors. What does traditional mean when it is clear that societies and culture change over time? Where do we draw the line for "traditional"? Nor are all people in industrial societies "westernized." And various industrialized societies clearly do not share the same values, as the studies below will show. But this division *will* set apart in the reader's mind more unfamiliar societies from those that might, at first, appear to be more familiar to most readers. We expect the traditional societies to be quite different from ours, and they are, but there are also surprising commonalities. In the same way, many expectations about some sort of common parenting style in industrial societies will be shattered as each country tells a slightly different story.[7] In many cases I also tell a tale of transition for the more traditional societies. None of these cultures, even our own, lives in pristine isolation; we are all in a transition of sorts. These transitions are sure to resonate in the way parents shift their goals for their children. As Margaret Mead pointed out many years ago, understanding the way children are treated is one of the most telling ways to track societies.

"TRADITIONAL" SOCIETIES

!Kung San of the Kalahari

One year a fellow anthropologist brought me a present from her trip to Botswana in southern Africa. It's a tiny apron made out of an animal skin, light brown, buffed to suede, and sewn with about 200 tiny discs punched out of an ostrich shell. When I first pulled the apron out of the bag, a woody sort of animal smell, the smell I associate with Africa, filled my living room. Now, many years later, when I pick up that apron and hold it in my fingers like a prayer book, I have to shove my nose deep into the skin to pick up the odor—not a holy sort of action, but one that has its own sort of reverence. For me, an anthropologist, this bit of Africa is a touchstone because it was made by Bushmen, the !Kung San of Botswana, some of the last remaining hunters and gatherers on earth. In that small apron lies the history of a people, the feel of a lifestyle that all humans once shared, and it reminds me what makes anthropology such an intriguing field of study.

As noted above, agriculture and the settled life have been part of human history for only about ten thousand years. Before the agricultural revolution, all human groups lived by the subsistence pattern called "hunting and gathering," in which people lived on both vegetable foods and large and small game. Since the human line has been around about four million years, agriculture and the settled life that comes with growing one's own food is only a small fraction of our history; an industrialized lifestyle, in which only a tiny fraction of the population is involved in food production, has been the lifestyle of some humans for only about two hundred years. Anthropologists point out that for the vast majority of time our species has been in existence, we have been hunters and gatherers. More important, our bodies and minds evolved to aid us in hunting and gathering, which might explain why so much of our behavior is inexplicable—we have shifted from a subsistence pattern but our biological selves have not yet caught up.[8] It is almost impossible to look at a modern industrialized society today and make statements about what human nature is, or why people act the way they do. Because of that, anthropologists have turned to the very few societies that still practice hunting and gathering to gain some understanding of who we are and where we came from. No one claims that the hunters and gatherers of today are exact models of our hominid ancestors, but they offer the only living clues we have that might help us to better understand what it must have been like to make a living in the Pleistocene age. And this is why the !Kung San have been under the observant eyes of anthropologists for over thirty years.[9]

The Kalahari desert, spreading across the countries of Botswana and Namibia, overlays the western portion of South Africa. It is inhabited by any number of tribes that practice every sort of subsistence pattern, from cattle farming to working for wages. The San, known to most Westerners as "Bushmen," are a traditional people in transition.[10] In the late nineteenth century, the San were nearly exterminated by the Dutch. Those that survived fled into the Kalahari. Today they are economically assimilating into "black" Bantu-speaking populations from whom they used to be so distinct. Although some San groups might still roam the outback as hunters and gatherers, many more are now settled in permanent villages, taking up the ways of their agricultural neighbors, or working for others. When anthropologist Richard Lee went to Botswana in

1963 to find a group of traditional hunters and gatherers, he was struck by how much Western ways had already infringed on the traditional San life. And within ten years, Lee saw the building of clinics, schools, and trading stores, and the introduction of the transistor radio and Western dress. By the 1980s, bow-and-arrow hunting had become almost nonexistent, and most groups were cultivating some sort of grain as a staple. No one knows how many San still practice hunting and gathering, but clearly the traditional way of living is, for the most part, no more. Most San also had, or aspired to, ownership of livestock. As Lee describes his time with the San, "I was able to observe a foraging mode of life during the last decade of its existence."[11] Some might feel a sense of loss for the San way of life, but that would be unfair. All societies change, absorbing the ways of others, and who are we to say that the San must hold on to a lifestyle just because we think it provides clues to the past? People are not museums. The old life might be gone, but the traditions and goals of that culture have been so detailed by anthropologists that the San cannot but play a central role in our understanding of the parental style of hunters and gatherers in the recent past, and how it might have been for our ancient hominid ancestors.

For Westerners, the most distinguishing feature of the San is their language—it is full of clicks and clacks. The correct pronunciation of !Kung, for example, involves pressing the tongue against the front of the roof of the mouth and making a nasal sound at the same time. Their language includes four distinct clicks made in various parts of the mouth, and an array of tones—a calliope of communication. Physically, the San tend to be small in stature and light-skinned, with heart-shaped faces and almond eyes. But as with all people in all cultures, there is a wide variety in physical type, including some tall dark-skinned San.

Anthropologists have discovered that compared to a horticultural, livestock-based, or industrial lifestyle, the work life of a hunter and gatherer is less time-consuming. On average, adults work two or three days a week gathering food, and children and the elderly do not work at all. Even when the hours needed to maintain tools and other domestic chores are added in, these hunters and gatherers have far more leisure time than any people on earth. Women do most of the gathering and they contribute 55 percent of the group's caloric needs and 60 to 80 percent of the food by weight. San eat over one hundred species of plants, but their major staple is the mongongo tree, and they utilize both the fruit of the tree and its nuts. Only men hunt large and small game, and the meat they bring in contributes 45 percent of the calories but far less bulk than vegetable foods. Meat is, however, the favored food.

The San move from place to place relative to food and water. During the dry season, they might camp near a permanent water source for months; but during the wet season, they move when the food in the immediate area has been exhausted and people have to travel too far from camp for resources. Land is not "owned" but recognized as belonging to those who have lived in the area the longest. A typical area of usage covers about 250 square miles, but the use of an area is not exclusive since people are either "residents" or "visitors," and both have access to the resources. Group composition is fluid and people might join several different camps during the year. But these camps are not random aggregations of people. At the center is an association of older people, often relatives, who have learned by experience that they can live and work together. Fluctuations in camp demography are the result of the comings and goings of their extended families and friends. Although there is some sort of hierarchy, one built on earned respect, both men and women are of equal status and power and the society is neither matrilineal nor patrilineal, but bilateral. When someone marries, either the bride or the groom will join the other's family.

The layout of a camp echoes what is important in San life. Small grass huts used mostly for storage and afternoon naps huddle close together in a circle with the openings facing inward. Everyone sleeps outside at night, close to the fire; there is no concept of privacy. Each morning, some women leave the camp to gather for some hours and some men take off on a hunting trip. Others stay at home tending to domestic chores. Food is shared in a reciprocal manner so that no one

goes hungry. Beyond the usual ties of kinship, the group is also connected by a complex system of gift giving, called the *hxaro*, by which
individuals are joined in a mutual long-term pact of exchange. There is
also a complex system of naming and attachment, which bonds people
when they are named the same. While a camp might have fluid membership, the fluidity is braced by a solid network of economic attachments
and social bonds.

Women give birth on average every four to five years, which results in
an interbirth interval that is long compared with more settled people.[12]
Women often give birth in the bush alone, which is considered a sign of
strength and achievement.[13] Babies are never left at home when mothers
go out to gather, an odd fact in that there is always someone at camp
who could babysit.[14] But the mother–infant relationship is considered
sacrosanct, so babies stay with their mothers at all times. Women wear a
large multipurpose animal skin garment, the *kaross*, which functions as
both a cover-up and a holding device. Babies sit in a special sling within
the *kaross*, a soft palate lined with grass. This sling is nonrestrictive and
allows the baby to wiggle around, moving its arms and legs at will.[15] It
also assumes constant mother–infant contact; anthropologist Melvin
Konner found that San infants have more than twice the amount of
passive contact with their mothers than do babies in industrialized societies.[16] The sling is hung on the mother's hip, not on her back, and so
the baby has good access to the breast and sees everything from the same
vantage point as its mother. Elimination is managed easily by replacing
the grass in the *kaross*, or if the baby eliminates on the mother, it is
simply whisked off without comment. Being semi-nomads, they have no
baby toys to be hauled around. Instead, babies grab and play with their
mothers' jewelry, bright strands of beads on head and necks.

Although San babies cry, they do not do so for long, and none of
them cries excessively or inconsolably; more than 90 percent of their
total crying events during the first nine months last less than thirty
seconds.[17] Babies are fed when they cry and often when they do not cry.
San breasts are long and flexible, and it is up to the baby to manage its

feeding by holding on to the breast and sucking whenever it is hungry—called "continuous feeding" by Melvin Konner.[18] Interestingly, we in the West call this kind of feeding "on demand," but in fact there is no demand being placed here. As soon as possible, babies control their own feeding and there is no conflict between mother and child over the time or amount of milk allowed, until weaning, which occurs at about four years of age. Once a mother knows she is pregnant again, she will coat her breasts with bitter herbs and gradually wean the child.

The sling also assures that the baby is always positioned vertically, which San believe is imperative—babies left in a horizontal position will never develop good motor skills, they believe. There is evidence that this line of thinking is correct.[19] Early on, San babies surpass their European peers in motor skills. It is possible that San children are genetically superior to Western babies in their motor skills, but testing shows that all babies in all cultures are born with basically the same motor skill potential. The difference is in both how babies are physically managed and how parents believe motor skills are acquired. San parents believe that most skills will be learned passively—but not motor skills.[20] Sitting, standing, and walking, they feel, must be taught and encouraged, and so San parents invest time in making sure their babies are physically adept early on. The sling allows for lots of wiggle room and babies are never placed down on their backs and left alone to flail about. Perhaps most important, parents practice many physical skills with babies and make sure they acquire these skills as soon as possible. As a result, San babies excel in motor-coordination tests and appear generally smarter in motor-cognition tests because they move better and concentrate harder than their Western peers.[21] This concentration on motor skills certainly makes sense, given the San lifestyle. Nothing in their life is physically passive, and physical ability is important. It is interesting, however, to note that this focus on the physical comes at such an early age and is so ingrained in parenting practices.

San babies grow up in a "socially dense" environment—there is always an adult or a pack of children around and babies are never alone.

Exploration begins at about seven months of age when babies begin to spend some time off their mothers.[22] By the time they are eighteen months of age, San children are spending time in the home camp with other children. This is not a peer group as such—camp membership is so small that it would be unlikely that there would be children of the same age in the same group. Instead, San children are part of a multi-age group, and older children serve as teachers to younger children. The transition to a child group is complete by the time a new sibling comes along, when the child is about four or five.

In a comparative study of hunter-and-gatherer San, and San who had adopted a settled life, changes in the role of children stand out.[23] This is not a surprise. When the subsistence style changes, everybody's role shifts. The most telling sign of social change comes from the altered layout of "camps," now modified for permanent living sites. Huts are built farther apart and they no longer face each other in a community circle. Instead, each structure opens up onto a corral, signaling the importance of cattle over neighbor. Daily activity has changed as well. Parents are off in the cultivated fields or off working for others, and not for just a few hours and not for just a few days a week. On another level, the interpersonal atmosphere is not the same. People do not come and go, and some social interactions are less fluid. The home group is no longer a mix of adults and children, but more a peer group of children alone with some elderly. Children of these settled communities are left on their own while most of the adults are away, and they tend to wander far from home. So far, these kids have not been put to work, but as the value of livestock, land, and possessions grows, it is likely that children will become necessary contributors to household economic production. The mother–infant bond is still strong, but baby-sitters will probably become necessary as mothers spend more time in the fields.

On a deeper emotional level, what was once open and connected in San society is now private. In the hunter-and-gatherer lifestyle, camps were interconnected, fluid rather than private, and based on reciprocal exchange. But in the settled lifestyle based on an economy of ownership and work, new notions of privacy, stable nuclear families, and difference in division of labor become important. The switch to a settled life means, by definition, ownership of goods, which in turn promotes privacy and results in monetary-based work to acquire those owned goods. Ownership also means a loss of the routes or necessity of gift exchange, the disintegration of sharing, and a need for social and physical privacy. In other words, the society now operates on an entirely different value system.

The parental goals of the traditional San are social integration, mobility, and sharing. These goals are reflected in the way babies and mothers interact as a single unit until such time as children can be left at home with camp members. Mobility is encouraged. Social exchange is integrated into every facet of life. The San who have opted for a settled life are experiencing a shift not simply in subsistence pattern but also in parental goals. Ownership and privacy are now paramount, and work, rather than leisure for social interaction, is paramount. As in any social transition, children are often affected the most. For the settled San children, the new way of life means more time without adults and without the prospect of work and involvement in household production, and ultimately a change in the way parents raise them. These children appear to be pushed to develop skills that will enable them to become economically productive adults, rather than scholars of the bush.

The Ache of Paraguay

A hunting-and-gathering lifestyle is not limited to the arid plains of Africa. On the other side of the globe, in the New World, various tribes of South American Indians have been living off the land for probably 150,000 years. Most of these indigenous groups now inhabit the forests of the Amazon Basin, moving across country boundaries through dense patches of tropical forest. Further south, in Paraguay, indigenous groups live in a more mixed forest that rises out of the plains to elevations of three hundred meters. The forest is different here—not the dripping wetness of Amazonia but a more wooded arena, a land not so much subject to the deluge of rain as vulnerable to changes in temperature. There are few animals here, and little species diversity; but a reasonable living can be gleaned from animals that poke about during the day and are easy to catch, combined with the gathering of a wide variety of fruits and vegetables. The forest still has the usual dangers—jaguars, biting insects, poisonous snakes, falling out of a tree—but it also offers up a million ways to make a meal. For thousands of years, bands of people, now called the Ache, moved about this patch of forest.[24] They have become one of the most intensely studied groups of traditional people. Their history is important not only because they tell us something about life in the forest and about hunting and gathering, but also because they have only very recently moved from being forest hunters and gatherers into more sedentary people living on reservations. One of the most notable teams to study the Ache is Kim Hill and Magdalena Hurtado of the University of New Mexico; Hill has lived with and observed the Ache for the past twenty years, and Hurtado for sixteen years. Together they are trying to understand how the Ache lifestyle change is affecting how the Ache live, how they die, and who they are.

Until recently, the Ache were not particularly interested in what the outside had to offer. They were not interested in the other groups of aboriginal peoples close by, in the Spanish colonists or Jesuit missionaries who came in the seventeenth century, or in the Paraguayan settlers who moved into their forest rather recently. They were, by all accounts, isolated "savages" who chose to keep to themselves. Accounts portrayed them as running naked through the woods, moving camp every few days, living in small groups, and fiercely rejecting any intervention from outsiders. They did not visit or trade with other groups, and they married only other Ache. In the early 1960s, however, some populations of Ache began to settle down on a private ranch. Harassment by Paraguayan colonists had made the traditional forest life a living hell—their land was stolen and their lives were in danger. As a reservation was established at the ranch, more Ache moved in, and that move proved fatal. Within a five-year period, half of the two bands died from contracting respiratory infections. Nonetheless, the reservation was moved to the north of Paraguay during the late 1960s and repeated attempts were made to "bring in" or pacify a large group called the "Northern Ache." By 1978, when anthropologist Kim Hill began his studies, there were still two uncontacted bands of about 35 people each, but most of the Northern Ache had settled on the reservation and were practicing a combination of a horticulture and forest-trekking life. Despite the epidemics that had killed a large portion of the population, the Ache themselves chose, finally, not to rely solely on the forest. But this is not to suggest that they have changed their Ache ways completely.

The Ache are of particular interest to anthropologists because they represent a certain kind of hunting and gathering, a particular social system. Before settling down, their patterns of movement, their ways of finding food, and their interactions with each other offered additional clues to understanding how early humans might have lived long ago. The Ache are also interesting in their own right, not just as evolutionary hominid models but because the way they survived in a forest habitat (and how they have recently adapted to a reservation) adds to our understanding of the endless number of ways people find to stay alive and reproduce. In the forest, the Ache lived in small bands of fifteen to seventy individuals. Several bands were loosely connected into what Hill calls a "group." As in other societies of hunters and gatherers, band and group membership were somewhat fluid but based on kinship and friendship. "Almost every adult who had reached the age of forty before contact had spent some time with almost every other adult in the population (about 250 adults total)," claim Hill and Hurtado.[25] People were extremely comfortable with each other, frequently touching, and at ease. As Hill and Hurtado put it, "Among the Ache there were no revolutionaries, no visionaries, and no rebels."[26]

The description of forest life here refers both to the time before settlement and to the current subsistence pattern which combines settled horticulture with long treks into the forest. These treks basically present the same restrictions, opportunities, and dangers that living in the forest presented only a few years ago. For example, daily life in the forest is centered around the quest for food. Men hunt about seven hours a day, catching slow-moving armadillos, fast monkeys, and small mammals. Women gather for about two hours a day; women with small children tend to stay in the camp. Men and women spend most of the day separately but the band comes together in the late afternoon to socialize and to handle domestic chores. Both meat and gathered food are shared, with meat being doled out to each family according to family size. Camps are only temporary social and sleeping places, small cleared areas without structures, and groups move almost every day from resource patch to resource patch; they are essentially forest nomads.

Perhaps the most striking feature of the Ache, to the Western mind, was (and still is even on the reservation) the variation in mating patterns. Sex is not exclusive for either males or females. Girls have sex before they reach menarche; women have sex with any number of partners during a pregnancy; and any Ache mother can name at least two males who might be the biological father. Most couples are married monogamously, but polygyny and polyandry are accepted as well. Other men and women are married and divorced several times, a pattern called "serial monogamy" by behavioral ecologists. Although the Ache are ostensibly matrilocal— that is, married couples sleep near the bride's family—the couple might end up anywhere. Hill and colleagues found that all first marriages ended in divorce and were of rather short duration, and that this first marriage was followed by a series of marriages. As a result, women typically have children fathered by different men. "Paternity is essentially probabilistic to the Ache and they treat it as such," says Hill.[27] Since contact and settling on the reservation, the rate of marriage change has decreased, probably under the influence of missionaries.

Women used to give birth publicly, that is, at the edge of camp while everyone looked on. Babies are born with a full head of hair and so those without hair, as well as those with clear disability and breech births, were buried. The child is immediately held by a specially designated *tapare* or godmother who looks after the child for the first few days and maintains a special relationship with the child throughout life. Males are also godparents; a designated male cuts the umbilical cord, signaling his special relationship with the child. Ache children do not lack for fathers. Besides the man who conceived the child—a man who might or might not be the mother's husband—men who had sex with the mother during the previous year become secondary fathers as well. Ache recognize the connection between sex and conception but also believe that other males contribute to the growth of the child's "essence" when they bring a woman meat; these males have a responsibility for the child as well. Add genetic kin to this network of godparents and secondary fathers, and any Ache child is enclosed in an envelope of attachments, guardians, and social connections. This network of connections provides support, but it also requires sharing of resources and thus eliminates the possibility of economic stratification in Ache society.

Parenthood, especially motherhood, requires an intense investment. Ache women have an average of eight live births, much more than the San or other South American Indian groups. For the first year of life, mothers sleep sitting up with their infants in their laps, hunched over to protect the baby from danger. Infants are also carried in a sling on the back, and suckle at will. Anthropologists found that during the first year, infants spend 93 percent of their daylight time and 100 percent of the night time in contact with their mothers.[28] Even toddlers over one year of age spend 40 percent of daylight time being held by their mothers, sitting on their laps or standing right next to them. Not until three years of age do children spend much time away from their mothers, and even then they are still no more than a few meters away and are constantly monitored. Hill recorded interviews with adults who told him about tying their children by a leash to a tree to keep them from harm.

Ache mothers with small children spend significantly less time foraging the forest, and have to rely on sharing by other females, and meat brought in by males. Although Ache children grow quickly at first, they are undersized due to malnutrition. Breast-feeding continues until the next sibling is conceived, usually two years later. Mothers supplement their diet with armadillo fat and insect larvae. Still, breast milk and supplemental foods do not meet the needs of growing forest children. Although Ache children do not differ from their American peers in personal and social skills, they are significantly further behind in some gross motor skills. For example, they walk nine months later than American children and more than one year later than San children.[29] Ache children also acquire linguistic skills later, but they are better at food awareness. Researchers suggest that the dangerous environment of the forest, where just about anything can happen, compels parents to discourage physical exploration. Even today, when so much time is spent living on the less hazardous reservation, forest treks expose babies to the same risks as before settlement. On the reservation, parents continue to pull babies back from attempts at exploration; and babies echo this pattern, exploring with hesitation and easily jumping back into their mothers' laps.[30]

Babies ride in slings until eighteen months, when they are taught to ride on the top of carried baskets, ducking and weaving as the overhanging forest canopy threatens a knock on the head. Older children and toddlers are carried piggyback by fathers and other relatives. But by five years old, Ache kids are faced with a major crisis second only to weaning—walking through the forest on their own two feet. As Hill describes it, "Children scream, cry, hit their parents, and try everything they can think of to get adults to continue carrying them. Often, they simply sit and refuse to walk, prompting older band members to leave them behind. This tactic leads to a dangerous game of 'chicken' in which parents and children both hope the other will give in before the child is too far behind and may become lost."[31] And so parents must force the physical independence that is required for a life in which the group is always on the move.

By three years old, Ache children begin their lessons in botany. They gather with the women foraging for fruit and insect larvae and pick up small animals. By eight years of age they can easily read the signs of a trail and can navigate between neighboring camps on their own. By ten years of age, boys carry their own bows and girls babysit and do domestic chores. By the age of thirteen girls gather almost a full adult load of forest foods, although boys at this age contribute little to gathering. In a sense, children this age are independent of their parents—still tightly connected to the band, but not as physically or nutritionally dependent. And so they sometimes hang out with other bands and sleep with relatives in other camps for long periods, especially if their biological fathers are gone, or are dead.

The intensity of parental investment in this culture was highlighted by the regular practice of child homicide, a practice that has ended with reservation life. But in the past, when an adult died, at least one child was thrown into the grave, alive, to accompany that adult to the afterlife. These children were typically orphans or those without relatives at the graveside to save them. Other cultures practice infanticide on deformed babies, twins, and unwanted girls; but the Ache even killed older children, those who had few protectors in the group to save them. Along the same lines, old people or sick people were often left behind during forest treks, or were killed or buried alive—a practice that makes economic sense for a culture always on the move.

Life on the reservation is now perceived as "easier" by the Ache; they also comment that the forest diet is better and life in the forest is less stressful.[32] But the dangers of the forest are many, not to mention the encroachment by Paraguayan colonists, and so staying in one area clear of these dangers, where food can be cultivated or bought, makes for an easier life. The Ache remain the poorest people in Paraguay, if material goods and income are the standard of accounting. Also, vulnerability to infection has shifted the danger from the forest to the risks of civilization; there may be lower mortality for adults, and lifespans may have lengthened somewhat, but children still die at a high rate from diarrhea and the settled population is at high risk for respiratory infections and communicable diseases. On the reservation, the Ache have built permanent houses with funds gained by selling off some of the forest timber to which they now have legal rights, and they have planted crops such as cotton for cash and maize for eating. These homesteads are separated from each other, and so the old idea of a communal temporary camp is gone. Also less in evidence is the sharing of food, a sign of the declining importance of social interdependence.

Nowadays, the Ache hang out near their fields when the crops need daily care, and take off into the surrounding forests on treks when they have time off from horticultural labor. This is not a life of luxury. The effect of the settled life on children is that children spend less time with their mothers. More significant, they are weaned earlier and thus their mothers ovulate sooner, decreasing the already short interbirth interval. As yet, no one knows what the impact of a settled life will be on how Ache parents treat their children. Before, the forest and the need to be on the move created a parenting style that began with years of close monitoring, followed by a push to physical independence. The Ache infancy model was a "folk pediatric model," with the greatest investment oriented toward keeping the child from danger. Once the danger point had passed, children were encouraged to stay close but make it on their own. By definition, the reservation life calls for a new parental script. Mothers are off in the gardens and children are at less risk, except for infectious diseases. Ultimately the most important change may be the move toward early weaning, which will increase population size and place a burden on older children to help out. Like the San, these children are sure to find life in the future not filled with play around the campsite, but work in the fields or at home. More than likely, mothers will also have to curtail their close proximity to their infants for the simple reason that they cannot physically carry more than one infant at a time. With westernization, then, comes different parental scripts that have nothing to do with the dangers of the forest and the need to walk alone.

The Gusii of East Africa

Most people expect Africa to look like either the dense jungle of Tarzan movies or the endless open plains seen so often in animal documentaries. What they don't expect is the topography of the Scottish Highlands. And yet there it is on the western edge of Kenya, a high rolling plain that sends fingers of greenery down to the savanna below. This is an incredibly fertile place—the land is rich, rainfall is plentiful most years, and crops grow on a yearly cycle. The Gusii, a reasonably self-sufficient group of Bantu-speaking people, have lived here for thousands of years, tending cattle and growing crops. Each Gusii holds allegiance to one of seven Gusii tribes; these tribes remain relatively cohesive and separate, until outside forces at times require that they band together against a common enemy. Within each tribe, there are patrilineal clans that trace descent through males. These clans acknowledge a common ancestor and a spiritual totem animal. This network of clans and tribes and their various permutations are an anthropologist's dream—just about every social interaction can be charted by the rules that govern the social fabric. For example, there are rules of exogamous marriage whereby a man of one clan must marry outside his own clan and into certain others. Economic interactions over cattle and land are governed by who is who and where they belong. The Gusii live on kin-based plots of land where extended families, a man with several wives and their children, tend gardens and herd cattle. There is no "village life," no town. Instead, a map of the individual homestead showing a man's house and the houses of his wives and their children echoes what is important in Gusii life— family, kin, clan, and tribe. As anthropologist Robert LeVine points out, this kind of residential cluster, based on kinship, is confusing only to the Western mind, which sees residence as an outgrowth of socioeconomic status rather than social affiliation.

Colonial British rule arrived in 1907 and initiated a new social order that imposed a centralized government. The state edict translated into a few administrative centers where people came to do business, but did not in fact disassemble the traditional way of a homestead based on family affiliation. The greatest change for the Gusii has come more recently with a shift in the economic base. With a rapid increase in population size, and a concurrent decrease in available land for crops and new homesteads, men and boys now either leave the home plot to work on large plantations or move to large cities and seek nonagricultural employment. Women are now solely responsible for growing vegetables and caring for sheep, and they are left home alone for long periods, as the sole parents. Women and children have also taken over care of cattle, an occupation that was once the province of men. Because the workload falls so heavily on those at home, the Gusii have become less cattle-oriented and more inclined to focus on crops. Crops are no longer grown just for homestead use, but are now often exported to markets across Kenya and have become a source of cash. And yet cattle are still bargaining chips and retain their status as objects of value. Cattle are inherited, sold, used to pay for wives, and stolen. They may be tended and milked by women and children these days, but the business of cattle is still a male activity.

In the early 1950s Robert and Sarah LeVine chose Gusiiland for their study of child development.[33] They were part of the Six Cultures project developed by Beatrice and John Whiting (see Chapter Two) and so the LeVines initially went to Gusiiland to gather comparative data on parents and children. Forty years later, the LeVines and their colleagues are still involved in studying the Gusii. In the 1970s they returned to expand their original study from one community to six. They were also interested in how the culture had changed under Western influence. This work represents one of the most intense research projects on a cultural group—and one of the longest-lasting. It is also one of the most informative about how parental goals are molded by a society, and how those goals change through time.

All adult Gusii want children; for both men and women, having children is an essential part of life. For a Gusii, childlessness is considered a supernatural punishment, a product of bad behavior and witch-craft. Women expect to give birth every two years, which results in a birthrate much higher than in other places in Africa.[34] Boys are in high demand because they will remain in the homestead as adults, caring for their aging mothers and perhaps expanding the homestead land. Girls are in demand because they are exchanged for cattle when they marry, thus bringing honor and prestige to the homestead. Gusii children grow up in a polygynous household but are attached to one biological mother, sur-rounded by both full and half siblings. Children are an integral part of the economic and social functioning of the extended homestead because they tend cattle and sheep, care for siblings, and do chores.

The primary parental goal of Gusii parents is infant survival. And for good reason—only 50 percent of children born alive reach maturity. The Gusii maintain that since infants are lighter-skinned than adults, they are especially prone to the "evil eye," vulnerable to witchcraft and bad spir-its. Babies are considered weak and vulnerable, unused to a cold climate, unable to fight off outside forces, and in need of special protection. For the Gusii, then, parenting until weaning should first and foremost ensure that babies are kept from harm, protected, out of danger. This goal then translates into intensive and highly responsive child care that includes constant carrying, feeding on demand, immediate response to distress, and sleeping with an infant.

During the day a Gusii baby is always carried, either by its mother, an older sibling, or a "child nurse" who is usually a young female relative. When a baby frets, the mother immediately soothes it, most often by feeding it. The object of the feeding and soothing is to quiet the baby, not stimulate it; there is no petting or fondling by the mother, just a breast produced for suckling. Nursing is considered the best way to quiet the baby and make it content, and mothers mechanically offer the breast whenever the baby is upset; there is no battle over feeding schedules or the amount of milk the baby consumes because the goal is to use nursing as a way to keep the baby content. As a result, Gusii babies at three months old cry half as much as babies of the same age in industrialized countries. Babies are rubbed with butter and kept clean of debris normally picked up during the day. According to the Gusii way of thinking, these bits and pieces picked up off the ground might easily soak into a child's delicate skin and cause harm. Infants rarely touch the ground until weaning, when the most dangerous time has passed.

Gusii babies are never left alone and Gusii mothers cannot imagine leaving a baby in a room by itself, or leaving it alone to cry. The first year is a time when all the baby's needs are met, but without infant training per se. The child nurse or *omoreri* teaches the infant to climb up on her back, and the child is carried around all day. Often the nurse is within a short distance of the mother working in the field and will hand the baby over for a feeding when it frets. If the mother is away, the child nurse will feed the baby a gruel made of meal.

Although the atmosphere is one of constant care, there is little demonstrative affection between parent and child as it is defined in Western culture. Mothers do not kiss and cuddle their babies and in fact appear comparatively aloof. Most striking to Western eyes is the fact that Gusii mothers do not interact verbally with their infants—they soothe and nurse, but consider conversation with infants a waste of time. A Gusii baby's world is one of constant tactile and visual sensation; verbally, Gusii babies learn by watching and listening to others rather than being encouraged to respond to verbal cues or engage in verbal exchanges. The one bit of training Gusii mothers and child nurses do undertake is to instill early on that some things in life deserve to be feared; such fear is considered a virtue.

A secondary goal of Gusii mothers and fathers, after basic infant survival, is to rear a compliant, obedient child who will easily fit into the extended family and be a productive member of the homestead. Once weaned—a process that is assisted by painting the breast with bitter herbs, ignoring the pleas of a hungry child, or even slapping it when it reaches for the breast—the child is expected to contribute to the household. Children are considered low-status family members, who must watch others and learn to imitate them; there is no concerted effort to teach children anything. Because they are expected to pick up on how things are done by observing other members of the household, infants and children are present at all family events but they are never the center of attention. The Gusii believe that to praise a child for the accomplishment of tasks is to encourage disobedience and selfishness. Not all children faithfully follow the rules and the Gusii discourage their disobedience by scaring them with tales of ghosts and witches. Other children are given a slap or a lash with a cane to encourage them to become obedient members of the group. In other words, a good child is an obedient child.

The Gusii parental script is one of intense protection and physical care during the first two years of a child's life, and a molding for obedience during early childhood. These goals, say the LeVines, have been adaptive to Gusii socioeconomics, or at least Gusii ways, until very recently. A fear of harm, disease, death, and the "evil eye" is a reasonable pressure that has molded the Gusii mothering style for generations. Mothers are only responding to the reality of bringing up an infant under vulnerable conditions; their model of infant care is "pediatric," in LeVine's words, because it focuses on infant health and survival. At the same time, these concerned mothers must return to their gardens as soon as possible, and so they must somehow navigate between the pressure to invest heavily in babies who are at risk in a vulnerable environment, and the pressure to get back to work. Use of child nurses and weaning at two years is the Gusii compromise. The mother–infant interaction pattern of little verbalization also helps the child make the transition away from the mother to the extended family. But early weaning also means women without natural birth control are apt to be pregnant again rather quickly. And with improved hygiene and medical care over recent decades, and the decrease in infant mortality, the population growth in Gusiiland is understandable. A reproductive pattern that was adaptive under harsher conditions now results in larger and larger family sizes, smaller plots available for crops, and even more pressure on mothers and fathers to fill hungry mouths.

The second goal of Gusii parents, to encourage a child to be obedient and fit quietly into the homestead, also makes social and economic sense. Each homestead is an economic unit; extended families grow crops, herd animals, and bring in wages with outside work. This system is family based, whereby individual members are part of a larger whole rather than responsible for their own subsistence. Children in this system are economic assets, assets that cost little or nothing to raise. Even at a very young age they can care for other children, and they are soon part of the subsistence machine of the homestead as they help in the fields or tend livestock. Childhood for the Gusii is not considered a carefree time as it is in industrialized nations, but a time of responsibility and learning.

In recent years this family social system, with children as integral members in domestic production, has been altered by the state. Children now go to school and they are not available as often for helping with younger kids, herding animals, or helping in the fields. As a result, various far-reaching changes in Gusii socioeconomics have taken place, underscored by the changing role of children in society. Very soon, one might expect, the style of parenting will follow suit. Researchers might hypothesize that as the values of the society change, parenting styles will reflect those changes. Perhaps mothers will take up the verbally interactive style of the West to encourage competition in school. Perhaps independence, rather than interdependence, will be encouraged. Like all societies, the Gusii are constantly changing, and it seems likely that parental styles and the very heart of childhood will soon reflect a move away from an integrated homestead and tightly knit bonds toward a more Western pattern of independence and individual achievement.

"INDUSTRIALIZED" SOCIETIES

Japan

The Japanese—as a people, a culture, and an economic entity—are endlessly fascinating to Western industrialized societies. Superficially, much about Japan is like the West: Japan is a first-world country, highly industrialized, and in global terms economically successful. And yet Japan does not quite fit the model of a first-world country—the Japanese have achieved modern economic success not with a philosophy of personal ambition and individual achievement, but with a sense of collectivity.[35] As a result, the Japanese command respect for their achievements but are viewed with suspicion by the West, because they have achieved modernity and economic success in another way. A broader picture of "industrialized" societies must include the Japanese way, as well as the Western way. A look at Japanese parenting demonstrates that children in Japan, too, are subject to different cultural and ideological values even though they boast a similar economic base and share much of the same popular culture.

Anthropologist Robert Smith, who has studied Japanese culture for decades, believes that Japan is different from the United States because the Japanese think about people and society, and the relationship between the two, quite differently than do Americans.[36] Among the agricultural, artisan, and commercial sectors in Japan, the household is considered a unit of production and consumption, and all members are involved in, and responsible for, the productive life of the unit. Although notions of family have been changing in recent years toward the conjugal unit as the focus of family, the productive model still holds true in Japan. More important, any unit—be it a family or a work group—is seen as part of a collective. In a sense the Japanese attitude toward "collectivity," rather than "individuality," simply applies the values of a small hunting-and-gathering group to a national level. And the collective attitude about a work group, be it farm or large corporation, is echoed in family life as well. Instead of favoring individual ambition and personal success, the Japanese expect individuals to do what is best for the group; group success in the end is seen as what is best for each individual. As Smith points out, it is not that individual Japanese have no sense of self or personal ambition. It is just that these individual values have been incorporated into a larger sense of a social self that is connected to others. People are seen as social creatures, and it is assumed that each individual is happiest and most successful within the social realm. And so individual freedom and personal success are less emphasized than working together to achieve success for the group; the expression of "self" has a lower priority in Japan. "So far, at least," writes Smith, "the Japanese have elected to forego the assertion of the right to the expression of untrammeled personal freedom in the interest of the maintenance of public order and the service of the common good."[37] In other words, "collectivity" is a choice the culture has made, and the Japanese have clearly demonstrated that this path to economic and social success works well.

What is most surprising about Japanese parenting is that parents share a collective attitude about how babies behave and how they should be treated.[38] In America, beyond the broad need for independence (see next section), every parent seems to have a personal take on children and parenting and every generation purports to have a new way to parent (see Chapter Six on the fashion of breast-feeding over time). American parents also view their babies in different ways. In Japan, however, the relationship between mother and child is viewed the same way by all—a baby is pure spirit, essentially good by design, and in need of being incorporated into the maternal self. Japanese babies and older children sleep between their parents to symbolize their position as a river between two banks, a being that is intimately connected to each parent as a river is to its riverbed.[39] This consensus view of parent–infant symbiosis has been around for hundreds of years in Japan. Both two-hundred-year-old baby care manuals and today's government pamphlets state that mothers should be responsive and gentle, and communicate frequently with their babies, to entwine the infant to its mother and bring the baby into the family fold. Japanese mothers are not interested in making sure their babies become independent, but rather in making sure they become part of the mother, a connected social being; she sees the baby as an extension of herself and wants to foster and intensify the connection.

Scholars trace this attitude to beliefs in vogue more than a thousand years ago, when babies were considered more godlike than mortal, and adults felt that by pleasing babies they would please the gods.[40] And from this grew a parenting style that is indulgent, one that caters to the baby's wishes and whims. Although the Japanese do not think the same about everything, this attitude toward infants is a strongly accepted consensus view, one that has been strengthened by generations of geographic and political isolation. And today, the strategy to integrate rather than individuate fits nicely with Japan's social values for collectivity. To a large degree, this consensus attitude that fosters mother–baby interdependence may cultivate, at the most basic level, Japanese homogeneity.[41]

The contrast with Western parenting is clear, and irresistible to child development researchers. If parenting is inextricably connected to how people turn out as adults, the difference between Western and Japanese cultures—so similar in their economics and modernity but so different in their ideology—should have roots in different parenting styles. Since the 1960s, Western scientists have drifted east to collect data on Japanese parenting in order to contrast it to Western parenting. In the 1960s, child development researchers William Caudill and Helen Weinstein went to Japan to collect data to contrast with the United States. They expected mothers in the two cultures to treat their children differently, and as a result they expected babies to behave differently because of these dissimilar mothering styles.[42] Since Japanese mothers seemed to be interested in integration of children into the larger social fabric of life, they expected Japanese mothers to spend more time with their infants to develop a mutually dependent, symbiotic relationship. They also knew that the Japanese distrust verbal skills,[43] and that Japanese social interaction relies on individuals anticipating the feelings of others. And so they expected Japanese mothers to emphasize physical contact over verbal interaction as a way to focus on the nonverbal. Essentially, they assumed that the Japanese mother would foster a more passive and contented baby, as opposed to a more stimulated, verbal American baby.

Using a sample of thirty Japanese and thirty American babies and their mothers, all from urban middle-class households, Caudill and Weinstein studied the children at three to four months of age, two and one-half years of age, and again at six years of age. They discovered that all the mothers dealt with the biological needs of their children the same way; they fed them and diapered them at the same rate. There was, surprisingly, no difference in the amount of time the mothers talked or played with their kids. But the quality of the interaction differed. Japanese mothers were more soothing in their talk and spent more time in bodily contact. As a result, Japanese babies were generally more subdued.

This research has been repeated several times since, and some of the original findings hold true while others paint a more complex picture. In a study comparing Japanese, French, and American mothers, Japanese and American mothers fared equally on rates of social interaction; Japanese babies were at least as active if not more active than their American peers.[44] In another study, mothers in both cultures kissed, looked at, and chatted with their babies at the same rate, although American mothers actually held their babies more than Japanese mothers, which might say more about changing styles in maternal behavior in America than anything about cultural differences.[45] Still, American mothers were more often engaged in stimulating their babies with play, exaggerated facial expressions, and fussing with them.[46] Other studies have documented subtle differences in what is important to mothers in the contrasting cultures. Japanese mothers, for example, expect early mastery of group skills such as self-control and courtesy, whereas American mothers expect their children to master verbal assertiveness and social skills, such as sharing with others, early.[47] More striking to Western parents, Japanese mothers see infant and child dependency as an indicator of a good and healthy bond between mother and baby that fosters emotional security, rather than something pathological that has to be "dealt with," ended, severed.[48]

Japanese parents seem different from parents in Western cultures because they are different. Parenting attitudes echo other attitudes in Japanese society. Instead of an "individualist" society, Japan—for historical, cultural, and political reasons—emphasizes the collective in society. Parents underscore and emphasize that approach as mothers bond with their babies both physically and emotionally, integrating babies into society as a whole. And still the country manages to be highly successful. We cannot assume that in a capitalist nation, children and adults must be out for themselves. As the Japanese have shown, orientation toward the group, rather than the individual, can lead to an economically modern nation.

The United States

The point of cultural anthropology or ethnology has always been to explain foreign cultures to the West—that is, to North Americans and Western Europeans. Only recently have Western anthropologists turned their gaze to their own countries. There are two reasons for this. "Traditional" societies are disappearing, and so there are fewer exotic societies to document. Also, most Western cultures are in reality a patchwork of cultures; within each modern society there are endless subpopulations for cross-cultural study. But not too long ago, few studies of modern industrial Western societies and cultures existed—it was assumed that the West was the standard to which all others were compared.[49] And yet, looking at one's own society is one of the more fascinating learning experiences. Anthropologists and child development researchers often initially try to explain the "other," often ending up revealing the "self" as well.

In picking a culture to represent "the West," I could have chosen Canada, France, Italy, the United Kingdom, or any other familiar culture. I chose the United States because most often the comparative work in child development and ethnopediatrics uses some segment of American parents for comparison. Therefore, there is more material on parenting in the United States than in any other Western industrialized nation. I also hope this is a rather objective view of general parenting practices in the United States, or at least one segment of the United States. It would be foolish to say I could write about all Americans, because by definition we are a multicultural society. The point here is to present the consensus view that guides much of what parents experience in this society; no matter what, all American parents experience the same reflection on how things "ought to be" through pediatricians, health care workers, baby books, and friends. And so while the descriptions that follow are certainly prejudiced, they are also the standard by which American parents tend to be judged these days; so far, there is little evidence that other ways to parent are fully accepted in American culture. As the population changes, as the various parenting techniques of subcultures are absorbed into the American mainstream, this standard will change; but I am guessing that all parents in America—even the most recent immigrants to American shores—will recognize in these descriptions the context in which they now raise their children.

The chief, overriding parental goal of American culture, whether stated overtly or not, is independence. In every study in which American parents were compared to other cultures, even other industrialized nations, American parents expressed over and over again the need to make a child independent and self-reliant.[50] This goal matches neatly with the economic, social, political, and geographical structure of American society. For example, one way for a capitalist economy to work is to stress individual achievement and personal success. These are usually measured by income, economic status, and the accumulation of material goods. Such measures of success are gained, in this culture, by singular rather than collective effort. Socially and politically, American culture honors those who achieve on their own, as if this were the most natural and normal—in fact the only—way to proceed through life. And geographically, Americans have continually encouraged private ownership and private lives. The independent self-reliant individual is one of the strongest ideological threads running through American culture and history. It also colors everything that American parents do to socialize their children, from how parents talk to children, how they treat them, and what they expect of them.[51]

The American family is a conjugal unit, not an extended network of kin, and parental privacy is an important element of family life. Parents generally feel solely responsible for how their children turn out, and kinship beyond the nuclear family does not particularly influence family life.[52] Attitudes about becoming a parent reflect the structure of American society. Because they have few responsibilities and don't add to household production, children are seen as a cost rather than an asset. Childhood is considered a time for learning, when children are trained by parents and educators to gain skills that will eventually allow them as adults to achieve on their own. Children are not expected to work, but rather to learn. Parents see themselves as teachers rather than protectors, and parental investment in terms of resources and time is expected to increase over time.[53] This investment pays off when children eventually leave home as young adults and start their own independent households. As such, American children are not seen as resources but as burdens and responsibilities that require heavy investment until such time as they are independent.[54]

Most American parents believe in an inborn temperament, a set of personality traits that can be molded somewhat by parenting and society. As ethnographers John and Ann Fisher discovered in their study of white middle-class parents in a New England town in the 1960s, parents in this culture think of babies as bundles of potential; they believe the job of a good parent is to uncover that set of latent abilities and talents and then encourage the "good" potential while discouraging the "bad" potential.[55] "The parent, ideally, acts as a kind of pleased observer who watches the child unfold," write the Fishers. Confirmation of this take on parenting can be heard in most parental conversations in America: What is the baby good at and how can we, as parents, foster that "talent"? The idea that each child has a special set of potentials concurs with the ideology of individuality—each child is unique and therefore independent, different, not part of a crowd, and will therefore be a success based on his or her unique set of talents. And so for American adults, having children is just like any job; it is a responsibility and a task that needs to be worked at, and one which can ultimately be judged a success or a failure.

During the earliest months of a baby's life, American parents are mostly concerned with daily maintenance of the child, including feeding, clothing, and keeping it clean. Parents are also concerned with developmental stages, and use the child's developing cognitive and motor skills to mark these stages. All parents are expected to know "norms" for these stages and to measure their infants against the average. By and large, American parents gain information about norms from their pediatricians, usually white middle-class male doctors—although this is changing—with little advanced training in child development.[56] After pediatricians, American parents turn for advice to child-care books, then friends, and only occasionally to family.

Physical contact with infants is comparatively minimum; mothers rarely carry babies. Gusii African babies, for example, are in physical contact with someone at least twice as much as white middle-class American babies.[57] Instead, infants are usually placed upright in hard plastic seats or laid down on their backs. The supine position, parents believe, gives the baby room to wiggle and move its arms and legs and explore its body. Only half of American babies are breast-fed, and when they are, breast-feeding on average lasts only about five months. Most breast-feeding and bottle-feeding is done on a schedule, usually about every two hours or less, and mothers are encouraged by pediatricians to regulate this schedule. Babies are expected to cry a lot, and parents feel it unnecessary to respond to all crying bouts. Control over the baby is a major issue for most parents; responses to both crying and feeding are guided by a hope of controlling the baby's behavior and a fear of spoiling or indulging what are seen as the baby's manipulative ways. Socialization is not a primary concern, and American babies tend to spend most of their time alone, sleeping solitary in a crib or sitting in a playpen or plastic seat. Many parents feel that social time is stressful and that infants need time alone to recover.[58] Very quickly, babies learn that social interaction is spaced between times of solitude.

Sleep is also a major concern of American parents.[59] How long and how hard babies sleep is used to determine developmental maturity by both parents and pediatricians. And babies are judged as "good" when they sleep through the night (see the next chapter). Other cultures, in contrast, have fewer concerns with sleep, but focus on different issues such as food or motor skills.[60] Once their babies are off the bottle, American parents think they should eat what and when they want, and as a result of unscheduled feeding and rigid sleeping schedules, babies are generally removed from the family social context; babies have different mealtimes and different bedtimes than other family members.[61]

Compared to parents in other cultures, American parents are extreme in their emphasis on verbal stimulation.[62] American parents talk to their babies both in "baby talk" and adult speech, and the mode of talking is mostly questions. They respond to 20 percent of any vocalization the baby makes (as compared to Gusii mothers, for example, who respond to only 5 percent).[63] They use a high-pitched voice and gyrating facial expression to get and hold a baby's attention; American parents believe that such stimulation will encourage learning and cognition.[64] Mothers tease, encourage, and stimulate the baby with words because they know such verbal and facial expressiveness is not only acceptable for adults in the culture, but a desirable communicative skill. Parents, especially mothers, see their primary role as one of teacher, the person responsible for making her child ready for later schooling and a life of personal achievement.

These white middle-class parental values are not necessarily shared by the myriad subgroups that make up American society. But these values are the ones that are imposed as the standard. In fact, child development researcher and anthropologist Edward Tronick spends much of his time at Children's Hospital in Boston, Massachusetts, enlightening pediatric residents on the fact that their parenting values are not the only ones available. The Hispanic mother, for example, may feel very comfortable leaving her baby with a ten-year-old sister in a safe environment, and it is not up to the doctor to judge these values, only to assess the health of the baby and make sure the environment is safe.[63]

Every culture has its ideal smart, well-functioning child. This ideal grows from historical, social, and political roots, and it is so ingrained in the culture that few question its validity. In America, that ideal is a highly verbal, independent, emotionally controlled, and self-reliant child. Social skills are seen as just that—skills to help one get along and be successful in an individualistic society.

A LESSON IN VARIETY

All mothers and fathers are evolutionarily designed to attend to infant signals, but they respond in all sorts of ways, ways that are culturally and personally molded.[66] Parents adjust these scripts, that is, adapt them, when the social and economic environment changes; and parental styles evolve when different risks are perceived. As Robert LeVine has so cogently pointed out, parents of a community redefine "custom" as these styles change through time. Everyone defers to religion, ethnicity, or common sense as an explanation of why parents do as they do. In fact, economics—that is, shifting subsistence patterns—may have more to do with parenting than most groups realize.[67] Think about the growth of single-parent households in the West. Even twenty years ago, single women were frowned upon as parents, and this made economic and social sense. But as women have gone into the workplace and have earned their own money, as they have gained economic independence, the subsistence base of the society has changed. Single parenthood, then, reflects a change in the socioeconomic subsistence base of adult individuals (both men and women) in this culture. It's not that the values of the society have changed, just that these values can be more easily achieved by one person than was formerly the case.

Parents in different cultures believe they have some influence on the development of their child, but how much influence varies from culture to culture. Some parents think that their job is first and foremost to keep the child alive, and that only later, when the dangers have passed, training can begin. Others believe that much of how a child turns out as an adult is destined from birth. And every parent, every adult member of a society, has an opinion on how kids should be brought up "right." American parents think they must encourage and teach their children from day one. Gusii mothers believe such encouragement produces a spoiled, self-centered adult. Probably both sets of parents are right. Every act by parents, every goal that molds that act, has a foundation in what is appropriate for that particular culture. In this sense, no parenting style is "right" and no style is "wrong." It is appropriate or inappropriate only according to the culture.

CHAPTER FOUR

A
REASONABLE
SLEEP

Two-month-old Jenny Calhoun lies in the crook of her mother's arm. As Jenny twitches in her sleep, ten thin wires taped to her face and bald head wiggle in all directions, giving her a Baby Medusa look. Jenny's mother, Amy Calhoun, opens her sleepy eyes in the dimly lit room, staring blankly into the tiny face only inches away. The matching wires on Amy's head nod toward the baby as she unconsciously reaches out and pats Jenny reassuringly a few times. Amy adjusts the infant's blanket and they both drift back into a deeper level of sleep. Two rooms away, anthropologist James McKenna watches the needles on a twelve-way polygraph jump in tandem as Jenny and Amy move physically, change their sleep levels, and then drift off.[1] The polygraph charts graphically what McKenna sees on the video screen—needles jump in response to electrical output, marking scratchy lines across a roll of paper. And even a novice can see that the lines for mother and baby follow a similar pattern. The pattern of brain wave activity, heart rate, muscle movement, and breathing are similar because the pair is experiencing a mutual arousal, moving together up, across, and then down through various levels of sleep. An elfin grin spreads across McKenna's face—he's seen this pattern often, but it never fails to amuse him to be able to watch nature so clearly play out the mother–infant bond, even in sleep. This work, along with his background in primate behavior, has convinced McKenna that most of our notions about infant sleep are culturally constructed and dangerously at odds with the biological and emotional needs of babies. "If you have a baby," McKenna says whenever he has a chance, "sleep with it."

Back in 1978, Jim McKenna and his wife had a baby, a son named Jeffrey, and Jeff's birth was a major turning point for McKenna in more ways than one. Up until 1978 McKenna was known for his work on Indian langurs monkeys, large gray monkeys famous for their *laissez-faire* mothering style—babies are often grabbed off their mothers by other troopmates soon after birth and passed around like so many dolls. But while McKenna was conversant with the parenting ways of monkeys, he had fewer ideas about how to parent his own son. One problem was sleep; like any newborn, Jeff would fuss and fidget and not go to sleep when he was supposed to. McKenna soon discovered that one way to get Jeff to sleep was to nap with him. "I'd lay down with him and breathe as if I was asleep," recalls McKenna eighteen years later, breathing in and out, pumping his chest up and down in front of me as if his baby Jeff were still bundled on top of him. "I noticed he was so responsive to these breathing cues. And then I wondered why I was so surprised—here was a primate baby, undeveloped at birth, selected to be responsive to parental contact and care." Based on his naps with his baby son, and pushed by an anthropological mind that shoots out in all directions when engaged in scholarly pursuit, McKenna began asking questions about human infant sleep.

Why should Jeff sleep alone if he sleeps better with a parent? Is any human infant evolutionarily designed to sleep alone? How do most babies around the world sleep? And what are the consequences of solitary sleep versus co-sleeping? This work has become a cornerstone of ethnopediatrics, combining cultural history, ethnography, and biological measures. And it is set to radically change the way many people bring up their children.

SLEEP ACROSS CULTURES

People spend a third of their lives asleep. And we do not sleep in random ways. How we sleep, with whom we sleep, and where we sleep is molded both by culture and custom, traditions handed down through generations. For most of human history, babies and children slept with their mothers, or perhaps with both parents. Our distant ancestors lived in small bands which subsisted by hunting and gathering, and it is safe to assume that these bands did not have separate sleeping quarters for parents and children in their temporary shelters. It wasn't until two hundred years ago that a few cultures began to construct dwellings with more than one room, and even today, such sleeping privacy is rare except in more affluent societies.[2] The majority of people today around the world still live in one-room shelters where all activities, be they conducted awake or asleep, take place.[3]

Anthropologist John Whiting found a simple association between climate and parent–child co-sleeping (among other behaviors).[4] Evaluating 136 societies for which he had information, Whiting outlined four kinds of typical sleeping arrangements for a household: mother and father in the same bed with baby in another bed; mother and baby together and father somewhere else; all members of the family in separate beds; and all members of the family together in one bed. The most prominent pattern across cultures, Whiting discovered, was mother with child and father in another place (50 percent of the 136 cultures). In another 16 percent, the baby slept with both mother and father. Many of these cultures, he wrote, were polygynous, so that fathers were moving among households and beds, and the stable unit was actually each mother with her children. Whiting also found a connection to cold weather. Men and women, that is, couples, routinely sleep together in places where the winter temperature falls below 50 degrees—presumably for warmth more than any other reason—but they often have separate sleeping arrangements where the climate is warmer. The sleeping place of babies, on the other hand, usually conforms to a different climatic situation—they "usually" stay with mother in areas with warm climates, but in colder climates, they are swaddled in blankets and strapped to cradleboards to minimize heat loss. These cultures, however, represent a small minority of the human population.

Where Babies Sleep

In almost all cultures around the globe today, babies sleep with an adult and children sleep with parents or other siblings. It is only in industrialized Western societies such as North America and some countries in Europe that sleep has become a private affair; the comparison of the latter pattern with that of other groups highlights one of the major ways in which the West stands out from the rest of humanity in the treatment of children. In one study of 186 nonindustrial societies, children sleep in the same bed as their parents in 46 percent of the nonindustrial cultures, and in a separate bed but in the same room in an additional 21 percent. In other words, in 67 percent of the cultures around the world, children sleep in the company of others.[5] More significant, in none of those 186 cultures do babies sleep in a separate place before they are at least one year old. In another survey of 172 societies, all infants in all cultures do some co-sleeping at night, even if only for a few hours.[6] The United States consistently stands out as the *only* society in which babies are routinely placed in their own beds and in their own rooms; in one survey of a hundred societies, only parents in the United States maintained separate quarters for their babies, and in another study of twelve societies, all parents but Americans slept with their babies until weaning.[7]

Babies in various cultures sleep in a variety of containers and on a wide array of surfaces—on a mat or soft blanket on the floor, in a hammock made of skin or fiber, on a mattress of split bamboo; or tucked into a hanging basket.[8] In most cases, the place babies sleep is consistent with—that is, no more special than—where parents sleep.

Anthropologist Gilda Morelli compared the sleeping arrangements and nighttime habits of parents in the United States with a group of Mayan Indians in Guatemala. The Mayan babies slept with their mothers in all cases for the first and sometimes the second year. In more than half the cases, the father was there as well, or he was sleeping with older children in another bed. Mayan mothers made no special note of feeding at night because they simply turned and made a breast available when the baby cried with hunger, probably while the mothers were still fast asleep. For the comparative U.S. group, three babies were placed in a separate room to sleep from the time they were born, and none of the eighteen subjects slept in the parents' bed on a regular basis. By three months of age, 58 percent of the babies were already sleeping in another room; and by six months of age, all but three had been moved out to a separate room. Not surprisingly, seventeen of the eighteen American parents reported having to stay awake for nighttime feedings.

Differences in attitude toward sleep in general were equally clear between the two cultures. American parents used lullabies, stories, special clothing, bathing, and toys to ritualize the sleep experience, whereas Mayan parents simply let the baby fall asleep when they did, with no folderol. When the researcher explained to the Mayan mothers how babies were put to bed in the United States, the Mayan mothers were shocked and highly disapproving, and expressed pity for the American babies who had to sleep alone. They saw their own sleep arrangements as part of a larger commitment to their children, a commitment in which practical consideration plays no part.[9] It did not matter to them if there was no privacy, or if the baby squirmed at night—closeness at night between mother and baby was seen as part of what all parents do for their children.

Conversely, the American parents who slept with their babies on a regular basis said they did so for "pragmatic" reasons (presumably for breast-feeding and comforting a fretful baby), although they acknowledged that co-sleeping seemed to foster attachment. But unlike the Mayans, they thought a close association strengthened by co-sleeping was worrisome and somehow emotionally or psychologically unhealthy.

They moved their babies out of the parental room as soon as possible, usually by six months; and they expressed the need to guide the child down a path of independence, as well as a desire for their own privacy. They also felt such separation would be less traumatic if done early rather than later. As one mother put it, "I am a human being, and I deserve some time and privacy to myself."[10] Many mothers have also been advised by pediatricians or child-care experts that sleeping alone in a bassinet or crib is more safe for the baby, and so they follow this advice assuming they are doing the right thing.

Differences in attitude among cultures can be clearly seen in work on immigrants from one culture to another; infant sleep patterns, it turns out, are one of the last traditions to change under pressure from the adopted country. In England, Asian parents—that is, people of Indian, Pakistani, and Bangladeshi origin—continue to sleep with their babies even when this is not the accepted pattern or the one advocated by British health care.[11] And in the United States, where solitary sleep is advocated by pediatricians and the larger society, ethnic pockets remain in which sleeping with the baby is the accepted pattern; minorities that live by nonwhite rules also regularly co-sleep. In one study of Hispanic-Americans in East Harlem in New York City, 21 percent of the children from six months to four years of age slept with their parents, as compared to 6 percent of a matched sample of white middle-class children.[12] Eighty percent of the Hispanic children shared the same room with their parents, and this sharing was not due solely to space constraints.

It is not only recent immigrants who differ in their sleeping arrangements with their children. For example, in a comparison of whites and African-Americans, 55 percent of the white parents and 70 percent of the black parents said they co-slept with their babies.[13] For whites, co-sleeping with their children took place primarily for those babies perceived to have sleeping problems—defined as waking during the night, or when mothers were not so pleased about taking on the parenting role and ambivalent about having a baby close. In this and other studies, co-sleeping in white families is usually a last-resort attempt to soothe a troubled child or fix a troubled parent–offspring relationship.[14] For black parents, co-sleeping was seen as a normal pattern and had nothing to do with fixing a troubled sleep history or a troubled relationship.

In Appalachia or eastern Kentucky, co-sleeping in infancy and childhood is the norm, as it has been for hundreds of years.[15] Although the people of this area are not an "ethnic minority" or recent immigrants, they do represent a cohesive population that has been resistant to change. Historians note that in colonial times on the eastern seaboard in the United States, several people slept in the same bed—it was the only way to sleep in such small houses.[16] But when new ideas about privacy began to appear in the nineteenth century, housing reflected those changes and suddenly there were private sleeping rooms, first in public houses and then in private homes. The people of Appalachia, descendants of that more colonial tradition, continued the communal sleeping arrangement and even now refuse to place babies alone even when there is plenty of room. Contrary to the advice given by pediatricians in the area, these mothers place their babies in the parental bed because they believe in their particular parenting ideology. As anthropologist Susan Abbott points out, "What it [co-sleeping] is not is some kind of quaint holdover from an archaic past, nor is it pathological in its constitution or outcome for the majority of those who experience it. It is a current, well-situated pattern of child rearing that is withstanding the onslaught of advice by contemporary childcare experts."[17] The point is to make a tightly knit family and keep children close. Seventy-five-year-old Verna Mae Sloane writes of motherhood in Appalachia: "How can you expect to hold on to them in life if you begin by pushing them away?"[18] Again, the ideology guiding co-sleeping in such cultures is one of attachment rather than independence.

Sleep as a Model of Life

Since parents control who sleeps where, it is their folk wisdom that dictates sleeping arrangements. As I discussed earlier, in those cultures in which the prime parental goal is to integrate children into the family, the household, and society, babies are held close at hand, even during the night. It is primarily in those societies (mostly in the industrialized West, especially the United States) where a premium is placed on independence and self-reliance that babies and children sleep alone. Underlying this unconscious societal goal is an even more fundamental assumption made by Americans and some other groups, that how we treat children from day one has a major effect on how they turn out as adults. This philosophy is not shared by all cultures. The Gusii, for example, see infancy as a time of dependence when the point is to keep babies alive, not to mold them. They believe a parent must wait until childhood for training. The Mayans see mother and infant as one inseparable unit and believe offspring are not ready for guidance until they can speak and reason, when they are older children. Newborns in their culture are not seen as susceptible to training, and, they feel, should just be cared for.

Sleep, in other words, can take on a moral overtone. And the basis for that morality is, of course, culturally constructed. American parents believe it is morally "correct" for infants to sleep alone and thus learn independence and self-sufficiency. They view child–parent co-sleeping as strange, psychologically pathological, and even sinful. Those in co-sleeping cultures see the Western practice of placing an infant alone as amoral and a form of child neglect or parental irresponsibility.[19] Parents in both kinds of cultures are convinced that their moral structure is "correct."

The difference in attitude also reflects the way different cultures view sleep in general. Mayans treat sleep as a social activity and think sleeping alone is a hardship, whereas Americans treat sleep as a time of privacy; sharing a bed is considered a sacrifice. Americans make a clear distinction between daytime and nighttime and the kinds of activities that can take place during each time of day, while the !Kung San think nothing of waking up in the middle of the night and spending a few hours around the campfire talking. There is no insomnia in their culture because no one is expected to sleep through the night. In fact, cross-cultural sleep research has shown that night waking is actually much less frequent in Western cultures than in others. And yet Western parents view those comparatively few bouts of alertness a baby may have during the night as much more problematic than parents in societies where babies' sleep is much lighter.[20]

But it is not just industrialization, or modernity, that has fostered nights of uninterrupted solitary sleep. As I mentioned earlier, Japanese children sleep with their parents until they are teens. Even when other rooms and other beds are available, Japanese babies and young children are placed on futons in the parental room. The Japanese see the child as a separate biological organism that needs to be drawn into an interdependent relationship with parents and society, especially with the mother.[21] Japanese prefer not to sleep alone; they do not expect, and probably cannot imagine being interested in, sleeping alone. Sleeping with someone other than the marital partner also de-emphasizes the sexual connection with night and beds that is so prevalent in American society. For the Japanese the concept of family includes sharing the night, and the model of the family tends to orient toward mother and children with the father on the outside, rather than the American version of the ideal nuclear family with mother and father as sacrosanct partners and children subordinate to that primary relationship.[22]

Other industrialized nations have set patterns of child sleep expectations. Dutch parents, as child development experts Sara Harkness and Charles Super found out, feel that children must be strictly regulated in sleep and all other matters. The Dutch also feel that when children have sleep problems it is because their routine has been interrupted.[23] Whereas American parents struggle to find short-term solutions to get their child to sleep through the night—car rides, loud vacuum cleaners, teddy bears with recorded heartbeats—Dutch children are all put to bed at the same early hour every evening and left to adapt. And if they wake up, they are expected to entertain themselves and get out of bed when the time is right. Dutch mothers follow through with this regulated schedule by making every day the same. They do not go dashing here and there with their children, or go on car trips. They do not believe in constant stimulation and excitement in an attempt to develop their babies' cognitive abilities. Instead, Dutch children and babies are presented with a stable environment, an environment that allows for little interruption or alteration. Like the Japanese, the Dutch tend to have a consensus view toward parenting. Regular hours in sleep and all else is the golden rule.

Helping the Baby Make It Through the Night

Infant sleeping patterns are used in some cultures, especially American culture, as a marker of developmental maturity. Does the baby sleep through the night? Why not? What's wrong with the baby or the parenting style? Sleep is often also a major topic for discussion with pediatricians, and an important subject for child-care advisors. Recently in the United States, for example, a method for helping babies sleep has been promoted by Richard Ferber. "Ferberization" involves understanding the natural sleep patterns of each infant, and working with the associations that young children form over sleep rituals.[24] The Ferber method has gained popularity for American parents because of the special role that sleep plays in this culture for parents. Both pediatricians and parents focus on sleep as one criterion for judging infant maturity, temperament, and personality.[25] A survey of American pediatricians showed that 92 percent believe in a regular time for bed, 80 percent believe in a ritualized and special bedtime routine, 88 percent advocate that the baby sleep in a crib outside the parents' room, and 65 percent suggest the baby receive no parental body contact at all during the night.[26] Because pediatricians are the major source of guidance for American parents, the message that is conveyed is loud and clear—solitary sleep is the proper way to raise your children. Backed by the medical establishment, this message takes on the aura of scientific truth; and American mothers, at least white middle-class and upper-middle-class mothers, by and large embrace this ideology unquestioningly.

But expecting babies to sleep for longer periods over time is not simply an American cultural construction. There are, in fact, good biological reasons to expect babies to change their sleep patterns as they develop. Newborn sleep is typically broken into short periods of sleep interspersed by even shorter periods of wakefulness.[27] At first, these sleep/awake intervals are randomly distributed across a twenty-four-hour period; the baby has no circadian or daily rhythm, since there was no day or night to adjust to within the womb. By three to four months of age, however, the environment has clearly dictated a nocturnal/diurnal cycle and the infant brain has matured enough to take in this rhythm. Although a baby increases its total sleep by only one and a half hours from the first week of life to four months of age, it will consolidate that sleep into longer periods. Most babies will sleep four hours at a time in the first few weeks and many of them, at least in Western cultures where such long sleeping intervals are encouraged, reach eight hours of continuous nighttime sleep by four months of age (supplemented by naps). And their brains follow that consolidation by showing more adultlike sleep patterns in brain wave activity at around three months. This development of consolidated sleep time is part of a general neurological development in which the infant begins to move its hands at will and follow people with its eyes. As child development expert Sara Harkness wryly puts it, all children eventually sleep like adults, it is just a matter of how long it takes them to achieve the adult pattern. In other words, obsessing on sleep and trying out different schemes to make the baby sleep through the night may push the matter past the biological potential of the baby.

What many parents need to know is that sleeping through the night—that is, for an uninterrupted six to eight hours—in childhood or in adulthood, is neither a biological truism nor a cultural universal. American babies, for example, usually wake during the night but they often self-comfort and fall back to sleep. Kipsigis African babies wake three to four times a night until they are eight months old.[28] And the amount of sleep that everyone gets is surprisingly variable. Harkness found that American babies sleep two more hours per day than Kipsigis babies. More surprising, she found that Dutch children sleep two hours more than American babies. Clearly babies, and presumably adults, sleep different amounts, and each culture helps determine how that sleep should progress. James McKenna, for one, has examined sleep patterns across cultures and come to some surprising conclusions: "We humans are biphasic sleepers, that is, we are designed to sleep twice in a twenty-four-hour period. The afternoon nap is part of who we are. And so no one should feel guilty about taking a little snooze during the day." The notion of a zestful awake phase during the day followed by a smooth unbroken sleep time in the night is probably more of a cultural fantasy than a biological imperative. It doesn't really fit with how humans, or other animals, manage the twenty-four-hour day.

SOLITARY VERSUS CO-SLEEP

Babies always get enough sleep, one way or another. Whether in a sling on its mother's back, hanging from a hammock in a mud hut, or nestled in a lace-lined bassinet in a pink-painted room, all babies manage to get what they need. But while the actual fact of sleep is also always the same—during sleep infants are unconscious and dreaming—the environment of sleep can be radically different for each child. Take the issue of noise. A baby sleeping alone enjoys considerable quiet, with few sounds penetrating its senses. A baby sleeping in a room full of people, even if they, too, are sleeping, is surrounded by noises—voices, and breathing. Think of the issue of touch. A baby alone feels only cloth and its own body; a baby in bed with another human feels skin, warmth, and breath.

Parents and child-care experts have always acknowledged that the sleep environment makes a difference; this is precisely why experts in the West advocate a solitary place with a quiet environment, because they are searching for a certain type of sleep. Ethnopediatricians are now focusing on the sleep environment for the same reasons—they, too, believe that sleep environment is crucial to infant health and development. But unlike most child-care experts, ethnopediatricians find that the usually recommended solitary sleep is exactly the opposite of what is the naturally evolved sleep situation for babies, and thus not what the baby really needs.

Why Do Some Babies Sleep Alone?

In every comparative study of infant sleep, Western industrial societies, especially white middle-class members of those societies, place their infants and their older children in single beds and often in their own rooms. This pattern sharply contrasts with most of human history. As stated earlier, until two hundred years ago all babies slept with adults and virtually all people slept with someone else. This was a time before the notions of "privacy" or "intimacy," concepts that have become cherished in American cultures. Middle-class houses in Europe reflected this lack of privacy and no houses had rooms that were functionally separate or sleeping rooms that were differentiated from living or eating rooms. Any room might be used for sleeping, cooking, entertaining guests, or conducting business, and little in a room was permanently fixed, not even the furniture. As architectural historian Witold Rybczynski writes, "The medieval home was a public, not a private place."[29] It was also a time of great poverty and squalor. Although the nobility of Europe may have had several houses and luxurious, spacious living quarters, the poor were stuck in one-room hovels.

It was also a time of death. Infant and child mortality were common; in the first Swedish census in 1749, for example, infant mortality was as high as 200 per 1000 births (20 percent).[30] Much of this infant death was due to problems during childbirth or disease, but many infants, especially those in urban centers, were thought to have been killed by "accident" while sleeping in the same beds as their parents. The cause was reported as "overlaying"—mother or father rolling over on the baby and suffocating it. Overlaying was considered such a problem that a device called the *arcuccio* was invented in Italy to protect newborns from menacingly sleepy parents. Drawings of the *arcuccio* look like lobster traps—wooden sides with large holes carved out to fit a nursing breast, roll bar over the top to hold up blankets or a tossing parent. Although overlaying was accepted as an explanation for a high infant mortality, many of these deaths were in fact highly suspicious.

From the sixteenth through the eighteenth centuries, most European countries enacted laws to prevent parents from sleeping with their babies.[31] They were, in essence, trying to prevent infanticide.[32] If there were too many mouths to feed, it was easy to suffocate a baby "by accident." As a result, the government needed to intervene.

The fear of overlaying haunts many parents in Western culture today. Most believe it is possible to roll over and squish a baby or suffocate it under a mound of blankets. But as infant sleep researcher McKenna notes, babies are born with strong survival reflexes, and they will kick and scream before they let anything clog their airways. The simple evidence that most babies around the world today sleep with a parent and they are not dying from suffocation should be enough to convince parents that it's pretty difficult to roll over on a baby and not notice. True, soft mattresses and plush pillows represent a very real risk of suffocation; also, if the baby is wrapped so tightly it can't express its natural instincts to push something away, there could be a problem. But Western parents who fear they will suffocate babies are wrong. In a healthy atmosphere, where parents are not intoxicated, on drugs, or obese, the chance of killing an infant by overlaying is zero. If this is true, why does the myth persist? The myth of overlaying persists because in many Western cultures there are also social, emotional, and political reasons to keep babies out of the parental bed. In the seventeenth century, the Catholic Church became concerned with the possible sexual vulnerability of young girls sleeping with their fathers. At the same time, European culture was developing notions of romantic love and redefining marriage as a conjugal bond rather than an economic or political unit. Suddenly the mother–father relationship took on a separateness within the larger idea of family.[33] When the relationship of mother and father became a sacred, private, sexually intimate bond, parental privacy was born. Children, although offshoots of the bond, were not allowed to interfere with the spousal union. Infants and children, on one level, were seen as a threat to that bond and to the patriarchy that established the father as the family authority. This view later led to the Oedipus complex in Freudian psychology—a drama that cannot be played out unless it is understood that mother and father have a special, private bond in the first place.[34]

Today, the myth against co-sleeping is perpetuated in the West by the child-care authorities—pediatricians and book authors. Here for example is the advice of British child-care expert Dr. Miriam Stoppard: "Some parents opt to have their newborns sleep with them because night feedings are easier to cope with. It shouldn't be a difficult habit to break after a few weeks."[35] It's not clear if the habit belongs to the baby or the parents. Dr. Stoppard recommends putting a large photograph of a human female face (perhaps Mom would do) in the baby's crib because babies like human faces so much and a photograph will easily substitute for a real face. Penelope Leach in *Babyhood* admits that babies sleep better when snuggled between adults. But Leach also notes that parents are often disturbed by the baby's fidgeting, and many are uncomfortable with an infant in the "marital bed."[36]

Dr. Benjamin Spock, the leading child-care expert in the United States for the past 40 years, has always advocated solitary sleep for babies—and no coddling, little comfort. T. Berry Brazelton, who has inherited Dr. Spock's mantle as the nation's pediatrician, agrees that babies need a routine with a quiet and solitary place to sleep. The cultural pressure to make the baby sleep alone is so strong in America that even when parents do sleep with their babies, they are reluctant to admit it, as if they were committing a crime.[37] And the reason seems to be theoretical and psychological and linked once again to the notion of independence. Although there is no specific evidence to support it, most parents in America believe that co-sleeping promotes emotional dependence, and in the overriding gestalt of American life, dependence is seen as negative. Adults may sleep together because their relationship is sexual, and intimate, and bed is the place for sexuality and intimacy in America. Moreover, interdependence between a couple is seen as the contemporary ideal. But children are not part of that intimacy or sexuality, nor are they considered part of that interdependence. Solitary sleeping fits with the ingrained perspective of the parental bond as closed, private, romantic, and exclusive. So underneath the fear of overlaying a baby lies a more strongly held parental goal for pushing children to be on their own, to find their own connections.

The path down which parents encourage their children begins soon after birth, and it is played out in sleep just as it is in daytime activities and interactions. Although there is no conclusive evidence that either solitary sleeping or co-sleeping has a direct effect on attachment later in life (sleep is, after all, only one part of how a life is lived), parents consciously choose one pattern over another. It would seem a rather benign choice, one that could reasonably be based on what is most convenient for parents. But startling new evidence suggests that solitary sleep is more than simply a parental goal—it could be biologically risky as well.

WHAT IS BEST FOR BABIES

The major point of studying infants across cultures is to gain some perspective about what might be the best way to raise babies of our species. All babies are born with the same needs—to be fed, clothed, cleaned, and cared for. But how parents go about those tasks is highly varied. It could be that whatever method a parent uses, babies will turn out all right. After all, babies are incredibly resilient to what the environment throws at them. All of us now in adulthood have clearly survived our infant years. Still, what babies eat, how they are fed, how they sleep, and how they are handled all affect their physical and psychological development. In previous chapters I wrote about attachment and bonding, and how studies of human and nonhuman primate infants have shown a physiological link between separation from mother and an increase in stress hormones along with a depressed immune system.[38] If an infant can be physiologically affected as a result of separation from its mother during the day, there may also be powerful effects from being separated during the night. Does it really make a difference from the baby's point of view whether it sleeps alone or with a parent?

Dr. Sandman

To answer such questions, Jim McKenna culled research from experts in physiology, infant neurology, and human sleep. Most importantly, he turned to sleeping mothers and babies to monitor their nocturnal dance. His experimental work on co-sleeping began in 1984 when, filled with questions about infant sleep, he walked into the first open door in the Department of Pediatrics at the University of California, Irvine, and bent the ear of Dr. Claibourne Dungy, a pediatrician. "My main asset was that I wasn't afraid to look stupid and ask questions," quips McKenna. Dungy quickly assembled "four people in white lab coats who stared at me skeptically," as McKenna recalls. One of them was Dr. Sarah Mosko, a psychobiologist, clinical psychologist, sleep expert, and most importantly a trained polysomnographer—a person who monitors sleepers with a polygraph; she had the skills to help McKenna set up an experimental situation that would tell him the difference, if any, between solitary and co-sleeping babies. They had little research to go on; up to that point, all studies of infant sleep had been conducted on solitary sleeping babies, as if that were the norm.[39] And so they had to pioneer an experimental protocol to test their hypothesis.

Bedtime in the Sleep Lab

McKenna and Mosko have since completed three studies of mother–infant pairs at the Sleep Disorders Lab at the University of California, Irvine, Medical School. In the first study, conducted in 1986, five mother–infant pairs were tracked for one night in the sleep lab. In the second study, eight mothers and infants spent the first two nights sleeping alone, but in adjacent rooms, so that the mothers could get up and feed babies as they would at home. On the third night, mothers and babies slept in the same bed—an unusual event for all but one of the mothers. In the most recent study, fifty Latino mother–infant pairs slept one night as they normally did, solitary or co-sleeping; the next night in a randomly assigned condition, be it the same or different from how they slept at home; and the third night in the opposite condition from the second night.

Mothers and their infants reported to the Sleep Lab at 8 P.M. The sleep room, with a comfortable bed and blackout curtains, provided subjects with a comfortable sleeping atmosphere. Before they settled down for the night, a wire each was taped to the skull of the mother and the child to record electroencephalogram (EEG) brain wave signals. Another wire, placed close to one eye orbit, monitored eye movements, and another wire on the chin measured muscle tone. Respiration was checked by measuring the air that passed by a bead placed on the nose, and by chest wall movement. Cardiac beats were monitored by a wire close to the heart. An infrared video camera was positioned so that it recorded movements of mothers and babies throughout the night. Contrary to expectations, the mothers reported that they slept extremely well in the lab. "These are sleep-deprived new mothers," says Mosko. "They usually say the time in the lab is the first reasonable night's sleep they've had since the baby was born."

Impulses from the wires traveled to the recording room where inked needles recorded messages through a twenty-two-channel polysomnograph, a lie detector machine used to draft the architecture of sleep. Later, Mosko read the pages and marked out sleep levels in thirty-second intervals. She determined whether each subject was sleeping at a certain level, or was wakeful, or was experiencing a transient arousal (when a person moves into lighter levels of sleep but not to full wakefulness). Arousals in infants appear as abrupt increases in slow, high-voltage brain waves drawn as spiky peaks on the polygraph. Similar EEG changes could be marked out for mothers. When undergoing an arousal, mothers and infants also showed other physiological changes such as blinking and chin movement. McKenna, with his animal-behavior background, scored the videotapes—when the baby lifted its head, the mother opened her eyes, and so on. The two scientists eventually compared mothers and infants sleeping alone and together, interval by interval.

These data help differentiate the five possible levels of sleep a person traverses during the night. Rapid Eye Movement, or REM sleep, is the most active—the eyes flicker, the chin moves about as muscles tense and relax, brain waves change, and breathing and heart rate become erratic. REM is also a dreaming state, although dreams can occur in other stages. There are four non-REM levels, called 1 through 4; deep sleep occurs in levels 3 and 4. For babies, researchers combine levels 1/2 and 3/4 to distinguish broad categories of lighter and deeper sleep. A good night's sleep is not necessarily determined by the amount of time spent at any particular level, and people vary in individual patterns of sleep, but the number of cycles through the various levels a person travels at night seems to be important for a satisfying sleep.

How Do They Sleep?

For all three McKenna and Mosko studies, the results were the same. When sleeping together, mothers and babies are extraordinarily in sync. This is the synchronized nocturnal dance that McKenna predicted from his early naps with son Jeff, but the footwork continues to surprise both of these researchers and the other colleagues who have joined their team. The most obvious result is that the sleepers are physiologically entwined; the movements and the breathing of one partner, mother or baby, affect the other. When one partner arouses, the other too moves through sleep levels. This echoing of sleep pattern even includes transient arousals, those fleeting moments of moving quickly up to lighter levels of sleep and then back down again. Why might this be important? Each time the baby responds to an arousal by its mom, an extra arousal from the baby's point of view, the response sets in motion a cycle that gives infants additional practice in breathing. Even healthy babies experience apneas, pauses in breathing, several times during the night. Apneas are the result of an arousal and a large gulp of air; the baby doesn't breathe because it doesn't have to yet. As the infant returns to sleep, the reason to breathe kicks in again. And so when the mother moves through levels of sleep and the baby moves with her, the child gets more practice at navigating through the nocturnal storm.[40] Since babies are born so neurologically unfinished, it makes sense that the external environment, even during sleep, would be so helpful in their "learning" how to sleep safely through the night.

McKenna and Mosko also discovered that co-sleeping babies, even when they are more used to sleeping alone, sleep differently when with their mothers. The babies seem to spend a greater percentage of their sleep time in levels 1-2 and less time at the deeper levels, exhibit more REM sleep, and are awake longer. In other words, they are more often moving among sleep levels, and they sleep lighter.[41]

Christopher Richard, Mosko, and McKenna have also found that most co-sleeping pairs spend the entire night facing each other.[42] Even if mothers normally put their babies face down on the solitary night, they position the baby on its back or side on the co-sleeping night and instinctively in a position so that mother and baby are *en face*. Babies seem to know this is what they want; on the co-sleeping night, even if they are on their backs and have a choice of where to look, they move their heads to face the mother. This might, at first, seem like a potentially dangerous situation. Indeed, the researchers have shown that adult women breathe out a hazardous amount of carbon dioxide at close range, especially when a blanket forms a pocket before an adult's face.[43] But an atmosphere of CO_2 in the face might also be beneficial for infants because it changes the immediate atmospheric environment for the baby and triggers the brain to breathe. Other studies have shown further physiological benefits for co-sleeping babies. Work with preterm infants has shown that skin-to-skin contact increases infant skin temperature, and since babies have trouble staying warm in cold climates this is an advantage as long as they don't get overheated.[44] Such contact also stabilizes infant heart rate and reduces crying and sleep apneas.[45] If nothing else, co-sleeping clearly makes for a very different external environment than sleeping alone.

But the most startling result of McKenna's research can be observed, even by the novice, on the videotapes. No one can miss the fact that co-sleeping results in more attention by the mothers. When McKenna scored mothers' co-sleeping behaviors and compared them to what mothers did when they slept in a different room and got up at night to attend the baby, co-sleeping mothers exhibited five times the protective behaviors toward their babies. They repeatedly kissed, touched, and repositioned the baby. They readjusted blankets and comforted the baby when it fretted. And sometimes these mothers, as the polygraph showed, were not even conscious. They reached out and cuddled their offspring instinctively, keeping them from harm's way.

Co-sleeping babies, then, are under constant physical supervision, and are just a whisper, a pat, and molecule of carbon dioxide away from the person who is looking after them. Solitary babies, although fed when they cry and picked up when they whimper, never receive this kind of intimate treatment during the night.

Why Is Co-sleeping Important?

No one knows *why* animals sleep, but we do have a pretty good idea *how* sleep occurs. Like most physical states, sleep involves a number of biological or physiological mechanisms. Sleep is controlled by the primitive brain stem at the base of the brain where differentiated cells send messages to and from the heart, the lungs, muscles around the diaphragm and ribs, and hormone-producing organs—all systems that monitor and regulate the choreography of sleep. During sleep, just as during periods of wakefulness, adult humans shift through periods of controlled neocortical-driven breaths and automatic brain-stem-initiated breaths.[46] Adults are able to manage the shift between these types, but infants do it less easily. Infants are born with neurologically unfinished brains, and they don't develop the ability to easily navigate types of breathing until they are at least three to four months old. And the sleep patterns of newborns reflect this. As I discussed earlier, they are unable to consolidate periods of sleep and don't distinguish between day and night; they also spend more time in REM sleep than adults do.[47] When sleeping with its mother, a baby reacts to her movements and goes through any number of changes in sleep stages, far more than when the infant sleeps alone, practicing the repeated hop from one kind of breathing to another. Left alone, babies must steer through night sleep with little training, and no external environmental stimuli or cues. Most babies eventually develop the skill to shift between types of breathing as their brains develop with the nerves, becoming more mylinated and thus connected and hence more adultlike, ultimately managing night breathing just fine. But for some babies, this shift among types of breathing may be harder; they could benefit from the external metronome of parental breathing. Co-sleeping, with all its entwined movements through various levels of sleep, and its physical checkpoints, may be exactly what nature intended to make sure babies survive through the night as well as learn how to sleep and breathe on their own.

For McKenna, the attachment between mother and infant so clearly seen in the physiological realm is presumably echoed in the psychological. Although we think of the infant as independent of its mother at birth, because the mother is no longer involved in regulating its physical being, there is still physical entrainment. Some might wish their babies were independent, but babies, as this sleep research shows, clearly need to be in contact, connected, and part of an adult biological system while they develop and mature at their own biological pace.

Most parents in Western culture, by opting not to co-sleep, have thus altered the physical parent–baby entrainment state during sleep hours. But it is important for parents who have done so to realize that they have opted for this setting because of *cultural* reasons, not out of biological appropriateness. What these well-meaning parents do not realize is that they might also be putting their babies unnecessarily at risk.

Co-sleeping and Sudden Infant Death

Sudden Infant Death Syndrome (SIDS) is the leading cause of infant death in the United States, and it has been identified in most societies across the globe. A baby goes to sleep, apparently healthy, and dies without warning.[48] SIDS is not a disease per se, but a syndrome, meaning the etiology is complex and the cause of death might be attributed to any number of physiological origins. Signs often point to respiratory failure, an inability to control the cycle of breathing during sleep, or perhaps an inability to breathe again after a sleep apnea. To McKenna and others, it is no coincidence that management of breathing ability comes developmentally at three to four months of age—just at the same period when babies are most vulnerable to SIDS. Also, some babies in cold climates die of SIDS during winter because they have been wrapped tightly in heavy blankets, and are subject to hypothermia. In general, the cardiovascular system collapses and the baby never recovers. SIDS is named as the cause of death when there is no accident and no disease has been diagnosed. All that the parents know is that something went terribly wrong with the baby, and for some reason the baby did not make it through the night, or through a nap. Warning signs that something is wrong are rare; some SIDS babies have had a slight cold, and others have shown respiratory problems, but most often parents and physicians have no indication that a particular baby is vulnerable. SIDS happens more often to male than female babies, and to lower birth-weight infants compared to those of normal birth weight (18 percent are premature infants).[49] The most striking feature of SIDS is the age at which it occurs. Ninety percent of SIDS deaths occur before six months of age, most commonly at three to four months.

The odd distribution of SIDS across cultures is surprising. The United States has the highest rate, with 2 per 1000 live births, nearly one per hour. The Sudden Infant Death Syndrome Alliance points out that more children in the United States die of SIDS in one year than all the children who die of cancer, heart disease, pneumonia, child abuse, AIDS, and other conditions combined. It is confusing that the United States and Canada have unexpectedly high rates of SIDS, especially as they are industrialized nations where nutrition is decent and prenatal health care is adequate. In contrast, SIDS is lowest in Asia; the SIDS rate in Japan is 0.3 per 1000 births; 0.03 per 1000 births in Hong Kong (a rate 50 to 70 times less than in the West); and virtually unknown in China, although there may be serious reporting problems in this case.[50]

Researchers speculate that the low rate in Asia may be due to environmental factors, such as crowding and a socially stimulated atmosphere, as well as the fact that babies not only sleep with adults but sleep supine rather than prone, which seems to guard against SIDS. The possibility that environment or parental style might be involved in SIDS rates is confirmed by studies of Asian immigrant populations in the United States. In a comparative study of SIDS among Chinese, Japanese, Vietnamese, and Filipino groups in Southern California, the rate overall was 1.1 per 1000 births, half that of the non-Asian population. More convincing, the rate of SIDS among those immigrants was highest in those groups that had been in their adopted country the longest and had presumably adopted Western child-care practices.[51] In Britain, where the mix of cultures is different from that of the United States, Asians from India, Bangladesh, and Pakistan have low rates, as do those families from West Africa.[52] These differences in SIDS rates by culture, and the surprising fact that SIDS rates are so low in areas where infants are at greater risk for malnutrition, disease, and low birth weight, begs an answer. If the incidence of SIDS does not decrease with good prenatal care, good nutrition, and good hygiene, what might be the other risks?

The Child-Care Environment and SIDS

"Infant sleep evolved against a background of being jerked up and down in the back of a sling," points out anthropologist Jim McKenna. "There is a physicality in that relationship and we can't go on assuming that there are no physiological consequences to sleeping alone. For the extremely altricial human infant, social care *is* physiological care." McKenna is convinced by his own lab work and the information on SIDS across cultures that the Western pattern of putting babies to sleep alone in their own bed and in their own room is not only odd, it goes against the grain of how babies were designed to be cared for.[53]

The idea that the environment, specifically parental care, might be involved in SIDS is a controversial subject. No one wants to blame parents, and clearly there is some primary biological reason that some babies do not survive infancy while others do, no matter where they sleep or how they are treated. But recent dramatic changes in the SIDS rate do underscore the importance of child-care practices in preventing SIDS. Originally advisors said that babies should be placed face down when they sleep so that the child would not choke on its own vomit. But a connection between the supine position and low rates of SIDS began to appear, and the rates of SIDS began to drop once parents were advised to put the baby face up rather than face down. There has been, for example, a 90 percent reduction in the rate of SIDS in the United Kingdom from 1981 to 1992 since the new sleeping position was advocated, and a 50 percent reduction in the Netherlands, Australia, and New Zealand. The drop in the SIDS rate has been much less dramatic in the United States because this change in pediatricians' recommendations has been less publicized and less well accepted. But most pediatricians now realize that the prone position does not allow the baby to kick off its blankets when it is too hot, negating the baby's natural instincts to regulate its body temperature. And it is not just the baby's movement that is affected. It appears that babies sleep differently when they are on their stomachs; they sleep longer and spend more time in non-REM sleep, and have fewer and shorter arousals.[54] In other words, they sleep hard. And this may be why pediatricians recommended the prone position in the first place—the goal in Western society had been to make babies sleep like logs. In the supine position they fidget and wiggle and sleep much lighter. What no one realized was that light sleep is essentially much better for a baby just learning *how* to sleep.

More intriguing, the prone/supine data may help to explain why non-Western cultures are not as subject to SIDS as some Western cultures. By definition, babies in non-Western cultures both sleep with their mothers and breast-feed on demand during the night. When babies sleep with their mothers, as McKenna's lab work has shown, mothers always put them on their backs. This position makes it easier for breast-feeding and for checking the baby, and the babies are freer to move about. Breast-feeding by itself is also known to protect against SIDS, presumably because frequent nighttime feedings hold off hypoglycemia, as well as ensuring that the mother is in attendance.[55] Mothers, of course, do not really choose the supine position because it prevents SIDS but because it seems natural. In the last five years or so, the simple act of changing an infant's sleep position from prone to supine has significantly lowered the rate of SIDS. Because the decrease was achieved with a simple change in parental care style, a new avenue for SIDS research—behavior rather than physiology—has opened up.

Following McKenna's lead, scientists in Britain asked if the different rates of SIDS among British Caucasians and Asians might be attributed to child-care practices or home environments. Although everyone in Britain has the right to decent health care and shares an overall culture, the researchers thought there might be differences in micro-environments which would provide some clues to the differing SIDS rates. They conducted a study of twenty Bangladeshi parents and twenty Welsh parents, all from the same socioeconomic class and living in the same area of Cardiff, Wales. They found that the babies in the Bangladeshi households lived in extended families, in "busy social and tactile environments."[56] The Bangladeshi infants were rarely left to cry or left alone, and infants and children always slept with an adult. Child care, the researchers concluded, is a public and communal business for the Bangladeshi household. Welsh babies, in contrast, were urged toward independence, left to cry at times, and spent much of their sleep and awake time alone. Also, child care for the Welsh was the province of one person, usually the mother, and others rarely interfered or participated. And so the researchers concluded that a social environment, as opposed to a private one, must have something to do with lower rates of SIDS among the Asians.

Others have been more skeptical, and they still see some risk in bringing a baby into the parental bed. One study from New Zealand tried to make a connection between bed-sharing and SIDS and they found an association among minority Maori groups.[57] But the study had not factored out alcohol and drug abuse, obesity and smoking, all of which are implicated in SIDS. And as McKenna points out, just because some SIDS infants die in the parental bed is no reason to assume that co-sleeping is the cause; there are other more likely potential risks. In fact, another study of bed-sharing and SIDS in two hundred families from various racial groups in California, where 22.4 percent of the cases were from bed-sharing households, found no association between co-sleeping and SIDS.[58]

Although the laboratory data may be new, the facts have been around for a long time—almost all human infants for the past million or so years have slept in contact with an adult. And even today, in most places in the world, infants spend their first year co-sleeping. Although many parents in Western culture strongly believe in independent sleeping for their infants, data from other cultures, along with an awareness of the potential risks of sleeping alone, might convince others to reject their own cultural traditions and try something else.

How Should We Sleep?

McKenna and his colleagues, even with reams of data and stacks of videotapes, do not believe that solitary sleeping per se causes SIDS. They also do not believe that if all babies were to co-sleep, SIDS would be eradicated. They do believe that for some babies who are at risk, a co-sleeping environment might provide a more positive physiological environment for traversing the night. More to the point, their data so far suggests clear benefits to co-sleeping, as opposed to the mountain of myths that stop parents from sharing the night with their young ones. Instead of the simple act of bringing infants to bed, Western culture continues to press for the perfect night of infant sleep, which means the infant sleeps alone. This involves a special room for the baby, elaborate cribs and soft mattresses, and sleep-enhancing toys such as bears that broadcast the sound of the human heart—an environment that is a far cry from the way our ancestral babies lived 1.5 million years ago. The new data do not advocate that we all go back to sleeping in mud huts, placing the baby on an animal skin on the floor; but just as clearly there are ways to combine what modern technology and scientific knowledge have to offer with what is best for infant biology. McKenna cites a good example. Many parents in the West use radio-transmitted walkie-talkies

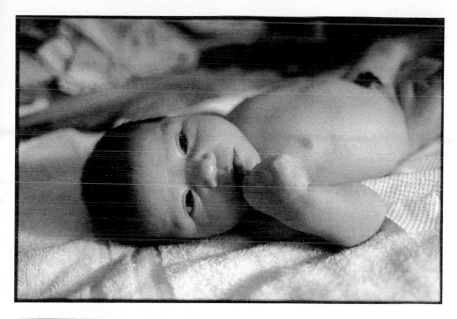

Human infants are born
neurologically unfinished and,
compared to other mammals
and other primates, highly
dependent on caretakers.

(© DEDE HATCH)

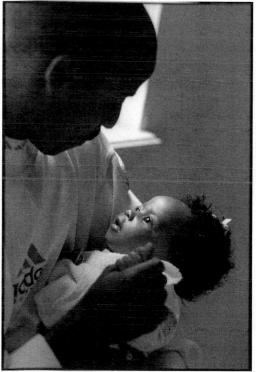

The infant–caretaker relationship,
by biological necessity, is
physiologically and
emotionally entwined.

(© DEDE HATCH)

The entwined relationship between adults and infants is fostered by various signals and responses, innately coordinated by both parties. (© DEDE HATCH)

The major job of babies is to regulate their internal state. They do so by sleeping, feeding, and communicating in both positive and negative ways. (© DEDE HATCH)

Cultural ideology often drives
parental decisions. In America,
where independence and self-reliance
are favored, babies are often put on
a feeding and sleeping schedule.
(© DEDE HATCH)

Among the !Kung San of
Botswana, where infants are an
integral part of the hunter-and-
gatherer lifestyle, infants are
held at all times, fed relatively
continuously, and sleep with parents.
(MELVIN KONNER, ANTHRO-FOTO)

Efé pygmies of Central Africa believe in a communal approach to life, and their child-care practices, with many men and women helping out with each baby, reflect this communal approach. (MICHAEL K. NICHOLS, NATIONAL GEOGRAPHIC)

All cultures believe their way is "best." Westerners are often shocked to see young girls in other cultures care for tiny babies, but those in non-Western cultures are just as surprised that Western babies spend so much time alone. (STEVEN L. RAYMER, NATIONAL GEOGRAPHIC)

All babies cry. They do so to communicate when their internal state is out of balance, requesting aid from adults who can help make it better.

(© DEDE HATCH)

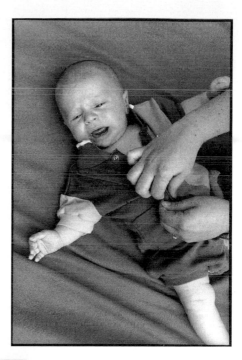

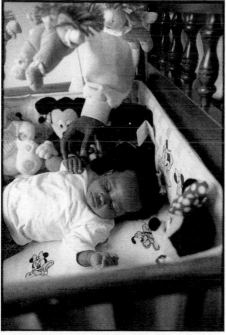

Babies in all cultures, except the industrialized West, sleep in the same room as adults and usually in the same bed. Many parents in the West, however, believe babies must learn independence and so place them in their own beds.

(© DEDE HATCH)

In most cultures—and over most of human history—babies spend almost all their time carried in a sling on the side or back of adults. In this position, babies see the world as adults do; the rhythm of adult walking is also physically soothing. (© BRUCE COLEMAN, INC.)

In Western industrialized nations, babies spend large amounts of time physically distant from caretakers. (© DEDE HATCH)

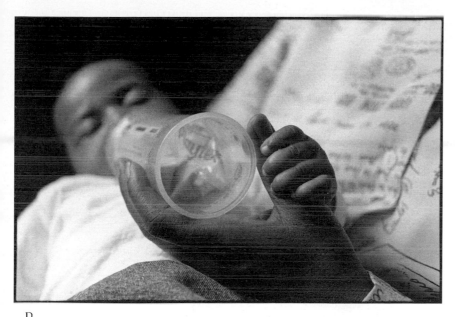

Bottle-feeding presents a possible trade-off for cultures where sanitation and decent medical care make this a reasonable option. Mothers may gain help feeding the baby, as well as physical independence, but they lose many immunological benefits for the baby. (© DEDE HATCH)

In all cultures, mothers supplement breast-feeding with other foods. (© DEDE HATCH)

There is wide variation in the duration of breast-feeding across cultures. Recent research has demonstrated major advantages of breast-feeding not only for the baby's health but also for the mother's health.

(© DEDE HATCH)

Grinning when we talk to them, crying in distress when left alone, sleeping best when nestled close beside us, babies teach us that growth is a cooperative venture.

(© DEDE HATCH)

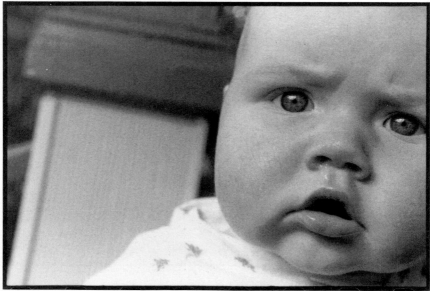

to let them know when the baby is crying and fretting.[59] From an evolutionary and biological perspective, these devices are ludicrous, for in most societies the baby would be sleeping with a mother or caretaker who would hear and feel every fret and cry. At the very least, McKenna suggests, walkie-talkies should be turned around so that babies can sleep among the normal noises of the household. Technology, in this case, has improved things for parents, but it has not improved the environment of our babies.

Infant needs and parental responses to those needs constitute a dynamic, co-evolving system, a system that was, and is even now, being shaped by natural selection to maximize infant survival and improve parental reproductive success. Culture may change, and society might progress, but biology changes at a much slower rate. Babies are still stuck with their Pleistocene biology despite our modern age, and no amount of technological devices or bedtime routines will change that.[60] What babies need from parents is to be part of that interactive parent–baby system that evolved for good evolutionary reasons, and which is a biological necessity even today.

CHAPTER FIVE

CRYBABY

The baby is obviously a newborn, delivered only hours before. He's been brought to the nurse's station for a test that involves pricking his heel with a lance and drawing blood—not a happy moment for someone who recently traversed the tight squeeze of the birth canal and weathered the bright lights and relative coldness of birth. But this baby seems content, for the moment, lying in a clear plastic hospital bassinet. He is dressed in a disposable diaper and sports a shock of thick black hair that sticks straight up from the top of his head. His newborn status is clear from the bump of his umbilicus and the fresh and wrinkled look of his skin. He wiggles about, flailing with arms and legs and moving his mouth in a sucking pout, looking around for he-doesn't-know-what. Then suddenly a mirror at the side of the bassinet catches his attention and he is momentarily arrested by the vague reflection of his own movements. Although sight is unfocused this early in life, the flash of pudgy legs and arms and the dark blotch of hair moving about make for intriguing images even for a newborn. And then comes the lab-coated arm, the lance, the prick of skin on his heel, and the baby screams. He is transformed from a peaceful kind of "alert-awake" state, as infant behavior researchers call it, to genuine distress.

As I watch the video of this change in infant state with Dr. Ronald

Barr, a pediatrician and researcher who studies crying and fretting at
Children's Hospital in Montreal, I shift uncomfortably in my seat. I find
it difficult to watch this sudden explosion of crying; my natural instinct
is to pick the baby up, hug him and rock him back and forth. Barr has
seen plenty of babies cry, but I know that he studies infant crying not
because he likes watching babies wail, but in hopes that he can suggest
ways to make them cry less. Barr is tall, with long dark hair and a
cheerful smile and a deep laugh, but his most distinctive feature is his
voice—it could soothe even the most ill-tempered baby. I imagine him
during an experiment with these crying newborns, talking softly to one
of his tiny subjects and seeing their eyes grow wide and their heads turn,
captivated by that voice. But at the moment, his voice isn't having much
of a soothing effect on me as he narrates through the experimental part
of this procedure. After the routine blood test, Barr steps in and quiets
the baby in an unexpected way—he has discovered that if you excite
brain sensors other than the pain sensors, the baby is no longer upset
that his heel has just been pierced.

On the screen, the arm of an assistant comes into the picture and a
few drops of water mixed with sucrose, a simple sugar, are placed on the
baby's tongue. The results are dramatic—the baby immediately calms
down. He looks confused, then preoccupied; most important, he's
stopped screaming. He now looks about, moves his mouth as if he were
testing the properties of some fine wine, shoves a fist in his mouth a few
times, and stops kicking.[1] The subject is now happy for a few minutes,
until the calming effect of the sucrose wears off and the pain from the
lancet registers in his brain again. When that happens, as Barr knows, the
baby's state will shift again from alert-awake into something more unpleasant, and someone else will have to figure out what to do next—feed
him, pick him up, offer him the breast, or perhaps sing him a lullaby.

Babies, like adults, experience all sorts of biological and mental states.
Sometimes they are awake, alert, and calm, and other times they are
stressed-out and crying. And for babies, regulating their internal state is
the most powerful thing they do.[2] The move from sleep to activity, the

slide from happiness to inconsolable crying, the sudden jump from screaming anger to quiet-awake—these are the physical and behavioral properties that make up a baby's world, and babies are very good at navigating their world. And since infants can't communicate their inner state with words, as older children and adults do, they use various other communicative signals to let caretakers know how they are. Babies, as any parent knows, do not only cry; they also smile, gurgle, and look about attentively, make unhappy faces or wave their arms in curiosity or frustration. They fidget and fuss, they reach out, they make eye contact. And just about everything they do indicates how they are doing.

How a baby feels is of critical importance because, for the first few years, human infants are extraordinarily dependent. They can't tell their mothers how wet their diapers are or that they are hungry or they need to be held and comforted. All they can do is cry. As a result of this speechless communication, most parents spend much of their time trying to decipher infant signals and figure out, hour by hour, how their baby is doing. Is he happy? Is she hungry? Why is he crying? What exactly caused that smile?

This constant checking on infant state, especially during the early months, is also powerful in the long term because, over time, parents form a sense of what their child is like in terms of temperament and personality. Some people are just lucky, they think. Their child is an angel, he never cries, he rests passively wherever he is. Other babies are brought into the pediatrician's office by frustrated parents at the end of their rope because their baby cries excessively. Is it because he has colic? Is something physically wrong? Or is this baby just naturally difficult? Most parents believe that differences in personality, ones that can be demonstrated within a few months of life, are inborn—that is, genetically configured. Parenting might have some effect on this given personality, this approach suggests, but the assumption is that kids are basically born the way they are, that personality and temperament are inherited and thus largely unchangeable. One parent might proclaim, "Our son Johnny, from the day he was born, was always patient, happy, and optimistic, just like his dad. And our Kimberly, the wiggler and crier as a baby, is now active, a fussbudget, and a social creature just like her mom." Today's approach to parenting suggests that people are born one way and that the environment—that is, family life—only slightly influences those hard-wired tendencies. Parents can discourage "bad" traits and encourage "good" traits, but there is only so much they can do.

However, work by Barr and other ethnopediatricians on infant state is showing that such facile statements about inborn temperament and personality are not so easily proven. The caregiving style of parents, the ideology that guides parenting choices, the day-to-day interactions between baby and caretaker, and the parents' own approach to life, all have profound effects on what kind of person their child becomes.

THE EVOLUTION OF CRYING

Crying is the earliest and most compelling of infant signals," writes Ronald Barr, and surely there is no sound on earth more piercing than the cry of an infant.[3] The ability to cry was hard-wired into human babies long ago as a potent signal to get adult attention. Like other primates, human infants needed to be able to send a message of distress to motivate action on the part of someone more able. The same kind of vocal signals are found in Rhesus monkeys, for example, which have very distinguishable distress noises called "coos." During a coo, the lips protrude into an "oh" and produce a plaintive series of cries when the infant is separated from its mother. Monkey and ape babies also shriek and scream and produce a deep-throated geck noise, all as signals to others.[4] These signals, of course, have evolved in primates and other animals because they work; the sounds bring the mother closer. Animal babies call when something threatens or frightens them, thereby making it known that, from the infant's point of view, something is terribly wrong. For humans, nothing compels a parent to do something more quickly than a child's piercing wail. And that's why crying is, in Ronald Barr's nomenclature, a paradox. It is a signal that evolved to broadcast an infant's unhappiness and motivate a parent to address the cause of its distress. But that same signal can, very easily, send parents over the edge. For example, reports of child abuse and child homicide often contain comments about a parent's or caretaker's ultimate frustration with a crying infant, and their claims that they just couldn't take it anymore.[5] And so what evolved as an adaptive signal can be destructive under certain circumstances, which doesn't make evolutionary sense at all.

The answer to the paradox of incessant crying lies, new research suggests, in understanding the exact nature of crying and the system in which it evolved. The environment in which we react to babies' cries today may be entirely different from the environment in which human cries first evolved.

The Nature of Crying

Although newborns have a plethora of vocal signals, parents pay most attention to crying, presumably because they are attuned to sounds of distress—and because the sound itself is so disturbing. Crying has been described as a rhythmic pattern of vocalization characterized by short bouts of breathy expiration, a long intake of air that sounds like a whistle, then a short rest before the cry begins again.[6] Physically, body systems such as heartbeat and lung intake, and the muscles of the larynx that modulate sound, are involved in the production of crying sounds.[7] Mentally, crying involves the central nervous system and the autonomic control of internal state as perceived by the infant's brain. In a sense, the baby is pushed and pulled by uncomfortable mental arousal—resulting from, say, pain, wetness, or hunger—and the automatic desire to inhibit that unpleasant arousal.

Crying is clearly the highest state of infant arousal, on a scale that runs from deep sleep to full alert. Although sometimes babies cry a bit when asleep, a full-scale cry pushes the infant to the alert side of the scale. Crying also exercises lung capacity and muscle movement. And as the baby wiggles about and tenses his arms and legs, the body generates heat which in turn contributes to thermoregulation and keeps the infant warm (or makes it too warm). All these processes obviously take caloric energy to produce and can be considered "exercise" of a sort. Most important, if crying works right as a signal, it will bring on food and touch from adults.[8]

Crying, according to infant-vocalization expert Peter Wolff, appears as part of a baby's behavior within half an hour after birth; it remains structurally consistent until between the second to the sixth month, depending on the baby, when the crying repertoire expands. At that point, three kinds of cries can be distinguished. First is the "angry" cry, when a large volume of air is forced through the vocal cords. The second is the "pain" cry, which comes in a sudden onset, without upbuilding or moaning, and includes long periods of the baby holding its breath. The third kind of cry is the "frustration" cry. Researchers can easily get a baby to perform this cry by putting a pacifier into its mouth and taking it out again. Eventually, the baby will issue a painlike cry to which it adds a long inspiratory whistle. This third type of cry is very familiar to parents; the name "frustration" probably applies both to the baby and the adult.[9]

Some parents perceive a shift in their baby's crying at about three months from "expressive" crying, when all cries sound the same regardless of what's going on with the baby, to more modulated "communicative" crying, with particular messages encoded within different types of crying.[10] This shift makes sense because there are a host of physical, especially neurological, changes in infant brains that kick in at three months (suggesting once again that human infants are, perhaps, born three months too early, in many biological respects). Ronald Barr explains that the cry begins in life as a relatively undifferentiated reflection of infant state and then becomes, through learning and reinforcement, more a matter of communication between the baby and its caretakers.[11]

Babies also fuss, which is an arrhythmic expression of unhappiness, a strained kind of pulsated crying full of pauses and intakes of breath. As any parent knows, fussing, while annoying, is not the desperate, demanding signal of more hearty crying. The average Western infant cries twenty-two minutes per day in the first three weeks of life and thirty-four minutes per day until the end of the second month, when crying gradually decreases to fourteen minutes per day by twelve weeks of age.[12] This crying curve, with frequent crying during the first eight weeks of life and then a decrease over the next several weeks and months, is found both for Western babies and babies from other some cultures such as the !Kung San. Although the crying curve, with a peak between six and eight weeks, is thought to be a human infant universal, a study of Korean infants did not show the same patterns. More universally, infants seem to cry more in the evening than any other time of day, but there has been little comparative work on the exact pattern across cultures.[13]

Early on, babies cry for food or physical contact, or out of frustration. Mothers often hear the frustration cry as a "fake" cry because the baby isn't hungry and there's nothing physically wrong with it. But there is, in fact, no such thing as a fake cry. The baby is crying for engagement of some sort—for personal interaction and social contact, or because it is bored. Babies also laugh during the first month of life, which spectrographically looks more like a cry than a chuckle and is probably related to conflicting emotions or rapid shifts in state.[14]

Some of this crying and babbling is clearly a precursor to language through vocal experiment and learning.[15] By the second month of life, crying, fussing, and any vocal outbursts become vocal practice sessions. While whining, especially, infants invent new sounds. Soon vocalizations rapidly diversify and the baby begins to conduct private conversations with itself, listening to its own voice. When parents talk baby-talk to infants (and studies show they do so in every culture[16]), spectrographic analysis reveals that although babies can't necessarily mimic the "ma-ma" and "da-da" sounds thrown at them for many months, even early on they do try to answer back in imitation using a limited vocal repertoire. A squealing baby, in fact, can be stopped dead in its vocal tracks by a sudden stream of baby-talk because the baby is determined to make the same sound.

In more affluent Western industrialized nations, parents assume crying is first and foremost linked to hunger. In fact, some women in these cultures often end breast-feeding and turn to bottle-feeding because they believe excessive crying by the baby means he is not getting enough nourishment from the breast.[17] But researchers know that early crying has a broader range of functions. It can be stopped by various methods, and food is not always the solution. In the 1960s, an era in America when parents were advised to let babies cry, Wolff ran a series of experiments to figure out just why these kids were so unhappy.[18] He tried a pacifier to determine if oral gratification, without nourishment, would calm a screaming baby. It worked. He next tested a series of newborns with wet diapers. Wolff put clean diapers on half and put the wet diapers back on the other half. Both groups were quieted and didn't seem to care if the diaper was wet or not. Wolff concluded that babies simply like the stimulation and physical sensation of being changed. He then questioned the idea that babies cry when they are cold, and so placed some infants in cribs heated to 88 degrees and others in cribs set 10 degrees cooler. Those in the cooler cribs cried more frequently, indicating that warmth, too, can reduce crying. Wolff investigated this notion further by layering some babies in clothes, covering others in various positions with blankets, and lightly swaddling others. Their reactions varied; some cried when covered tightly, others liked it tight. Finally Wolff tried the classic parental response to a crying baby. Using a group of crying babies who had to be artificially fed by tubes into their abdomens for medical reasons, he fed them this way until their stomachs were full and waited to see if satisfying their hunger would quiet them. Surprisingly, a full stomach did not stop these infants from wailing. Wolff also discovered that simply picking them up worked perfectly well as a cry-stopper, even if they were hungry and waiting to be fed. In general, he concluded, picking up a baby, giving it a pacifier, or feeding it—not for the nutritional value but for the physical contact—worked best.

As most parents intuitively know, crying is not just a signal of hunger. Even in newborns, it communicates much more—the need for touch seems to be especially important; and clearly a crying baby is announcing its internal state and calling for some sort of change.

The Function of Crying

The first cry after birth, points out pediatrician T. Berry Brazelton, functions to reorganize the infant from its intrauterine life without lung breathing to an extrauterine cardiorespiratory system.[19] The passage through the birth canal, the relative coldness of the air outside the mother's body, the lights, all these stimuli on the skin and body trigger a cry that kick-starts a new kind of interaction with a new kind of environment. Part of the initial function of crying is to expand pulmonary function over the first few days of life. The newborn's lungs, which used to be flat and filled with liquid, are adapting to taking in air and breathing.

As a distress signal, a cry means someone should do something to put the baby and its environment back into equilibrium. It is remarkable that an organism so unused to regulating tension in utero, and unable to display a reaction except for kicking and turning about in a tight space, is suddenly adapted, right at birth, to vocalize its internal state. "The infant expects a response from the environment," explains Brazelton, "And [he] cries for the mothering that will relieve his condition."[20] In other words, infants don't cry without a reason. Although it may be incomprehensible to parents at the time, the baby's internal regulating barometer is falling, and crying is the signal of that change in state. That barometer might have changed because of hunger or fatigue or a need to be reassured and touched, but it is a clear signal something is out of whack.

In the beginning, an infant's cry is automatic, a straightforward announcement of a need. But within a few months, it develops into an efficient feedback system between infant and adult. Parents sometimes feel manipulated by crying, and they are correct in this assessment. The baby is biologically designed to manipulate adults to take care of it. But obviously this manipulation is unconscious on the part of the baby, a system selected over evolutionary history to produce the necessary care. Nor can the "manipulation" be controlled or regulated. Ignoring the baby's cries might force the baby to finally fall asleep, but it will not, in the end, break the crying–feedback cycle which is so hard-wired into the infant. The biological function of crying is to signal, and as in any signal, it has import only if it affects the recipient. When parents ignore a baby's cries, they are not, from the baby's point of view, holding up their end of the baby–parent biological system. As a result, there is a gap in the signal–feedback loop. Within the perspective of an evolved adaptation, parental decisions to ignore a baby's cries then go against the grain of natural selection and are at odds with the function of the signal in the first place.

Is There Such a Thing as Colic?

Colic, as it is conceived in Western minds, is a pathological reaction of infants to some internal distress that causes them to cry excessively and uncontrollably. Most parents assume there is something physiologically wrong with the baby—intestinal gas, or some sort of physiological or developmental immaturity—that makes their baby more unhappy than the norm. The label "colic" has been applied to 10–20 percent of Western babies. It is known to happen during the first few months and then go away, and is described as long bouts of inconsolable crying that most often occur during the evening.[21] Clinically, however, the word *colic* is applied only if the pattern follows what pediatricians call the Wessel rule of threes—if the crying goes on for more than three hours, over more than three days, and over more than three weeks.[22] Parents recognize colic when the baby scrunches its face as if in pain, retracts its lips, and makes a square mouth while crying. The baby seems out of control and on a crying jag that can't be interrupted. In response, parents typically walk about helplessly trying to comfort the baby who may tighten its muscles and arch its back in apparent fury. These bouts of colic come on unexpectedly; they seem to both start and stop spontaneously, and often nothing seems able to stop the wailing. Eventually, the baby just stops on its own.[23]

Faced with an inconsolable infant, parents often call the doctor or even go to the hospital emergency room only to learn that there's rarely anything physically wrong with the baby.[24] In a few cases a physiological cause can be diagnosed, such as a reaction to an immunization or the onset of a serious medical condition. But most often, physicians are unable to find a medical cause—that is, physical pathology—that might account for the baby's extreme discomfort.

Traditionally, parents in Western culture think there must be something wrong with the baby's diet or digestive track; perhaps they are feeding it the wrong formula, or it has excessive gas. But studies show that there's really no relation between food and the far end of the crying continuum. Most Western babies are adequately fed, and all-night crying is clearly not caused by hunger. It is also not the result of food type. There is no difference in the number of infants reported as excessive criers among bottle-fed and breast-fed infants.[25] For bottle-fed infants, it is always possible that the baby might be allergic to a specific antigen in cow's milk or formula, or that the baby might be unable to efficiently absorb lactose, the primary sugar in milk. But allergy to milk or formula or the inability to digest the properties of milk are very rare conditions. Only about 10 percent of all infants have some sort of milk protein intolerance and even fewer have trouble with carbohydrates.[26] Contrary to what most parents believe, distended bellies and gas are most often the result of swallowing air during crying, rather than incompatible formula.[27] And yet 26 percent of formula-fed infants go through a formula change in reaction to parental complaints about crying. Parents feel the formula is too rich, too weak, has too much carbohydrate or protein or not enough, and so they struggle to change the formula in the hope of reducing the baby's dissatisfaction. Often parents report a decrease in crying after changing formula, but apparently a perceived decrease in colic is largely a placebo effect for parents who desperately want to believe they have solved the problem.[28] In most cases, a baby's crying decreases not specifically because the formula is more suited to it, but because the baby has passed the crying peak and is settling down into a later developmental stage.

Often, unbeknownst to tired and frustrated parents, the baby doesn't warrant the "colic" label at all. When studying two groups of babies, Ronald Barr and colleagues found that the babies parents described as "colicky" and the ones that parents didn't describe as troubled criers were often similar in their crying profiles.[29] Based on parental diaries of infant behavior and state, some of the so-called colicky babies actually did not warrant the Wessel clinical label of colic; in fact, their profiles were much like the other groups of infants that served as controls and had not been considered extreme criers by their parents. When parents are isolated and inexperienced, or when their tolerance level is lower than other parents, the baby might appear to be colicky when it is actually quite normal in terms of its amount of crying. Physicians can relieve parental anxiety somewhat by pointing out that what seems excessive may be actually normal. For physicians faced with this situation, there are pitfalls in either direction. Once their baby is pronounced "normal," its parents might be more liable to ignore its cries. On the other hand, applying the "colic" label to a baby might encourage parents to see the infant as sickly, vulnerable, and prone to problems.

In reality, colic is only the extreme end of the normal crying continuum. Since most infants follow the usual crying curve, increasing their crying around six to eight weeks and decreasing it thereafter, in reality only a small percentage of infants can be medically labeled as colicky.[30] And of those, an even smaller percentage, less than 10 percent, actually have something physically wrong with them.[31] Colic, in Ronald Barr's words, is something infants *do*, not something they *have*. And it is, in fact, most often a symptom of a mismatch between what babies cry for and what they receive. Research on soothing supports this notion; it appears that caretaking is both the most likely initial cause and the most effective strategy for relief of excessive crying.

How to Soothe a Crying Baby

Because physiological causes of colic, such as allergy to formula or intestinal blockage, are rare, physicians most often rely on behavioral suggestions to help parents deal with excessive crying.[32] Pediatricians suggest changing feeding schedules, bouncing the baby, rocking, changing position. They suggest distracting the baby with sights or sounds—a drive in the car, the hum of music. And, indeed, research shows that some techniques work better than others. More interesting, some babies are more "soothable" than others.[33] The most widely prescribed tonic is to promote suckling, either with a pacifier, a bottle, or the nipple.[34] And yet research has shown that oral gratification or a full stomach is not the point. Well-fed babies are often the loudest criers; changing formula does nothing but pacify parents; wiggling a rubber stopper in a screaming baby's mouth often has no effect. A series of studies with monkeys by Harry Harlow shows that given the choice, an unhappy primate infant will choose the comfort of a soft cloth-covered mother substitute over a wire mother that delivers milk and the opportunity for suckling.[35]

What seems to work best is simple human contact. Peter Wolff long ago demonstrated that picking up a baby works better than anything else to stop any baby from crying. In another study, infant researchers Bell and Ainsworth showed in the 1970s, with a sample of twenty-six infants, that consistent and prompt response by the infant's mother is associated with a decrease in the duration of infant crying.[36] Urs Hunziker and Ronald Barr recently took this idea even further when they experimented with different infant carrying schedules to test whether or not carrying could have a proactive effect on crying. They recruited a group of parents with newborns and asked half of them to carry their infants at least three hours per day beyond feeding time. The other subjects were not told to carry their infants any more than they normally would. When the babies were twelve weeks of age, the mothers were asked to bring in diaries in which they had noted when and how long their babies cried. The researchers found that the control mothers carried their babies on average 2.7 hours a day and the mothers involved in the experiment carried their babies about 4.4 hours per day, an increase of only 1.7 hours per day. The diaries show that during the peak crying period at eight weeks of age, both groups of babies cried with the same frequency, but those that had been carried longer cried 43 percent less in duration than those carried a shorter time per day; the frequency of crying was the same but the duration was almost half as much.[37] The infants who were carried more also reached their crying peak on the early side, at four weeks, and leveled off at six weeks. Interestingly, when this same procedure was later tried on babies already labeled as "colicky," it didn't work as well. Even though half of the 66 colicky four-week-olds were carried 56 percent more (2.2 hours longer) than the other colicky babies, they didn't cry less.[38] Perhaps longer carrying would have been effective if it had been done from birth, but either one month of age is perhaps too late for differences in parental style to have much effect on crying or these babies labeled as colicky were just not as susceptible to being comforted in this manner.

Although type of food and total amount of food do not seem to dramatically affect infant crying, the timing of food and the way food is delivered do seem to be of prime importance in staving off crying. Comparing members of the La Leche League, women devoted to relatively continuous breast-feeding, and a group of mothers following the more traditional American pattern of feeding on a schedule with hours between feedings, Barr and his colleagues explored the possibility that the length of time between feedings might have an effect on crying.[39] Observing these two groups at home, and through daily diaries kept by mothers, Barr and Elias found that the quietest infants were those who were fed at short intervals and whose mothers quickly responded to their crying. Interestingly it was the combination of feeding and response, and not just food, that was so effective; the infants of mothers who fed in short intervals but were slow to respond, and of those who fed with long intervals between feedings but responded quickly, all cried a lot. In other words, it's not just the constant availability of milk that makes a baby happy, it is also an engaged mother who responds quickly.

Pediatricians and child experts suggest trying one soothing technique after another. But the best answer, according to this research, is a particular parenting style. What crying babies seem to need most, or what decreases their crying, is a caretaking package that puts their world right. And some babies seem to yell louder than others for a change if their world is not in balance.

Crying Across Cultures

There is extensive scientific evidence that the accepted Western caretaking style repeatedly, and perhaps dangerously, violates the adaptive system called crying that evolved to help babies communicate with adults.[40] In America, for example, we are used to seeing children cry in public. It is accepted, and expected, that babies will at some point cry endlessly. As a result, many adults on public transportation or in public places will move away from parents with small children in tow, to get away before the screaming starts. The situation is strikingly different in other areas of the world. Even to the casual visitor in less developed nations, it becomes apparent that babies in non-Western cultures rarely cry; I have never heard an African baby or a Balinese baby cry during my many trips to both those sides of the world. And this casual observation has been confirmed by ethnopediatric research. In a study comparing the amount of crying by babies from America and Holland with crying by infant !Kung San, Ronald Barr found that babies in all three cultures cry with equal frequency—that is, they begin to whimper at the same rate. All the babies, regardless of culture, also produce a similar curve of crying over time with a peak at about two months. But there is a dramatic difference in the duration of crying across cultures; Western babies cry much longer per bout, and the total amount of time spent crying each day is longer in both Holland and America.[41]

Berry Brazelton also found that Mayan Indian babies in Mexico were most often in the quiet-alert state, and he recorded no periods of intense crying.[42] In a study of 160 Korean infants, another researcher found no infants that could be classified as colicky, no clear crying peak at two months, and apparently no cluster of evening crying.[43] The Korean sample is especially intriguing because although these infants share much of the socioeconomic status of other developed nations, caretaking in Korea is apparently more physically engaged than in Western industrialized nations. For example, Korean babies at one month old spend only two hours, or 8.3 percent of their time, alone. In contrast, American infants spend 67.5 percent of their time alone. In addition, the Korean babies are carried almost twice the amount of time per day as American babies. And Korean mothers virtually always respond immediately to infant cries, whereas American mothers typically ignore crying much of the time. In another sample, Bell and Ainsworth found that mothers in America deliberately do not respond to 46 percent of crying episodes during the first three months of a baby's life.[44] Presumably Korean caretaking accounts for the lower amount of crying and the lack of colic.

Pediatricians and child-development experts are well aware that there is high variability among children in terms of crying, and that the frequency and duration of crying varies for any individual child over time. The fact that there are clear population differences is more startling. These studies show that although crying itself is an infant universal, the way in which that crying manifests itself is not hard-wired, but easily influenced by the environment. The notion that all babies cry a lot at night is false. The belief that colic is just one end of a normal crying continuum, and that it is something that must be inevitable, is also erroneous.

Crying is highly influenced by an infant's immediate environment. As difficult as it might be to explain this to a sleep-deprived American mother who is spending yet another night rocking a baby that cannot be comforted, our caretaking style seems to be the root of infant discomfort. But the solution is not a simple matter of rocking or feeding. Nor does it mean that one mother is somehow a better parent than another. New research merely indicates that Western babies typically cry for long periods, and even develop "colic," because the accepted and culturally composed caretaking style is often at odds with infant biology. When an infant cried inconsolably for hours, when its tiny body arches in frustration, when its fists punch the air in anger, we see the clearest example of the clash between biology and culture. The baby is responding to an environment that has been culturally altered, and for which it has not been biologically adapted. And this is the trade-off. The infant is biologically adapted to expect the constant physical attachment and care within which the human infant evolved millions of years ago. But in some cultures, such as the industrialized countries of Europe and North America, parents are opting for a more independent relationship from their babies. They choose to place babies in cribs and car seats rather than carry them all the time, to feed babies in intervals rather than continuously, and to respond less quickly to infant distress. Although this style provides parents with some freedom from the demands of the infant, it also comes with a cost—a crying baby who is not biologically adapted to the cultural change.

Crying as an Evolutionary Adaptation

About 1.5 million years ago our human ancestors, looking much like us today, scratched out a living in the various savanna and woodland niches of Africa. They most likely lived in small groups, keeping close to kin; and although there is no evidence of language as we understand it today, there was certainly a sophisticated system of communication. It was a time that some anthropologists call "the environment of evolutionary adaptedness," often shortened to "the EEA." Although the human species evolved from previous hominid forms—that is, from Australopithecines—and before that shared a common ancestor with today's chimpanzees, the EEA is often the focus for figuring out the human condition because it's the period when our genus, Homo, appeared. Over time there were several species of Homo, starting with Homo habilis and then Homo erectus, and eventually Homo sapiens, but all of these species had what we now consider the major hallmarks of humans; they were large-brained and they walked bipedally. It was during this period, anthropologists assume, that the constraints and pressures that formed the modern version of us—Homo sapiens sapiens—exerted their greatest influence. In many ways, people living today are still operating with bodies and minds that evolved during the EEA; we have changed very little physically since then, although our world has certainly changed as a result of culture, technology, and civilization.[45]

More to the point, human babies have not changed much from the time of the EEA. Although various accouterments of society and material culture make adult life easier and give it more structure, babies are still cultural novices, unable to utilize the benefits of culture or conform to its demands until they grow and learn. When we think of infants with bodies and minds that evolved during the EEA, crying takes on new meaning.

Crying evolved to serve the infant's purposes: to assure protection, adequate feeding, and nurturing for an organism that cannot care for itself. By definition, crying is designed to elicit a response, to activate emotions, to play on the empathy of another. The "other" is usually the mother or father or a related caretaker. The caretaker has also evolved the sensory mechanism to recognize that infant cries are a signal of unhappiness, and thus be motivated to do something about it.[46]

This kind of symbiotic relationship certainly made sense in the EEA. Even back then we were a large-brained species whose infants had to be born early in their physical development because of the constraints of the bipedal pelvis. As a result, human babies could not yet talk and thus had to communicate by other means. In the EEA, crying probably promoted survival because it kept the mother close, resulted in the infant's being fed as she held out the breast to quiet it, and kept parents attentive against predators.[47] A quick cry, then, made evolutionary sense, at least in the EEA. At the most fundamental level, crying is an adaptive strategy because it keeps a baby alive and well fed and therefore ultimately passes on genes and improves a parent's reproductive success.

It might also have an added evolutionary advantage. When a baby is allowed to feed continuously, ovulation in the mother and conception of the next sibling who will take over breast-feeding is delayed (as I discuss more fully in Chapter Six). And so the combination of crying and the continuous feeding that results from crying is also an effective adaptive strategy on the part of the infant; infants who evolved with these traits had a better chance of survival than those who did not.[48] In this scenario, the infant is not simply a helpless or passive recipient of parental largess, but an active initiator of a synergistic relationship with the parent.

In some cultures today, the fit between infant cries and survival has been altered and crying has become, as in the case of colic, a maladaptive trait that no longer promotes survival. Any trait can become maladaptive when the environment changes; what once was "good" now becomes neutral or "bad" because it is no longer effective under the new conditions. When crying is continual and annoying to the point of placing the infant in danger of abuse or neglect, it is a clearly maladaptive signal. And that may be what has happened in our modern age. It is not that babies have changed, but rather that the environment in which babies send their signals has been altered.

Colic, as Ronald Barr puts it, is a sign of discordance between the infant and its total caretaking package. Frequent short intervals of crying make sense—they remind the mother to feed and pick up the baby. But long spells of crying make no sense, especially when the mother decides to delay her response. For example, in strictly scheduled feeding regimes, wailing will not bring a feeding any closer, no matter what the baby expects the signal to achieve. And endlessly crying does not endear a baby to adults and promote cuddling. In fact, such constant crying can have exactly the opposite effect for the infant; he is sometimes placed in another room to give everyone—that is, adults—some relief. As the baby screams and the caretaker withdraws, the entire system only grows more and more out of whack, becoming a negative feedback loop which in turn makes the baby scream even more loudly from anger and confusion. And no wonder that parents are mystified, desperate to find a physical cause. It is a paradox—everything is fine in terms of food and diapers, and most child-care experts would say that the parents are acting appropriately, yet the baby continues to cry.[49]

In a sense, points out Ronald Barr, the Western industrialized pattern of not responding quickly to babies, of interval feeding, and of forcing the baby to spend so much time alone, is a kind of ongoing experiment to test infant survival in a new environment. Clearly, babies do survive; Western babies do, in fact, grow up seemingly fine. More significant, this "experiment" proves that the parental emotional bond can be formed even when there are long periods of separation between infant and caretaker.[50] Colic and long bouts of screaming are simply the negative side of the separation trade-off.

TEMPERAMENT AND SYMBIOSIS

In addition to crying, babies' wakeful states range from inactive-awake to laughing joy. And each baby, as any parent knows, has a distinct personality. To some parents, that personality is clear from the earliest signals. Some mothers even talk about the activity level of their babies during pregnancy and from that movement predict how active or passive their child will be.[51] But, of course, whether or not a baby's personality is set from birth is unclear. In many societies it is assumed that personality does not form until much later in life—until the child can talk and hold a conversation, or be trained. Babies in these cultures are viewed as blank slates, personality-less beings in the process of further development. But in other cultures, especially America, many believe each person has an inborn basic nature, one that might be molded or influenced, but which is essentially persistent through time.

In the clinical sense, personality is really a complex of thoughts, feelings, emotions, and actions, a combination of genes and environment that describes how a person both sees the world and interacts with it. The idea of an inborn "type" or personality has been fostered, in the public's mind, by work in behavioral genetics. With reports in the paper every day about the discovery of the gene for this or that disease or mental disorder, and with the sometimes startling pronouncement of the similarity in personality between twins even after years of separation, the public has been bombarded with the idea that genes are primarily responsible for who or what someone is. What the news reports fail to explain is that when researchers suggest that some behavior or personality tic is heritable, they really mean genes can account for 30 to 60 percent of the variation you see in that trait. In other words, personality—even those parts of it that might be highly tied to genes—is still a complex mixture of biology and life experience.

The debate over the strength of genes in determining personality is especially critical for parents. Such knowledge not only labels infants and perhaps prejudices their care in either a positive or negative way, but there is always the possibility that parents might abdicate their parenting responsibilities if they believe their input has little effect. For example, a parent may decide that a baby girl is a screamer, just born that way and there is nothing a mother or father can do about it. Or if an infant son is always passive in his early responses, parents may fail to engage him, thinking such responses are fixed forever. And so every report that underscores a biological basis for personality has the potential to discount the influence of parenting because parents are led to believe "she was just born that way." Lost in the popular news reports on genetic discoveries is the fact that most of this work is narrowly focused and is not tested on a variable population. Also lost is the fact that no one is saying personality is hard-wired and unchangeable. Although people are born not as blank slates but with a certain brain chemistry and genetic complement, it is the experience of life that molds this biological given into a person. It is impossible to say that a particular personality trait or behavior is purely genetic or purely learned—everything is a mix of both. To favor either end of such an argument is inappropriate.

The ethnopediatric view is especially important when studying personality because it takes into account both heredity and environment. Only work that bridges lifestyles and varying parental caretaking, as well as the adaptive evolutionary scenario, can really help us to understand what makes people what they are.

Temperament

Each of us has a personality. Moreover, it is relatively easy to describe the personality of others in words that anyone can comprehend. But it is a difficult task to explain exactly why one personality develops rather than another. In other words, we can describe personality but we cannot always explain it. As I indicated earlier, a person's personality is defined by that individual's interactions with the world—how he or she responds to other people and to various situations. Personality is the sum total of who we are and what makes us distinct in behavior and thought from other humans. Temperament, one component of personality, is that part which is said to be most grounded in biology, more encoded on the genes and inherited and thus less changeable by what happens during life experience.[52] Temperament is generally defined as mood, activity level, and tenseness; that is, basic attitude. Psychologists have focused on measuring temperament because mood and attitude are perhaps the most basic characteristics of a person. More significant to scientists, temperament is defined by visible reactions to stimuli and can therefore be measured.

Not long ago, temperament was thought to be tied to climate, or a particular diet, or perhaps part of the body fluids or "humors." There was even a time in psychology when body type—being fat or thin, tall or squat—was correlated with temperament type; endomorphs, the bulky people, were thought to be naturally jolly, whereas ectomorphs, the tall thin types, were supposedly hyperactive. Today psychologists think of temperament as a rather amorphous cluster of behaviors with biological underpinnings, a set of reactions that are inherited, mediated by the biochemistry of the brain, and automatic.

But no two researchers agree on exactly which behaviors should be included under the label "temperament."[53] In general, temperament is the part of the personality that is reactive, the part of oneself that takes in stimuli and then responds without one's even thinking. A person's temperament supposedly determines how he or she will respond at the automatic physical level to fearful or funny situations, or how that person deals with stress. Temperament is emotional rather than cognitive, the immediate reaction rather than the well-thought-out response.[54]

Psychologists believe that much of this reactivity of temperament is biologically based; a person is born with a certain brain chemistry that follows a particular reactive path most times that a certain stimuli is presented, and this reaction is automatic, occurring without thinking.[55] Presumably, each of us reacts at a personal threshold and we navigate through that reaction; we are able to dampen or control that response at a particular rate, which is also part of our temperament.

In the end, these various reactions make up the temperamental part of what we call personality, because we spend much of the day automatically reacting to stimuli.[56] For example, you might be walking down the street when suddenly a car swerves in your direction. You jump away. This jump is automatic because you do not consciously register the car and do not really make a decision to jump. It just happens. The reaction is so hard-wired that even if you know in your mind that the car will miss, you jump anyway. But perhaps your walking companion, who also saw the car, stands frozen in place. Her reaction is also automatic, but quite different from yours. The two of you have different reactions and therefore different temperaments. Given its complexity, temperament is a "rubric" rather than a simple trait; in other words, temperamental values reflect tendencies rather than discrete behaviors.[57]

Psychologists are interested in infant and child temperament because, based on the belief that temperament is largely hard-wired, it should be demonstrable and testable soon after birth. Even if personality in general takes years to form and develop, the part of personality that is more biologically based, such as temperament, should be there in an infant for all to see. For parents, an infant's so-called temperament is important for another reason—reaction (the major measure of temperament) is a big part of the communication their baby has with them: Show the baby a new toy and he screams. Put the baby down and he is fine. Pick the baby up and she gurgles in pleasure. Since babies cannot talk, these temperamentally based reactions are often the only signals parents have as to how the baby feels. And so these automatic responses form the parents' early ideas about their child's personality.

Often a baby is described as either "easy" or "difficult," based on how the baby usually fares through the day; that is, how it reacts. Easy infants are those that are rhythmic in their body functions, adaptable to new situations, mild in their responses, and mostly in a good mood. Difficult babies are irregular, slow to adapt, intensely responsive to all stimuli, and generally negative in attitude. In one study, parents, especially fathers, characterized their babies as easy if they slept for long periods and did not need to be carried much.[58] In other words, what the psychologists define as temperament is not how parents perceive it. However, parents and most psychologists now believe that temperament, no matter how it is defined, is encoded on the genes and translated through an inherited brain chemistry; and that each individual is born with a particular temperament which is the filter through which each one of us interacts with life. According to this thesis, temperament is the most basic "state" of the infant against which all interaction is measured. Or is it?

The problem is that the public hears about studies of single facets of temperament and from these studies assumes a child's whole personality is fixed from birth. It is an easy leap of faith to make—after all, the baby *is* acting a certain way and seems to be independently expressing something and reacting in a certain way. But labels can be applied too early and too exclusively. As noted above, parents sometimes even have preconceptions about their babies' temperaments prenatally, based on vague "feelings," and they tend to hold on to those labels after the child is born no matter how the baby actually behaves.[59] At a baby's birth, parents start out trying to identify who it looks like and they end up parceling out its personality as well. Americans, for example, assume that talents, behavior, personality traits, and attitude are all handed down like eye color and nose shape. And while there might certainly be some sort of genetically based foundation to the makeup of an individual—we are, after all, organic beings—no research so far has categorically shown that any particular gene or set of genes is alone responsible for a particular pattern of behavior. There are exciting hints and real possibilities pointing to biological influence for some categories of behavior, such as a tendency to be depressed or optimistic, but the data are not as clear as some might expect.

The Inheritance of Temperament

The most detailed studies of infant temperament have been conducted by psychologist Jerome Kagan. Kagan's objective has been to test for the persistence of one aspect of temperament—the continuum of inhibited–uninhibited in response to stimuli. His hypothesis is that this parameter of temperament, whether one is afraid or unafraid in novel situations, is inborn and thus will persist throughout a lifetime. Kagan states quite clearly that environment and experience can affect the development of this facet of personality; he also knows that the percentage of children who can be polarized as clearly timid or outgoing is rather small.

According to his work, 15 percent of Caucasian children in America can be classified as shy and subdued (or inhibited), and another 15 percent can be labeled as sociable and effectively spontaneous (or uninhibited). The inhibited children are characterized as cautious and emotionally reserved in new situations, while the uninhibited children are more socially easy and less fearful.[60] According to Kagan's work, these labels, defined by a battery of tests, are consistent from several months of age until these children are at least ten years old. That is, 30 percent of white middle-class American kids show reliable responses, either negative or positive, to novel objects and situations, suggesting their temperaments are naturally directed one way or another; and this particular facet of temperament persists from infancy through childhood, and presumably into adulthood.[61] The rest of the population, the 70 percent, lie somewhere in the middle of the inhibited–uninhibited continuum, in a gray area where they are either not consistent in their responses over time or sometimes afraid and sometimes interested.

Kagan's work stands on fifteen years of data, endlessly repeated tests, and sound reasoning about brain chemistry and the logic of automatic responses that should help the human animal approach or avoid novel objects and situations.[62] More recently a group of researchers has even found a possible dopamine receptor gene on chromosome number eleven that correlates with seeking out novelty, again giving genetic support to Kagan's hypothesis.[63] The possible genetic link to inhibition finds additional support in animal literature where behaviorists have shown that nonhuman primates and other animals behave differentially, in an inhibited or uninhibited way, to novel situations.[64]

But looking through the ethnopediatric lens suggests that a cautionary brake should be applied to any ready acceptance of a hard-wired temperament. Is the inhibited–uninhibited dichotomy really a human universal? Or is it affected by differences in culture and various styles of parenting?

Babies in the Lab

If temperament is inherited it should show up early, be distinct, and be consistent over time. To test this hypothesis, Dr. Kagan studied a series of babies periodically during the first year of life and then several more times until they were young children. At four months, testing begins as a subject is set up in a plastic car seat in front of a video camera and made to feel content. The baby's mother is close by; if the baby frets, her mother steps in to reassure her. Once the baby is settled, a research assistant dangles an object on a string in front of the baby's eyes—something new, something novel. Each baby, of course, reacts in a different way. She might reach for the toy and make noises. Or she might arch her back, become tense, and move her tongue in and out of her mouth, signaling an uncomfortable moment. She might burst out screaming. The same baby is then tested again with a mobile full of new objects, and then with a tape recording of an unfamiliar female voice repeating simple syllables like *ba-ba-ba*. At nine months, the same baby is tested again and this time an unfamiliar female comes into the room and personally presents the baby with objects. Sometimes the mother is there, sometimes not. The baby might get a robot, or a puppet, or perhaps a clown will show up.

The point is to test these kids with strange objects, unfamiliar sounds, and unknown people.[65] Again, about 30 percent of the infants and children reacted in an extreme way. And it is not just their body language that shows different reactions. Those who are classified as inhibited show greater heart rate accelerations when under the stress of novelty—that is, their physiology reflects their fear. And there is a tendency for kids to have the same sort of reaction to the same sort of stimuli when it is presented again in later months.

Kagan says that intense motor activity and crying during these tests indicates an inhibited temperament; those kids who are not very upset are less inhibited. Since responses at the extreme ends of the reaction continuum are consistent over the test months, these experiments speak to a biologically stable, hard-wired facet of temperament.

There is no doubt that what Kagan and his colleagues see in that lab is genuine—the videotapes of this work clearly show babies either cooing and reaching for novel objects or getting upset and shying away. But the problem, from an ethnopediatric point of view, is that the study situation follows Western—specifically, American—babies and therefore tells us little about how universally an inherited temperament might be expressed. One can only imagine attempting to perform this same test on !Kung San infants. First of all, a San mother probably would not allow a strange white researcher to take her baby out of her sight and put in a stiff plastic seat in the first place. And the notion of offering novel objects or unfamiliar people is ludicrous for a hunter and gatherer who grows up in the same social group handling the same objects over time. A Gusii baby, on the other hand, has been molded from infancy to be quiet and affable. More than likely, there will be little reaction from a Gusii baby. And a Japanese child might be more disturbed by being separated from its mother than by any toy dangled in its face. In other words, the test setup—the idea of testing novel objects and people, and maybe even the dichotomy of inhibited–uninhibited—is a white, Western, middle-class scenario. Such studies may not be applicable to all human babies. It works in Western culture to separate children on this plane of temperament, but studies of temperament in other cultures are few, and the ones that do look at babies are unclear.

Another possible criticism of Kagan's work is that by the time babies enter the test, at four months of age, they have already interacted with caretakers over numerous hours, and such interaction sets up a pattern of reaction in which environment has had a major influence. My discussion of the symbiotic nature of the infant–adult relationship in Chapter Two suggests that babies take in stimuli from the moment of birth and are molded by how adults care for them. Testing them several months later, then, cannot filter out the influence of parenting style regardless of a baby's inborn nature.

Environment has such an effect that broad cultural differences can sometimes be detected. In one study of temperament in Taiwan, a group of researchers asked 349 parents of young infants to fill out Carey's Revised Infant Temperament Questionnaire which asks about babies' reactions to stimuli.[66] Comparing their answers to those given by parents in the United States, the Taiwanese babies appeared to be, at least according to their parents' perceptions and the way they answered the form, more intense, less active, less adaptable, more negative in mood, and more responsive. On the surface, then, Chinese infants—at least those in modern industrialized Taiwan—seem quite different from babies in the United States. But there was also incredible overlap in the scores from both cultures; apparently there are "difficult" babies and "easy" babies in both groups, and most babies fall somewhere in between. Comparing twenty-four Chinese-American and twenty-four Euro-American two-day-olds, another group of researchers found that the Chinese-American babies did not get as excited as the Euro-American babies; they were not as red-faced when frustrated and didn't move through as many state changes during the exam. The Chinese-American babies were essentially more placid. This difference was demonstrated even more clearly when the babies were moved about—the Chinese-American babies didn't much mind being placed face down or having a blanket placed over their faces, but the Euro-American babies protested. Similarly, the Chinese-American babies were easier to console and were able to calm themselves much more quickly than the Euro-American babies.[67] Interestingly, the same researchers found that Navaho newborns were even more placid and subdued than the Chinese-American babies.[68]

But again, the confusing specter of the interaction of genes and environment rears its ugly head here. Who can tell what influences on temperament occur prenatally? Surely nutrition, maternal health, and activity levels influence the developing fetus. More than likely there are universally variable and inherited aspects of temperament and personality. Testing white babies in one lab in one culture, or testing on a few nonwhite babies in select cultures, is not enough to figure out how much of personality and temperament are inborn.

More important, it might be impossible to translate tests of personality and temperament into other cultures in any reasonable way. In Ghana, for example, researchers were interested in testing kids on perspective—that is, how three-dimensional objects end up on paper. They found that Ghanaian children simply could not identify a horizon line when it was drawn on a piece of paper.[69] It wasn't that the kids were stupid; they just didn't have any experience with drawing, painting, or looking at the world as represented by a flat piece of paper with things drawn on it. The whole concept of two dimensions was completely foreign to them. Once they had been initiated into the idea of paper and pencil and how objects appear when drawn, which took only a few hours, they quickly got it.

It might also be difficult to extend the categories of temperament across cultures when the categories mean different things in different environments. For example, "difficult" babies in Western cultures are those who do not sleep for long periods and those who cry. Under a different caretaking package, these reactions would not even show up. More important, there is no reason to assume that what is "bad" in one culture will end up "bad" in another culture. Dutch researcher Marten de Vries followed a set of Masai infants in Kenya during a period of great drought in the 1970s.[70] He labeled babies "difficult" or "easy" based on his observation and the application of Western categories of adaptability, intense reactions, regularity, and whether or not they were manageable. He also used the standard Western Infant Temperament Questionnaire, modified for the Masai (he had to delete questions about going to the doctor and add questions about being carried), to ask parents how they perceived their babies. He wanted to categorize the babies on a continuum of temperament, and so he concentrated on the ten easiest and ten most difficult babies as his subjects. Returning three months later, he sought out the parents of the twenty babies at the extremes but found the parents of only thirteen—Masai are, after all, nomadic people. The parents had been dealing for years with the destruction that a drought causes to people who make their living off the land, and all the babies were already malnourished. In the following three months, during some of the worst of the drought, seven of the thirteen infants he had located died. But interestingly, only one of the so-called difficult babies, as categorized by Western criteria, were dead, while six of those he labeled as easy were dead. De Vries surmised that traits we perceive as difficult under ample conditions might be more beneficial to survival during times of nutritional stress. A "bad" temperament might be evolutionarily advantageous under certain circumstances or in certain environments. In times of nutritional deprivation, it may be the fretful baby that gets the most milk, or is picked up most often. It is only in our affluence that we use the negative word "difficult" to describe the fact that the baby is evolutionarily designed to gain attention. The perceptions of temperament, in other words, are relative.

But the strongest caveat to Kagan's work comes from studies of infants and their parents. Although certainly temperament and personality have some sort of biological basis—behavior is, after all, mediated through the brain and acted out by the body—there is also no question that from the moment of birth, the input from parents influences even the very temperament and personality of an infant.

Symbiosis and Infant Temperament

A friend of mine was once staying with a family in India. The baby slept with its mother and, my friend reported with great surprise, the baby never wore diapers. The mother was so in tune with the baby that she might be standing with it in her arms and then suddenly hold the baby aloft while it peed, wipe it off, and then go about her work. "She just knew," said my friend. If we accept the scenario that until rather recently babies were always in contact with another person, this type of awareness on the part of the mother doesn't seem so impossible. But it also means that the mother's awareness becomes an intimate part of the baby's environment, and thus an influence on the infant's developing personality.

In a more evolutionarily appropriate infant–caretaker scheme, the infant is a social partner, part of a dyad.[71] Both mother and infant are interested in being in equilibrium, that is, in a stable and contented state. This goal is achieved by mutual regulation, by reciprocity, and by keeping tabs on each other.[72] This system nicely describes the infant–caretaker pair, and as I have presented in Chapter Two, there is a great deal of evidence that infants and those who love them are attuned to each other and have evolutionarily selected to be so. They are a biological system of interdependence that seeks the same goal—stability. The infant's part in the system is straightforward. It monitors its internal state and then announces any deficiencies, crying for food, warmth, or touch. Crying and smiling are signals of what is right or wrong with the baby's state, its equilibrium. And when there is a tilt in the equilibrium, the baby tells the other part of the dyad and seeks reciprocity. The problem comes when the other half of the dyad is not checking in, or is refusing to hold up his or her part of the system; the pact is broken and a mismatch occurs. A mismatch, an unanswered signal, is of course not always bad. Think of a tennis game. When one player lobs a ball off to one side of the court, it makes the other player run and reach out, which theoretically pushes the opponent to be a better player in the long run. This view might be applied to the scenario of one type of Western caretaking system—food, touch, and comfort come, but not on an EEA infant-requested schedule. The system is not perfect from the baby's point of view—perhaps a few too many balls are hit out of bounds, and needs are lobbed not when asked—but the interaction does follow some sort of game plan.

More serious imbalances occur, as several studies have shown, when there is no interactive system at all, when the mismatch is so great that if these two individuals were adults, they would divorce. Anthropologist Edward Tronick, who has worked both with Efé pygmy babies in the forest of Zaire and with American babies at Children's Hospital in Boston, describes such a scene. Imagine two mothers playing peek-a-boo with their babies. In one case the mother is patient, waits for the baby to look at her, and then responds to his giggles. In the other case the mother becomes impatient, hones in on the baby, demands its attention, and when he cries, she walks away.[73] In the first case the baby looks at the mother, responds by smiling, and she further responds by playing the game again. It is an emotional feedback system that reinforces each of the players to respond and signal. In the second scenario the baby and the mother are mismatched, but the onus of this mismatch must be placed on the mother, at least at first. Young infants can signal only with what they have—crying and body language—and perhaps this mother is unable to read those signals. So she gets in the baby's face, and when he signals his displeasure, she walks away. Tronick points out that babies have self-directed regulating systems that take over once their signals have not been read, and as a result the system is no longer in a state of equilibrium. When signals are missed, babies stop signaling; they withdraw; they suck their thumbs; they turn away; they try to right the system themselves by not sending out any more signals.

These signals and how they are responded to form an emotional feedback system. The infant is signaling emotionally and the adult is responding emotionally. And each member of the dyad is so attuned to the other that infants use the emotional state of the primary caretaker as a guide; the infant is emotionally reflecting off the parent.[74] The infant is not only able to regulate its state in order to exercise some control over it, but in turn the baby's mood also affects the caretaker because of the nature of the symbiotic relationship. Both individuals in the dyad modify their expressions relative to the other, and their emotions are therefore reciprocal and often synchronous.[75]

In studies of mothers interacting with their babies, Tronick found that 30 percent of the time that American babies are in face-to-face contact with their mothers, their expressions are coordinated.[76] But when mothers are depressed, the coordination is almost nil, or is misdi-

rected. Depressed mothers either look away from their babies more frequently, or display angry irritated faces and are inappropriately intrusive
and negative toward them. Sometimes a depressed mother's timing is just
off and the response comes too late or it is inappropriate to the initial
signal, and the mother and infant are stuck in a miscoordinated maze
where neither one is connected to the other.[77] In another study of fifty-
eight mother–infant dyads, researchers found that depressed mothers
accomplished the usual caretaking tasks as well as mothers who were not
depressed. But the unhappy mothers displayed fewer positive facial expressions and less vocal and visual contact, and their overall responses to
the baby were delayed.[78] Babies are intensely cued in to their mothers,
and in response to such cues will self-regulate by turning away, by
rocking back and forth, by pushing the mother away, and/or by sucking
their thumbs—thus exhibiting what psychologists call a "negative affect."
And then the mothers under stress, it seems, tend to have babies who cry
more, sleep less, and are more fussy.[79] A vicious cycle is in motion.
Although no one has followed these babies to see how they turn out as
adults, it is reasonable to suggest that such early unhappiness must have a
strong effect on adult personality and attitude.

Tronick and his colleague Jeffrey Cohn tested the effect of maternal
response through a series of experiments in which they asked mothers to
"fake" depression. Three-month-old infants were placed in seats and
their mothers then approached. For three minutes the mothers acted
normally, played with their babies, made their usual baby talk and funny
faces, which their babies responded to with positive sounds and happy
movements. And then for three minutes the mothers were asked to elimi-
nate all expression from their faces, talk in a monotone, not touch the
babies, and generally be unresponsive. The photographs of the babies'
reactions are startling. Once the mother acted depressed, the baby
quickly smiled and tried to engage her by reaching out, but she remained
unresponsive and the baby quickly became "sober and wary," in
Tronick's words; the baby looked away and even tried to orient its body
away from the mother as well.[80] What had been a rhythmic, coordi-

nated, and positive tumble through various levels of greeting, mutual responsivity, down time, and play again between mother and infant now became a stilted and jerky interpersonal interaction between miscoordinated strangers.[81]

After three minutes of this experimental protocol, the mothers were allowed to act normal again. Many of them expressed how difficult it had been not to respond to their babies' attempts to engage. More startling, however, babies did not switch back so easily. It took thirty seconds of coaxing for babies to lose their wary looks and engage with their mothers again.[82] And this after a mere three minutes of unresponsiveness. Imagine the lifelong effects for infants stuck with less-than-interactive partners. There's simply no dyad for reciprocity, and by default the "other's" mood, when it is the mother, becomes the infant's. It is therefore reasonable to propose, especially during this highly dependent, symbiotic stage, that the caretaker's mood and the ability of the dyad to connect form a compelling force behind infant state.

So when mothers are especially sensitive and responsive, when they are naturally empathetic and happy around the baby, attachment develops and the dyad functions well; this healthy attachment in turn serves the baby in other social situations. But when the mother, or the primary caretaker, is generally unresponsive, depressed, or incapable of empathy, babies eventually lose interest in regaining contact and turn inward.[83] They are more likely to exhibit negative responses and the attachment process does not go well. It is reasonable to predict that babies developing in such a system will not fare well in other interpersonal interactions.

Crying, Temperament, and the Infant State

This early feedback of signal and response, the dance of equilibrium, might help to explain why some babies have a happy and less fearful temperament while others are forever fearful and cautious. It might explain temperament with as much validity as genetic endowment. Going beyond the effects that genes might have, the work by Tronick and others shows that even from day one, the way babies connect to their caretakers has a powerful influence on how they see the world. One child might grow up self-assured with a positive attitude because even in infancy she experienced a state of equilibrium with a caretaker who was sensitive and empathetic—a symbiosis that was coordinated, smooth, and gave positive feedback. And another child might grow up with low self-esteem and a negative outlook on life because his signals were always misread or not read at all, and he spent his early months self-regulating, alone, to a stable state. Disengagement in adulthood and lack of a sense of self might find its roots back in the first few months of a child's life when he or she feels powerless to foster reciprocity and has to disengage from a mismatched caretaking dyad.

In a three-way comparison of hunter-and-gatherer cultures, the United States, and other nonindustrial societies, the heavy hand of culture clearly maps out how parenting traditions influence the parent–infant symbiotic dyad. Parents can respond only when they are in close proximity to their babies and in many cultures there is simply no one around to be part of the dyad. In all of ten hunter-and-gatherer societies studied today, infants are carried more than 50 percent of the time. In only 56 percent of nonindustrial societies are babies carried that often. In the United States, babies are typically in physical contact with their parents 25 percent of the day.[84] This pattern is consistent in other areas of caretaking as well. In hunter-and-gatherer societies, mothers sleep with their infants and respond immediately to their cries. Parents in other nonindustrial cultures do that as well, but less often. In other words, when culture and modernity intervene, babies are not attended to as quickly and spend more time alone. As a result, no one is there to respond even if the baby cries or fusses to announce a problem.

From a baby's point of view, the hunter-and-gatherer life is better because it supplies all the necessary ingredients and opportunities for a symbiotic parent–infant dyad. The point is not that we need to recreate the dynamics of hunter/gatherer societies, but rather that we recognize those parts of other lifestyles that are beneficial to infants and figure out ways to incorporate those lessons into the parent–infant tradition in our own culture, if we choose to do so.

In the 1950s, pediatricians, child-care experts, and parents in Western culture thought that picking up a baby every time it cried or feeding it whenever it was hungry was "indulgent." Today we know that what was once thought indulgent is better viewed as what is needed by the baby and part of the natural course of events. An infant and its primary caretaker are intimately entwined. The baby is communicating "intent" when it cries or gurgles, providing information about its state. It is not calling for attention, at least not in a negative way. The baby is merely communicating and asking for engagement; it is initiating a dialog. We now also know that neither genes nor environment alone are responsible for how a person turns out. A person may be dealt a certain kind of temperament, or various parts of personality, but from the moment that baby interacts with other humans, his or her self is molded by the surroundings. Humans, like all creatures, are part and parcel of nature, a combination of genes and experience.

CHAPTER SIX

FOOD
FOR
THOUGHT

One of the most important lessons about breast-feeding can be learned with a small balloon and a tube of lipstick. I was handed a bright yellow balloon, so I used M.A.C. Russian Red, Madonna's favorite lipstick, to contrast with it. I filled the balloon full of water, tied it shut, and then held it up over my head as if it were a breast and I was a hungry baby. After applying the lipstick, I opened my mouth as wide as possible and latched onto the balloon with my lips, taking a long noisy suck before releasing the balloon. A perfect "O" in Russian Red was painted on the end of the balloon. To complete the experiment, I tried again, but this time I squeezed the pseudo-breast like a sandwich, horizontally; after a good suck, the lipstick impression was much bigger, and much wider. It demonstrated that a minor adjustment in breast presentation made for a much better fit between my adult mouth and the water balloon. If I had been an infant and that balloon a real breast, the horizontal squeeze would have helped me take not just the nipple into my mouth but a large measure of breast tissue as well, giving me the opportunity to press on the area around the aureole and squeeze out more milk.

The point of the balloon experiment is to show that breast-feeding takes a certain amount of finesse both from the baby and the mother to work efficiently. And most of that finesse is based on common sense, as

Diane Wiessinger, a "lactation consultant," showed me. Knowing the American love of gadgets, and the need for visual aids when educating, Wiessinger's particular bag of tricks—a large canvas carry-all—is stuffed with the tools of her trade; and by the end of our talk, the floor of her living room and the chairs were littered with such items as a soft rubber shield that extends the nipple and helps trigger the sucking reflex by touching the far reaches of a baby's upper palate; a stuffed breast that opens up to a diagram of breast biology; a blue and yellow portable breast pump that can double-pump any engorged mother on the go; a rag baby doll dressed in calico ready to demonstrate what breast-feeding is all about; and a balloon with lipstick. Besides education about breast-feeding and positional tips, Wiessinger provides reassurance and support for her clients. Sometimes she offers a voice of approval in a culture devoid of generational support systems. "I am the replacement for everybody's sister and neighbor and mother and aunt, for the older women in the community," she explains.

I had come to Diane's house to ask why women have to be taught to breast-feed. From an evolutionary point of view, it would seem that breast-feeding should be one of the more instinctual behaviors, like eating or sleeping or sex. In most mammals, if mothers don't know how to offer their milk or babies don't know how to suckle, the infant dies. If the purpose of reproduction is to pass on genes, it would seem that feeding would be one of the more hard-wired biological behaviors. In explanation, Wiessinger offered this story: A female gorilla, born and raised in a zoo, gave birth to an infant. In an attempt to nurse it, the mother held her infant incorrectly, with the back of the baby's head toward the nipple. The keepers feared for the infant's life and took the baby away. During the gorilla's next pregnancy, the keepers tried an experiment. They lined up a group of breast-feeding humans outside the cage and allowed the mother gorilla to observe. When her next infant was born, the mother gorilla, too, turned the baby toward her breast and everything went fine.

The point is that breast-feeding is not necessarily an automatic response for any mammal, especially under less than natural conditions. It requires certain triggers and certain coordination between mother and offspring. And humans are no different from other species. Imagine taking a newborn calf or lamb or piglet away from its mother in order to wash it and do tests. Farmers know that any separation of mother and newborn farm animals results in rejection of the infant by the mother or an inability on the part of the baby to suckle. Although we recognize this situation in livestock, we have only recently become aware that human babies have the same sort of reflexes designed to seal the pact between mother and infant right after birth. As many pediatricians and hospital staff now know, the sucking reflex is strongest within the first thirty minutes after birth. Newborns placed on their mothers' bellies directly after birth also begin wiggling and moving determinedly toward the breast when left on the mother's body for twenty minutes.[1] "But," explains Wiessinger, "if you take the baby away and give him a bath and take his footprints and measure him and wrap him up and bring him back, he's lost the dance." This interruption in the loop can derail the whole process. In other words, breast-feeding is instinctually and biologically triggered, but it can also be behaviorally disrupted. For example, when the birth process became medicalized in the United States in the 1930s and more babies were born in hospitals, the number of mothers breast-feeding dropped. Also, some mothers were unable to breast-feed successfully. Their failure was, in part, probably due to the long separation of baby from mother for long periods in the hospital right after birth. Today, with birthing rooms and babies kept close to their mothers at all times, breast-feeding has been proceeding more smoothly.

Feeding an infant by any means is a complex interaction between biology and culture, yet it is an elemental interaction for the infant's survival. One of the things ethnopediatricians consider is how a human infant's instinctual reflexes operate and what the infant needs to stay alive. There is, of course, a great deal of behavioral wriggle room in this process. Because of this, ethnopediatricians assume that culture has interfered and influenced this process for as long as humans could alter or manipulate their world.

THE EVOLUTION OF INFANT FEEDING

Breasts were designed to deliver milk to babies. But breast milk is not the only way offspring can be nourished. Baby birds, for example, never suckle from the breast. From the moment they crack out of the egg, young birds are able to digest regurgitated insects their mother or father provides. Newborn fish must forage on their own for food as soon as they are mature enough to swim away from wherever they were deposited. Loggerhead turtle offspring are abandoned after the mother digs a hole in beach sand and deposits the eggs, waddling back to the sea. Once hatched, baby turtles must dig out from their sandy underground nest and instinctually flipper down the beach and out to sea, where they seem to instinctually know what to eat. But the group of 4,237 extant species know as mammals[2] have evolved quite differently—only the mothers can supply a species-specific liquid that provides nutrients for the young.

The Evolution of Breasts

About sixty-five million years ago, at the end of the Mesozoic era and the beginning of the Cenozoic, the niche once dominated by the dinosaurs was available for other creatures. The opportunistic could move into that niche now empty of large reptiles, and prosper in their place. Among these creatures that flourished were small egg-laying animals, a group that had been around for at least a million years and that sported specialized patches on their chests.[3] Sitting on their eggs, the mothers of these species gave off body heat through these warming pads. The patches also had a glandular function, secreting a liquid rich in lysozyme that coated the eggs with an antibacterial slime and destroyed harmful microorganisms.[4] When the eggs hatched, the new infants probably licked up some of that egg-coating ooze, which turned out to be immunologically protective once ingested.[5] It may be that the newly hatched babies were simply hydrating themselves by licking their mothers' chests for the liquid that had collected there.[6] In any case, those babies who licked up the fluid gained an advantage for their efforts in terms of survival—they either grew faster or bigger, or they were healthier than those who ignored the opportunity. Maternal ooze eventually evolved strong nutrient properties that could sustain a baby even when the mother was unable to bring back food to the nest or the infant was too weak to forage on its own. Thus lactation was born.

At first the mammary gland must have been a kind of sweat gland, an eccrine gland, a gland that excreted material to the outside of the body like those found in armpits that excrete water and electrolytes. In fact, the gland might have emitted distinctive and attractive odors that brought premammallian infants close to their mothers' chests. Eventually these chest glands changed into apocrine glands, tissue that can synthesize proteins, carbohydrates, and lipids rather than just excrete water.[7] We know that breasts, and the liquid they manufacture, must have coevolved with the infants' ability to find the nipple, suck, and digest what was ingested. Mothers must have already been adapted to stay close to their infants and engage in some sort of positive maternal care, and infants must have been selected to turn only to their mothers and what they offered.[8] Eventually these premammals began to give birth to live young, and most of them developed hair. But their most distinguishing characteristic, what set them apart from reptiles and birds, was their ability to lactate from specialized glands to nourish their young. Thus began the evolutionary path of modern mammals, animals in which the female members invest highly in each offspring by manufacturing and secreting for days, weeks, or months a fluid that is the sole food of their young.

This scenario—with egg-laying animals secreting specialized chest fluid eventually evolving into creatures that routinely give birth to live young and nurse them—is at best speculative, but it is the only scenario that can be reconstructed from the available fossil evidence.[9] It is also supported by creatures living today, an odd group of animals called monotremes. These are the egg-laying but lactating group that includes the duck-billed platypus. They provide evidence that live birth, or viviparity, came after lactation, and that nursing and sucking was selected for long before babies were born without shells.

Why did this system of intense maternal investment evolve? Clearly, there are other ways to feed infants, including leaving them to forage on their own or allowing others to help in the task. The answer is complex; it involves a nutritional, protective, maturational, and social advantage to mammal young. First of all, nursing is actually quite efficient, especially from the infant's point of view. When being nursed on maternal secretions, infants can stay in the nest, making them less likely to succumb to predators. Also, the infant need not expend any energy looking for food. From the mother's point of view it is more efficient as well. Babies with their less mature digestive systems and immature masticatory apparatus have to eat different food than adults do. For example, baby crocodiles, who do not nurse, eat entirely different things than adult crocodiles and so to support every age-class crocodiles must reside in a habitat of varied foodstuffs so that they can all obtain their nutritional needs. But if a mother can go out and forage and then internally synthesize that food into milk for its young, such a food source is probably more efficient in the end. In addition, mothers can exploit new areas, and even get by on marginally nutritious food, because as long as she eats the whole brood gets fed. Although it takes a certain number of calories for an adult female to synthesize milk, when times are rough and the food supply is low, it takes fewer calories for a mother to forage than for babies to look for food themselves.

In animals that do not lactate, infants must be born with the face, teeth, and jaws of adults so that they can forage on their own.[10] Teeth in particular are a problem because they do not grow in width or girth, like the rest of the jaw, and so most such animals have replaceable teeth that come in at each stage of jaw development. This puts intense selection pressure on growth and maturity for the infant. Because mammals do not need teeth to suckle, a late-growing set of "baby teeth" is enough.[11] When Mom is providing the diet after birth, teeth, which are energetically costly, can take their time coming in, and the whole facial architecture can develop after birth and later accommodate adult teeth when they appear.

And then there is the social bonding that takes place during nursing. Lactation and sucking require a physical bond between mother and infant, and this physicality initializes an attachment that can be beneficial for both in the long term in social species where interpersonal connections become so important to daily life. It also provides an opportunity for learning and behavioral modification. Lactation, then, appears to be a successful alternate route to developing offspring until they are physically and behaviorally able to forage and survive on their own.

The Hominid Blueprint

Humans, as primates and mammals, are designed to feed off mother's milk from birth. We can assume that from the time humans evolved into a separate species during the Pleistocene, 1.5 million years ago, babies fed only on mother's milk. There may have been some sort of supplementation—even infant monkeys poke around in their mothers' mouths and sometimes sneak already masticated food—but most likely, before there were clay vessels for holding and distributing milk and handy sources of milk from domesticated animals, babies survived solely on mother's milk. Given that breast-feeding was the only option, what style of breast-feeding might those mothers have used?

Human groups today that still hunt and gather in a manner that is likely similar to that of our early ancestors exhibit an intense style of infant feeding. Babies are almost always carried on their mothers' hips and have access to their breasts at all times. In fact, babies carried in this manner are soon responsible for wiggling into position and latching onto the breast on their own; the phrase "feeding on demand" has no real meaning in this case and perhaps should be called "on cue." Infants are not demanding anything and mothers are not giving in; the baby is simply feeding.[12] Infants of hunter-gatherers feed very frequently. !Kung San infants, for example, feed every thirteen minutes on average.[13] This pattern of frequent feeding, with the infant soon able to guide the process himself, probably echoes how the first human infants fed until they were able to walk, sometime during the first year or so.[14] Human infants long ago must have also been carried all the time; they probably slept with their mothers and fed frequently throughout the day and night. In fact, during 99 percent of human history this was surely the pattern of infant eating, sleeping, and contact.[15] The current pattern in some cultures of long intervals between feeding, no night feeding, and supplementation of mother's milk with other species' milk or artificial milk is very recent for the human species.

Although it is clear that early hominid babies were suckling continuously, there is no easy way to tell how long they were dependent on their mothers for milk. In the West today, solid food such as rice cereal is introduced during the first four to eight months of age; and from there, a steady progression of mashed and then chunky but soft foods are usually introduced, until eventually the child is ingesting more solid food than milk. In that way, the child is weaned easily—it seems to happen by mutual agreement (although at times the child must be physically prevented from using the nipple, and weaning becomes a noisy conflict between mother and child). Weaning in other cultures tells a similar story—the introduction of solid food and then either a gradual or abrupt cessation of mother's milk as the primary food source. In many cases, weaning is culturally mandated when the child is forced to stop nursing because the mother is pregnant again; many cultures have a taboo against nursing during pregnancy, although, in fact, milk production continues. Some cultures have a taboo against sex during nursing, and a mother will wean so that she can resume sexual relations. And in some cultures, such as America where it is culturally frowned on for a walking toddler to grab for the breast, early weaning is encouraged.

Different cultures have various standards about the duration of breast-feeding. Some are based on interactions between mother and father, others are based on who-knows-what. Anthropologist Katherine Dettwyler has suggested that there is a biological pattern among species that can be used to find the ideal human weaning age. One possibility is to use gestation length as a measure; the assumption here is that a mother of any species should nurse for the same length of time as gestation. If that is true, humans should nurse for about a year, taking into account the nine-month gestation period and the fact that compared to other mammals, newborn human infants arrive approximately three months too soon. Achievement of a particular weight, such as three or four times birth weight, is another possible standard. Again, nursing would last at least a year, on average, if tripling birth weight is the standard. Eruption of certain teeth is the best indicator of masticatory maturity, and this physical sign of readiness to move on to solid food could be used to signal an appropriate weaning time.[16] However, if eruption of the first permanent molar is the standard, human kids would nurse until they were five years old.[17]

The best predictive method may be to place humans within the context of other primates, who wean at anywhere from one to seven years of age depending on the body size of the species and the typical interbirth interval. Large primates, of course, have longer gestations and spend a longer time breast-feeding. For example, a macaque monkey that is about the size of a large house cat will nurse for at least a year and a bit more if there is no new pregnancy that year. But young macaques begin eating food from their mothers' mouths or foraging some on their own after several months. They just prefer to drink from their mothers and thus don't give it up until they are forced to do so; weaning in small-bodied macaques is complete by two years of age or earlier. Chimpanzee infants, which are much bigger animals, nurse for several years, at least four. Based on this primate trajectory, and the fact that human infants are born a bit too soon, Dettwyler suggests that human infants are designed to be weaned somewhere between two and a half and seven years old.[18] Interestingly enough, the cross-cultural data fit this prediction; only in the West are infants weaned before one year of age.[19] It is reasonable to suggest, then, that human infants long ago, back in the Pleistocene when they were carried at all times and there were no supplemental foods around, were suckling whenever they could in short but frequent bouts and for at least two and a half years, probably more.

Archaeologists have discovered that since the Pleistocene, humans have always suckled infants for several years. Using biochemical analysis of bones buried long ago, researchers have been able to estimate of a given human population when its children moved from breast milk to other foods.[20] In one group of skeletons from South Dakota dated between 5500–2000 B.C., children were apparently depending on food other than mother's milk by the time they were twenty months of age.[21] Recorded history also tells a similar story. Middle Eastern groups in 3000 B.C. were breast-fed for two to three years, which was the common age of weaning for Hebrew populations.[22] At another North American site near the Missouri River dated to the seventeenth century, researchers were able to determine that infants were breast-fed exclusively for one year and that weaning was between two and six years of age.[23] This work has been confirmed at other sites, where researchers have also found evidence that not so long ago there typically was no abrupt change from breast milk to other foods, as we often think weaning should be, but a gradual change.[24]

In all cases, this hominid blueprint of the way babies were fed for 99 percent of human history indicates breast milk as the primary or sole food until two years of age or so, and nursing commonly continuing for several more years.

THE BIOLOGY OF BREAST-FEEDING

The human breast, unique among the glands of the body, is a plastic organ. That is, once past the maturation to adulthood, all breasts change during the menstrual cycle under the influence of various hormones and even more if a pregnancy occurs.[25]

The Mechanics of Breast-feeding

During pregnancy, the mammary glands grow exponentially in a process called mammogenesis. The milk-manufacturing cells proliferate and mature, and by the end of the fourth month of pregnancy the breasts are fully functional. This mammary growth is promoted by estrogen, progesterone, and lactogen coming from the infant's placenta, as well as prolactin produced by the mother. Toward the end of pregnancy, high levels of progesterone actually inhibit the production of milk and it takes birth, and expulsion of the progesterone-producing placenta, for milk production to really kick in. Essentially, it is the infant's hormones that prepare the mother for nursing, first by pushing the mammary glands to grow and mature and then by inhibiting milk production until after birth.[26]

Each breast is composed of fifteen to twenty-five segments, or lobi, which constitute a lactiferous duct system. These ducts are embedded in fat and connective tissue and are fully supplied with blood vessels, nerves, and lymphatics.[27] Within each duct system are thousands of sacs lined with cells called alveoli that manufacture milk—a process called lactogenesis—by absorbing water, salts, sugar, and fat from the blood. Breasts are, of course, nicely designed for their function. The aureole, the darker area surrounding the nipple, contains apocrine glands that produce sweat, which both lubricates the nipple to prevent soreness and emits an odor that probably helps baby find the source of milk.[28]

During pregnancy, increased levels of both estrogen and progesterone are responsible for what one text calls "aborization," that is, extensive tree-like branching of the gland; the duct system sprouts more branches and the lines elongate.[29] Lactogenesis begins during the final five months of pregnancy—this is why women who miscarry might produce fluid from the breasts. About three months before birth, lactogenesis in the alveolar cells steps up production, but no milk is secreted. At that point, plasma progesterone and estrogen fall rapidly while prolactin levels stay high, and a milklike fluid called colostrum is produced and passed through the ducts. Colostrum is high in protein, low in sugar and fat, and particularly loaded with protective lysozymes and immunoglobulins; it is therefore exquisitely designed to protect a newborn. Unfortunately, in many cultures, colostrum—which is thicker than milk and a more yellow color—is considered not good for babies.[30]

Once lactogenesis is in full production, the milk pours through the duct system where it joins with milk from the other segments and eventually flows to an area right behind the nipple called the lactiferous sinus.[31] Think of a mountain range watershed upside-down. Traversing the range are reservoirs and small lakes that catch falling rain or melting snow, joined together by innumerable tiny streams and creeks, and they all empty into the tip of the upside-down cone. The tip in this analogy is the single nipple pore that projects from the end of the breast. But unlike the watershed, there is no cistern or holding tank here to collect runoff until it's needed. There is simply a direct and open line from milk-manufacturing ducts to the nipple opening.

Prolactin is the key hormone for initiating lactogenesis and maintaining lactation over time.[32] Prolactin drops after birth but remains above pregnancy levels and then rises again when the newborn first puts its mouth on the nipple—nerve endings in the aureole send messages to the anterior pituitary gland at the base of the mother's skull, which in turn manufactures and releases prolactin. At the same time, nerve endings also send messages to the posterior pituitary, and the hormone oxytocin is also released. Oxytocin is necessary because it contracts the myoepithelial cells surrounding the milk-producing alveoli; this ejects the fluid through the ducts and sends it on its way. As reproductive physiologist R. V. Short puts it, oxytocin serves today's meal while prolactin prepares tomorrow's.[33] The flowing of milk out of the alveoli and into the tip is called the "let-down reflex," whereby the sight of an infant's open mouth, the sound of its cry, or even the thought of breast-feeding can trigger the physical release of milk from the ducts.[34] Since there is no holding tank as such, the mother is then compelled to feed the infant as all this milk rushes out of the milk sacs and through the duct system toward the nipple. If the infant doesn't breast-feed within the first four or so days after birth, the level of prolactin falls and milk production eventually stops. This means mothers have only a three- or four-day window of opportunity to connect with their babies and get the nursing process under way.[35]

Once milk production is established, it is maintained by an efficient feedback system—the more the baby sucks, the higher the level of circulating prolactin, which means more milk and continued milk production. When the baby sucks less often and for shorter bouts, the prolactin level falls and milk production decreases—supply-and-demand economics at its best. Colostrum is replaced after a few days by more watery milk, and changes in milk composition continue until mature milk is established at about ten days after birth. Once mature milk has come in, the first milk to come out into the baby's mouth at each feeding is called "foremilk"; it is left over from the previous feed. Since human females do not have storage tanks for milk, such as cows, this foremilk changes composition the longer it waits behind the nipple. It starts out high in fat at the end of the previous feed, but that fat is soon absorbed back into the body and ends up providing only fifteen calories an ounce. Therefore, foremilk is low fat milk. Once the foremilk is removed, the hindmilk—which was higher up in the duct system—flows down after the let-down reflex; this is higher in fat, about twenty-five calories per ounce.[36] Since babies are sated by fat content in milk, quick feeds transfer mostly foremilk and little hindmilk and infants are still hungry when they are removed from the nipple. Longer feeds allow them to gain both foremilk and hindmilk, and to become sated both by fat and total liquid content if they are dehydrated, although rarely do infants completely empty the breast at any feed.

In fact, left to their own devices, babies will self-regulate and get what they need and no more.[37] This is easily demonstrated in cultures where infants have full-time access to the breast and they, not the mothers, regulate when they eat. Although in the West mothers are concerned that babies cry when the volume of milk might be insufficient, it is probably low fat content that signals a stop-feed. Interval feeding, with more low-fat foremilk and less high-fat hindmilk, and short-duration feeds that do not allow for enough hindmilk, produce watery and unsatisfying feeds for infants. And so they cry. Babies on schedules with hours in between feeds seem like they should be full because they have taken in a decent volume, but the fat content is low per feed. And so they are grumpy, hungry for something else besides watery fluid, and not really as satisfied as they would be with several feeds close together that would be lower in total volume, but richer.[38] Also, fat content in mother's milk is highest at night, and so when babies feed less at night, they are more inclined to be hungry and unhappy in the morning.[39]

Lactation experts describe breast-feeding as an interactive process between maternal biology and infant instinct. Milk is synthesized in the mother's breast ducts and is let down when she thinks about feeding. The mother also has a nipple erection reflex which pops the nipple out for an easier feed. But the baby plays a part too. Infants are equipped with a "rooting reflex." If you touch a newborn on the cheek, he will turn his head in that direction looking for a breast. This reflex is strongest twenty to thirty minutes after birth. Infants are also born with a sucking reflex which occurs when the nipple fills its mouth. The baby then automatically pushes his tongue toward the top of the mouth, squeezing the nipple and releasing fluid. And, of course, babies know how to swallow.[40] But the interaction between human mother and infant is less predictive than might be expected, given the intense need of the helpless infant and the biological directive of mothers to feed. Called a "practical art," breast-feeding, at least for humans, sometimes requires teaching, experience, and a frame of mind that allows mothers to coordinate with their babies.[41] For example, the let-down reflex may be susceptible to suggestion, both positive and negative. Because of that, emotional stress can interrupt nursing by preventing the release of milk. As experts put it, there is a difference between milk making and milk giving, and milk giving is especially influenced by outside forces and the mother's state of mind. Thus anxiety about breast-feeding can be a self-fulfilling prophecy when the let-down reflex is inhibited by this anxiety.[42] Also, babies need to be positioned just right so that the nipple is engaged correctly with the infant's mouth.[43] If positioned incorrectly, the baby is unable to press the area around the nipple efficiently and so it receives mostly water and not much fat at all. And when breasts are large, position can be a major cause when mothers complain that breast-feeding is not working for them.

Among mammals, breasts come in all sorts of shapes and sizes, and it seems that there is no relationship between shape or size and what the breast can do. For example, anthropologists argue about the evolutionary reasons for the fat content of the human breast—some believe protruding breasts have evolved to attract males while others believe the function of all that fat is to support nursing in times of scarcity[44]—but in the end, human females around the globe exhibit an astonishing range of shapes and sizes. In some cultures, especially in Western Europe and North America, big breasts are admired because they have been culturally associated with sex, leading men in these cultures to be attracted to them. But in many other cultures, breasts are seen as functional rather than as sexual adornments, which explains why being uncovered above the waist is not considered immodest for women in such cultures.[45]

Big breasts are partly a product of a high calorie fat-rich diet. Storing fat in breast tissue and on the hips and stomach, as women naturally do, is an adaptation left over from the leaner times of our ancestral hominids when decreases in the food supply would select for those females carrying more fat. In fact, primate lactation and pregnancy are well protected against times of scarcity. First of all, primates produce a lower peak of milk yield relative to body weight than do other mammals; other mammals produce four to fifteen times the milk that primate mothers do.[46] This translates into fewer calories needed for primates to lactate. It takes only a 14 percent increase in daily calories to support a human pregnancy (imagine a 150-pound female adult who needs only an extra 200 calories a day—a few pats of butter or a handful of M&Ms); and only 24 percent more calories to support lactation (a bag of M&Ms). Female rats, as a contrast, increase their energy output during lactation 300 percent. In response, rat mothers not only eat more, but they also give up any fat stores and even some weight of their internal organs during lactation.[47] Human females, then, with their lower caloric nursing needs per unit of milk and high body fat-storage capacity, have it comparatively easy. They can meet the demands of this low-cost lactation simply by eating a bit more or giving up some of that stored fat, or by moving around a little less. And so it takes a major drop in caloric intake or a major change in the quality of the mother's nutrition for breast milk to be affected. In a study of Burmese women, for example, there was no significant difference in breast milk composition between well-nourished and badly nourished nursing mothers.[48] And so human lactation, and pregnancy for that matter, are highly resilient to decreases in the quality and quantity of food, which explains why the pregnancy rate does not fall significantly during times of famine. It might also explain why humans were so successful in migrating out of Africa and across the globe thousands of years ago—the caloric needs of reproduction were not so limiting as they might have been for another species.

What Is Milk?

Our notions of mother's milk come from what we see, and for most of us the milk we see is cow's milk, a brilliant white liquid. But milk from other species looks quite different—kangaroo milk, for example, is pink. But whatever the hue, breast milk is species-specific; that is, the composition is finely tuned to the particular growth and maturational needs and digestive system of the young of each species.[49] For example, cow's milk is higher in volatile fatty acids than human milk, and humans do not digest volatile fatty acid that well. So while cow's milk is easy for baby cows to digest, it causes intestinal gas in human babies. Cow's milk is also higher in iron than human milk, but the iron is a type that is not easily absorbed by the human digestive system. Because of this, human babies absorb more iron when they drink human breast milk than they do when they drink cow's milk, even though cow's milk contains comparatively more iron to begin with.[50] Species-compatible milk is also easier to digest; it takes human infants twenty minutes to digest breast milk, and four hours to digest formula milk made from cow's milk.[51] Human milk also contains about one hundred amino acids, vitamins, and minerals, including salts and sugars, in a recipe made specifically for the needs of human infants.

Milk composition also offers clues to the intensity and style of species-specific maternal behavior. In species where mothers are expected to feed only occasionally and leave babies in a nest for long periods, the milk is high in fat and protein so that infants can be both nutritionally compensated (by protein) and satisfied (with fat) for long periods alone. When the milk is low in fat and protein, as it is in humans, it is an indication that breast-feeding is designated or intended to be more continuous.[52] Human milk is 88 percent water and 4.5 percent fat on average, depending on the style of feeding; interval feeding with long spaces in between produces lower-fat milk, while continuous feeding produces higher-fat milk. In contrast, for example, seal milk is made up of 54 percent fat, which is an extremely high fat content. Predictably, baby seals feed in long intervals; they also need high fat to grow thick layers of body fat to keep warm in a cold aquatic environment.

Nature's Protective Fluid

Babies are born with a certain amount of circulating antibodies that they acquire from their mothers through the placenta. But this immunity is fragile, and infants need exposure to the outside world and experience with immune reactions to build their own more sophisticated foundation for fighting off germs.[53] First colostrum and then breast milk, because they are both veritable drugstores of viral and bacterial protectants, form a nice transitional form of protection between prenatal life and later childhood, when the immune system fully develops at about five years of age. Interestingly, researchers have discovered the extent of this transferred immune system only during the past twenty years; this explains, in part, why artificial formulas that offer no immune value were thought to be as good as breast milk years ago.

Most important among this battery of transferred immunity is lactoferrin, an iron-binding protein that protects against E. coli and staphylococci, the primary causes of infant diarrhea and hence infant mortality.[54] Breast milk also has antiviral properties that physically devour invading germs such as those for cholera and ghiardia, which explains why breast-fed infants in areas with bad hygiene survive. Also critical in colostrum and human breast milk are the five categories of antibodies called immunoglobulins, which protect against infection and constitute a major wall of immunity for infants. This system is especially important because it operates within mucosa, the linings of the nose, chest, and intestines, the exact areas where infants are most vulnerable to pathogens.[55] IgA is a case in point. The secretory form of IgA, written as S-IgA, is found in the respiratory system and intestinal tracts of adults in areas called Peyer's patches.[56] When a mother ingests or inhales disease-causing agents, which she does every day, S-IgA molecules bind to that agent or antigen and render it mute; the specific S-IgA then becomes targeted to that specific antigen. In milk-producing females, this same newly fashioned IgA then travels through the maternal blood system and finds a home in the very cells that synthesize breast milk and are also sensitive to S-IgA. The specific S-IgA is then transferred in breast milk to the infant, who has been, by definition, exposed to the same harmful antigen.[57] Significantly, this system is initiated without any inflammation, which means babies are protected without irritation to their inner organs. Other antiviral and antibacterial agents such as oligiosacchrides and mucins are transferred via breast milk as well.[58] By four months of age, infants who are breast-fed are receiving about 0.5 grams of antibodies a day into their systems from mother's milk, and most of these antibodies find a permanent home in the infant's digestive tract or other areas. Since the major cause of infant sickness and mortality worldwide is intestinal and respiratory bacteria, transfer of immune properties from mother to infant through breast milk is just about the only protection most infants have against a virus- and bacteria-filled world.

There is also evidence that breast-fed babies mature their own immune systems faster and more strongly than babies fed artificially.[59] For example, colostrum specifically helps clear out the dark green myconium from the intestinal track right after birth and jump-starts the digestive process.[60] It may also be that breast milk immunities in general are helpful because babies do not have to fight the environment so soon, which frees the internal system to build early and quickly rather than being exposed and then having to build from that exposure. In other words, breast-feeding is an efficient way to transfer both nutrients and protective substances until such time as a child matures its own immunological system.

Why Breast Milk Is Good Today

In countries with adequate health care and good sanitation, artificial milk made from canned and powdered formula may be a reasonable substitute for breast milk. But when conditions are unsanitary, bottle-feeding presents a major risk to infant health.[61] When families do not have the facilities to sterilize bottles, or use disposable bottles and liners, the feeding apparatus itself becomes a vector for all sorts of viruses and bacteria. Also, because a bottle-fed infant by definition does not have the transferred immunities that come with breast milk, the infant is even more susceptible to those destructive agents. Infant death for bottle-feeders commonly results both from gastrointestinal infection—that is, diarrhea—and from respiratory infections. Even in Western Europe and

North America, where sanitation is better than in other parts of the world, bottle-fed infants exhibit two to five times the number of respiratory infections than breast-fed infants do. Other infant diseases such as bacterial infection of the blood, meningitis, and fatal necrotizing enterocolitis, whereby the intestines themselves disintegrate, are significantly higher among bottle-fed babies.

Breast-feeding also seems to be protective against Sudden Infant Death Syndrome (SIDS). In a study of 2,285 babies in New Zealand, for example, bottle-feeding appeared to double the risk of SIDS.[62] Others estimate that bottle-feeding multiplies by five the risk of SIDS.[63] At this point it is hard to tell if there is something particular about breast milk, or something about the overall manner in which babies breast-feed, that protects against SIDS. It might, in fact, be a combination of both. Breast milk is known to contain all sorts of immunological properties that not only protect a baby but help its internal organs mature. But breast-feeding also means that the mother must be highly interactive with and attentive to her baby, which might be protective in itself. Also, when a mother breast-feeds at night and when she brings the baby into her bed, as infant sleep researcher James McKenna (see Chapter Four) and colleagues have shown, that mother invariably places her baby in the supine rather than prone position.[64] From a practical view, the supine position lets a baby feed when it wants, but we now know that the supine position also protects against SIDS. And so it may be the whole maternal breast-feeding package—including the entwined maternal–infant behavior, the increased vigilance by the mother, and the properties of breast milk—that help to protect against SIDS.[65]

Breast milk may also have positive health benefits later in life. There is evidence that adult conditions such as inflammatory bowel syndrome, juvenile diabetes, breast cancer, and malignant lymphoma are connected to being bottle-fed. And chronic conditions such as asthma and allergies, or middle ear infections, are more common in children and adults who were bottle-fed. It is not that breast-feeding wipes out all these problems, only that it makes an already susceptible individual less at risk, or decreases the severity of the condition.[66]

Besides the obvious nutritional and immunological factors in breast milk, recent research shows that there are other benefits of breast milk over artificial foods. Breast-feeding with its hormonal storm of oxytocin and prolactin has an opiate effect on mother and infant.[67] In other animals, oxytocin is actually required for mothers to attach to their infants, but in humans the exact role of oxytocin as a direct initiator of attachment is less clear; it does seem to play a role in making them both relax, concentrate on each other, and therefore must at some level be involved in fostering the bonding process.[68] More startling, several studies have shown that breast-fed infants seem to score higher on cognitive tests as babies and as older children.[69] However, it is difficult to determine if breast milk alone is responsible for higher scores, or if a maternal style that includes breast milk as a component of the caretaking package explains the difference. One study looked at premature babies who were fed by tube, either mother's milk or artificial milk. The babies fed with mother's milk show higher I.Q. scores at eight months of age even though all the babies were reared the same for the first few weeks. Interestingly, this difference also had nothing to do with the education or socioeconomic status of the mothers.[70]

There may also be a down side to breast-feeding, and not just that clothing is awkward or that social disapproval gets in the way. Because mother's milk is produced in the body and passed on so efficiently, it not only carries "good" stuff but also "bad" stuff, including drugs. Today, there is a risk that breast milk may be a lethal fluid for the baby if the mother is HIV-positive. The HIV virus can be easily transmitted through breast milk and so a child that might be born HIV-negative might become positive if breast-fed. But in every case excluding the possibility of HIV infection, breast-feeding is physiologically better for babies, sometimes critically so.

Breast-feeding for Mother

The most noticeable benefit for mothers who breast-feed, at least those in Western culture who tend to gain excessive amounts of weight during pregnancy, is that breast-feeding is nature's easiest diet.[71] Nursing uses up an extra 500 to 1,000 calories a day if the infant is sucking continuously and taking in all the fat that is manufactured. Breast-feeding also releases oxytocin, which—during the first few days after birth—contracts the uterus and stops residual bleeding while the uterus returns to its former size.[72] There also appears to be a relationship between breast-feeding and breast cancer. Women who were never breast-fed themselves, and who never breast-fed as adults, are at higher risk for breast cancer than women who did both.[73] Although the mechanism of this protection is unclear, and other variables such as family genetics play a large part, it still makes sense that organs such as mammary glands that are designed to go through a series of hormonal and physical changes become vulnerable to cancerous mutations when those changes never occur.

The most startling effect of breast-feeding is its role as part of the entire reproductive package. Although pediatricians, gynecologists, hospitals, and mothers seem to think birth is the end product of gestation and the termination of the system of reproduction, the system is actually much more lengthy. It continues from conception to weaning and thus is biologically designed to go on for months or years in a process called "exogestation"—gestation outside the womb that is still intimately connected. We know this because of the profound effect that breast-feeding has on the female fertility system—continuous breast-feeding stops ovulation and prevents conception.

R. V. Short has called breast-feeding "nature's contraceptive," and like any contraceptive it has to be used correctly to work. Prolactin, the hormone that maintains lactogenesis, is a highly labile hormone and it appears that suckling, not the passage of milk, is responsible for fluctuating levels of prolactin. Pulling on the nipple inhibits the dopamine release from the hypothalamus, which in turn allows the release of pro-lactin from the anterior pituitary. But once the baby stops nursing, the prolactin level immediately begins to drop;[74] within two hours after a feed, serum prolactin levels of nursing mothers are back to baseline and within four to six hours the levels match those of non-nursing moth-ers.[75] The level of prolactin in the blood is important to the contracep-tive story because it is an indicator of how the ovarian process is work-ing.[76] It may be that prolactin directly inhibits the production of leutenizing hormone (LH), which is the hormone that bursts the ovarian follicle and makes ovulation occur. Or prolactin may simply indicate that the hypothalamus is stopping LH production.[77] In any case, there is an interaction between prolactin levels and LH, which then interferes with the ovulation process. Also, breast-feeding seems to interrupt the direct hormonal feedback loop between the ovaries and the hypothalamus; it slows the production of estrogen that normally occurs within the egg follicles of the ovaries. As a result of low estrogen levels, the eggs are underdeveloped and there is a concurrent absence of circulating estrogen, the usual trigger for LH release and the final stages of ovulation.[78] And so even if the ovulation process is working at all, it works badly, and conception is unlikely. The key to a reliable contraceptive effect is that the levels of prolactin and other hormonal inhibitors have to be consis-tently high for ovulation to be repressed.[79] So when women breast-feed only intermittently, or have long spaces between feeding bouts, or do not feed at night, their serum prolactin levels rise, other hormones kick in, and the risk of pregnancy rises; this period of "lactation amenorrhea" is highly sensitive to the maternal breast-feeding style. It's not the volume of milk that passes through the breast that makes a difference, but the frequency of infant sucking on the mother's nipple.[80] For lactation to have an inhibitory effect on the ovaries it has to be relatively continuous and occur at night as well as during the day. As soon as the baby is put on a schedule, or supplemented with bottles or solid food, the rate of suckling decreases and ovulation begins.

Within the past few years, we have had confirmation that not just

breast-feeding per se, but breast-feeding style is key to anovulation—
to the cessation of ovulation. And it took cross-cultural research in
cultures where women lactate long-term and do not use other methods of birth control to figure it out.[81] In the 1980s, !Kung San
women, hunter-gatherers from Botswana who have three- to four-year
interbirth intervals, were examined for clues to the relationship between maternal breast-feeding style and reproductive physiology. Anthropologists Melvin Konner and Carol Worthman showed that San
women breast-feed on average every thirteen minutes for the first few
years, and sleep with their babies and allow them to feed at will during the night. Blood work showed that prolactin levels of the mothers
remained high as long as they kept up this schedule, while estrogen
and progesterone, the hormones that guide ovulation, remained low.[82]
They also found that when San women decreased nursing after a few
years to less than six times a day, their hormone levels shifted and
the women would ovulate and conceive again. The interbirth interval
among the San is 4.1 years. With these longer interbirth intervals,
San families, even without artificial birth control, average around four
children.[83] Some of that relatively small family size can be attributed
to relatively late marriage and a sex taboo when women are nursing;
but surely some of it is due to intense and long-term breast-feeding
and the resulting alteration in hormone profiles that stops ovulation
and conception.

In another study of the Gainj of highland New Guinea, where the
interbirth interval is at least two years, researchers showed the same
relationship between continuous breast-feeding and prolactin levels. This
study confirmed the sensitive nature of the contraceptive effect of nursing. The reason the Gainj infants are born two years apart instead of the
San average of four years is because their average feeding decreases with
infant age, so that older infants feed less often; as a result the hormonal
levels move closer to non-nursing levels much sooner than among the
San, allowing ovulation to kick in.[84]

As these studies seem to indicate, continuous breast-feeding with short intervals is contraceptive; when breast-feeding stops, or is offered less than six times a day, the hormone levels return to prepregnancy levels and the birth rate goes up. This effect can be seen all over the globe, especially in areas where formula feeding has been introduced and encouraged. In Kenya, for example, where only 7 percent of the population uses artificial birth control, the rate of pregnancy has increased to about eight births per woman and is directly correlated with the decline in breast-feeding.[85]

And so it appears that the old wives' tale that breast-feeding makes for fewer children has genuine validity.[86] Before artificial feeding, in the hunter-gatherer world of our ancestors, the interbirth interval was probably around four years, as it is in the San. It evolved that way to allow mothers to invest heavily, and for long periods, in one offspring at a time. The problem may be that although the contraceptive effect of breast-feeding was selected for in our species, we are now sidestepping that advantage. As R.V. Short puts it, "The changing history of breast-feeding is the history of human population explosion. Our hunter-gatherer ancestors spent most of their reproductive lives in a state of lactation amenorrhea; there is much to be said for trying to replicate some of that magic."[87]

The Culture of Infant Feeding

In my living room, I have a bead-decorated Masai gourd that I bought in a shop in Kenya several years ago. I had no idea what it was normally used for, but I fell in love with its odd shape and beaded decorations. At the time, curious about its function, I turned to my Masai friend Thomas and asked what it was. "That is for babies," he said, "for drinking milk." Surprised, I pushed Thomas further: "But babies drink from their mothers, don't they? So why this?" My question, it appeared, was inappropriate; my friend blinked at me a few times, turned away, eyes down, and refused to answer. My cross-cultural gaff was a sign of naiveté—in every culture, in every society, there are situations when a baby cannot be breast-fed. In addition, in every culture there are mothers who choose not to breast-feed. In fact, artificial feeding has been part of human history ever since animals were domesticated and people figured out ways to make tiny vessels that could hold milk other than the infant's mother's milk.[88] In other words, there is cross-cultural variation in what babies eat and how they are fed.

Infant Feeding Cross-Culturally

The mostly widely used comparison to the Western pattern of long intervals between scheduled feedings are the !Kung San, the hunter-gatherers who feed their babies on average every thirteen minutes, almost continuously. It is true that the San are polar opposites to the Western pattern, but a broader look cross-culturally shows that, as in all matters human, there is extensive variability across cultures in the pattern and style of infant feeding. But in general, most in-depth studies of other nonindustrial societies, from the Amele of Papua New Guinea to the Indonesians of Central Java, reveal that mothers tend to feed on cue—what the West has disparagingly called "on demand," in short intervals all day long and at night as well.[89]

Women, of course, adapt their mothering style to their own circumstances and societal demands. For example, in the highlands of Nepal, where woman are working rice fields and tending livestock, mothers offer their infants the breast when daily tasks allow, and the schedule of breast-feeding changes as the work season changes.[90] Gusii mothers in Africa have young girls tend their babies, but they watch closely from the garden so they can return and feed when necessary.[91] In all cultures, women adapt their lifestyles to infant needs, and to an extent, infants adapt to their mothers' availability. For the mother who carries her infant in a sling on the side or in front, the baby is nestled close to the breast and does all the work reaching the breast. For the mother who must work in rice paddies, the baby is carried on her back, rocked and tended, but sometimes there just is no time to feed until all the workers stop to rest. And if food supplements are available, mothers tend to use them.

Culturally, breast milk also has symbolic power. In northwest Tunisia, for example, the Khmir people believe that mothers transfer power, a life force, when they feed their infants with their milk.[92] In the same way, the mother is held responsible for keeping that milk "good," and whenever a child is sick or badly behaved, people feel the mother's milk is at fault; this means the mother has done something wrong, such as offered the breast when she was tired or when she had eaten something foul, transferring that badness to her child. The same idea is fostered in Western culture when a mother assumes her baby is crying because of the mother's having eaten a particular food such as hot sauce or broccoli or chocolate. Although various substances such as nicotine and caffeine can be detected in breast milk, and various foods change the chemical composition of breast milk, there is no clinical evidence that small amounts of these foods affect babies. But mothers anecdotally report reactions by their infants when nursing after a certain type of meal.

Overall, mothers in nonindustrial societies expect to feed babies during the day and at night, and assume breast-feeding is a natural part of family life. Only in recent years, corporations that produce baby formula have moved into developing nations with advertisements and "clinics" that promote formula feeding as the primary mode of nourishment, and the result has been an increase in infant mortality due to disease and infection.[93]

Cross-cultural feeding patterns also show that no matter the method or style of feeding, mothers use some sort of supplemental food in addition to breast milk. For example, in Central Java, mothers supplement breast milk as early as three days after birth. In the highlands of Thailand, mothers begin supplements about two weeks after birth.[94] Quecha mothers in Peru breast-feed on cue, but they also give the baby tea and broth soon after birth; wealthier women in one community begin supplementing earlier and wean their infants earlier than poorer women, emphasizing the role of status and socioeconomic class on this decision.[95] Baby food might be a gruel made of grain or a watery soup or a mixture of bread and the milk from other animals. The ingredients of supplements have been passed on by tradition, but in each culture the types of supplements can probably be traced to the fact they were the only ingredients available in that society when first introduced. In India, mothers use a combination of clarified butter and honey to replace colostrum, which they feel is not suited for babies.[96] The Amele of Papua New Guinea use soup, juice, and a mash of bananas and papaya as occasional baby food. In the West, there is a history of supplementing mother's milk with milk of other animals and other women.

Infant Feeding in Western Culture

In the 1800s, more than 95 percent of infants in the United States were breast-fed by their mothers and children were not weaned until they were two to four years old.[97] Today, about half the infants born in the United States are breast-fed, and breast-feeding duration is relatively short, about four months for most babies. The choice to breast-feed in the United States varies according to education level, race, and socioeconomic class. White and Hispanic women who have some college education, are a bit older, and are middle- or upper-class in income, tend to breast-feed more often and for a longer duration than other women.[98]

At least half the new mothers who opt for the bottle over breast-feeding say they are not willing to make the dietary changes necessary to facilitate breast-feeding, such as giving up cigarettes and alcohol. Others must return to work and are usually unable to breast-feed during the day.[99] Some opt for the bottle because they want to share the feeding responsibilities and rewards with the father, and the bottle offers a reasonable option for them to do so. One study showed that most women know that breast-feeding is better for babies, but they see it as less convenient and less modern than working with artificial formulas.[100]

Moreover, artificial feeding fits our Western cultural notion of nurturing an infant in a precise and measured way.

Women in Western culture have always found convenient ways to feed infants when breast-feeding was not possible or preferred. Small vessels apparently used for artificial feeding have been found in archaeological ruins dating from 4000 B.C.[101] It is impossible to say who used these vessels and whether or not they were used primarily by sick or motherless children. But they do indicate that along with other technological developments, people figured out a way to feed infants with handmade vessels. There is also a long tradition of using milk from other species.[102] At first, using the milk of other species was a way to feed infants whose mothers had died in childbirth or were too ill from giving birth to feed. It was a way for parents to feed babies who were so sick that they could not suckle properly. Cow's milk is the replacement milk of choice in the West today only by accident—cows happened to be the animal close at hand. In other countries, goat's milk was more available. In fact, goat's milk is more like human milk, and better for infants, than cow's milk. Better yet would have been chimpanzee or gorilla milk, given our close phylogenetic relationship.[103] But the domestication of the cow made it the prime supplier of substitute milk in many Western countries.

Evidence of wet nurses—that is, lactating women hired to feed others' children—is as old as recorded history. In Egyptian harems in the second century A.D., for example, women frequently nursed each other's babies. In ancient Rome, wet nurses were an organized business.[104] In medieval Europe, wet nursing was common, both among aristocrats and among the merchant class, and passing babies to others for breast-feeding may help to explain why the wealthy had more children and at a faster pace than women in the lower classes who were nursing their own as well as other people's babies.[105] In the 1700s, employment bureaus existed for wet nurses in large cities in France and one estimate from 1780 claims that out of 21,000 babies born that year in Paris, only a thousand were actually nursed by their own mothers.[106]

By the nineteenth century it became more fashionable for women, even the upper classes, to nurse their own babies, but wet nurses were also acceptable. Handing a baby over to another lactating woman rather than giving it milk from another animal offers evidence that, even back then, mothers were aware that human milk was better for their children than the milk of some other animal. But cow's milk and goat's milk were also commonly used by some women to feed their newborns. Babies were also fed supplementary solid food, a gruel or pap made of bread or flour mixed with milk or water. This process, called "dry nursing," was common for foundlings and for the babies of mothers who had to leave their children behind when they worked for others.[107] The mortality rates for these infants were correspondingly high—from 50 to 99 percent.[108]

By the late nineteenth century, especially in industrial Britain where women were working in factories, artificial feeding again became common. The first artificial formula was invented by a German chemist in 1867 and was made primarily of cow's milk and flour with potassium bicarbonate and malt.[109] The product did not sell well, and it was not until condensed milk was developed that the commercialization of artificial infant food took hold. In the late 1800s, large corporations such as Borden and Nestlé began to advertise their safe, nutritious, and supposedly easy way to feed babies. By 1911 there were a hundred varieties of condensed and evaporated milk for sale, a cow's milk product for babies that needed no refrigeration. More important, pasteurization of milk and sterilization of feeding vessels made artificial and substitute milk a cleaner and safer alternative than it had been. As a consequence, infant feeding became a major business opportunity.

These and other manufacturers were soon producing a plethora of baby formulas—evaporated, condensed, and powdered, and all easily transportable. Artificial food was readily accepted by the public and also endorsed by the medical profession (some say in collusion with the corporations).[110] Even the name "formula" has the aura of science, offered and seen as something better, more modern, and healthier for baby.[111] Advised by their doctors, swayed by advertising, and pushed by the thought of convenience, mothers made bottle-feeding the norm. In the United States, for example, only about 20 to 30 percent of babies were breast-fed during the 1940s. Wet nursing was already out of fashion, and during the post–World War II baby boom, breast-feeding itself became unfashionable—out of date, even—and so uncommon that women who chose to breast-feed were considered odd.

In the 1980s, a backlash was brewing in the United States. The collusion between the medical establishment and the formula companies was revealed. A major U.S. boycott against Nestlé, the conglomerate that was strong-arming women in the third world to use their formulas, was initiated and was successful. UNICEF and the World Health Organization decried the switch to bottle-feeding and launched worldwide campaigns for a return to breast-feeding as the best way to feed babies.[112] And in affluent countries, the medicalization of the birth process, and by extension nursing, was also rejected by many; bolstered by a move for female empowerment, women began to choose breast-feeding again. Today about half the babies in the United States are breast-fed, up about 25 percent from the 1970s. But still, even today, women are sometimes asked to cover up their breasts when feeding in public; breast-feeding might be more fashionable for mothers right now, but it is still not always socially acceptable.

The point of this fluctuating account of infant-feeding styles in Western society is to show that breast-feeding, a behavior designed through evolution to nourish an infant, is both a matter of biology and a matter of culture in today's world. Think of any other human behavior—eating, sex, social interaction—all are subject to the whims of society and the evolution of culture. Behaviors, like clothing or jewelry, go in and out of fashion. Breast-feeding is no different from other behaviors in that there is a social consensus about how to feed babies, and that consensus changes over time. But treating the infant-feeding pattern as a fashion statement is a dangerous game. As history and cross-cultural studies show, when artificial feeding is more fashionable, more babies die, especially where artificial feeding is not practiced under sanitary conditions. This particular intersection of biology and culture has more at stake than mere superficial cultural behaviors.

More significantly, the breast–bottle controversy has moved far away from the question of what is best for babies. The decision for substitute milk is influenced by the pressures of corporations, their advertising, and their lobbies. The money game behind the production of formula has overpowered what might be best for babies here in first-world countries and for babies more at risk in third-world countries. It takes about $1,800 a year to feed an infant some kind of powdered or canned formula. In third-world cultures, and for the working poor in developed nations, the cost is crippling. It is also undefendable given that a free alternative is readily at hand. Where medical care and hygiene are poor, many babies fed on formula become sick and die. Some researchers claim that bottle-feeding in underdeveloped countries increases the risk of infant mortality tenfold.[113] And UNICEF estimates that 1.5 million babies die each year because they are not breast-fed.[114] Loss of natural immunities and the lack of adequate sanitation provide an environment in which formula-feeding is not the safest alternative for infants, and thus infant mortality increases.[115] In the West, where conditions are better and fewer babies die directly from formula-feeding, many more are sick with chronic health conditions. The U.S. National Institute of Environmental Health and Safety estimates that four out of every thousand infants in the United States die because they are not breast-fed.[116] The increase in respiratory and gastrointestinal disease, the greater number of inner ear infections, the additional allergy shots necessary, and the extra pregnancies and births that come from the loss of the contraceptive effect of lactation, all combine to increase health costs shared by all.

Interestingly, the third world seems to be more savvy about how corporations push formulas on expectant mothers. The dramatic rise in mortality among formula-fed babies in developing nations has induced some professionals to initiate changes to combat the invasion of Western infant-feeding practices. For example, in Papua New Guinea, a prescription is now needed to buy a baby bottle. In the Philippines, hospitals now forbid formula-feeding and promote breast-feeding.[117] As a result, fewer staff have been needed to prepare bottles and less electricity has been used to sterilize equipment. The hospitals estimated they saved over

$10,000 in one year from their new program. Most important, there have been rapid decreases in infant illness. Other hospitals around the world, such as one in Quito, Ecuador, have copied the Philippine initiative.[118]

Insufficient Milk?

Even when women do decide to breast-feed, they sometimes feel they are thwarted by their own bodies. "Insufficient milk" is cited as a major reason women in the West terminate breast-feeding after a few days or weeks.[119] The syndrome is fascinating because it is a clear example of a disease being "invented," defined, and then perpetuated by culture at large. In only about 5 percent of the cases is there something making it physically impossible for a woman to breast-feed.[120] Before bottle-feeding came into vogue, women rarely, if ever, reported a lack of milk. But when breast-feeding went out of fashion in the 1940s, this new syndrome appeared. The real cause of insufficient-milk syndrome appears to be a confluence of social changes—hospitals took over the birth process and separated newborns from their mothers, doctors recommended interval feeding, and artificial formula presented a reasonable alternative. It is interesting to note that insufficient-milk syndrome appears only in Western industrial nations and has yet to be found in other cultures.[121] Why do so many women in affluent countries say they have no milk for their babies?

Breast-feeding is initiated by instinct, pushed by the biology of milk production, and reinforced by the actions of the baby.[122] But there is also a psychosomatic element to breast-feeding. The let-down reflex, when milk flows from the ducts toward the nipple, is highly susceptible to anxiety and fear; and when no one is there to guide a new mother and she becomes anxious, this can set into motion a vicious cycle of failure. Beyond the problems with the let-down reflex, the physiology of breast-feeding can be interrupted by cultural style. When the baby is separated from the mother at birth, she misses the first and strongest impulse to suckle. When hospitals feed newborns with water or glucose from a bottle, they interrupt the initial bonding moments between infant and mother's breast. The scheduling of breast-feeding can also have a dramatic effect on milk production and on the feedback system between baby and breast. When women decide to feed on a schedule with long intervals of two or three hours in between, and then feed their babies in short bouts of under ten minutes, the lower fat composition of milk offered at each feed further complicates what should be a smooth process. The baby has been unfed for so long, has had a waiting period so much longer than its physiology was designed to handle, that it is extremely hungry and pulls hard on the nipple.

Many women experience nipple soreness, and believe that frequent nursing will exacerbate the problem. But the opposite is true—frequent nursing makes sure the baby is less ravenous and aggressive.[123] Also, and probably more important in this situation, foremilk has come up behind the nipple at the end of the last feed long ago and has since lost most of its fat. Now, as the first fluid to come out, this particular long-awaited foremilk is extra-watery, low in fat, and therefore not very satisfying for a hungry baby. It then takes a while for the hindmilk, still being manufactured and let down, to flow through the nipple and touch the infant's hunger button. And so feeding interval—that is, the style of nursing—alters milk composition and can make the situation difficult for even the most well-intentioned mothers. It is not that she doesn't have enough milk; it's that she simply waited too long and now the milk is of low quality and the baby knows it.

In other words, there really is no such thing as "insufficient milk." Demographic studies that compare breast-feeding across cultures and within populations attest to this. Even nutritionally deprived women, unless they are nursing during a major famine, have plenty of milk, and the composition of their milk is the same as that of better-nourished women.[124] Oddly enough, the greatest number of women who say they cannot produce enough milk are highly nourished, well-fed Western women. Lack of milk is, in fact, an urban phenomenon—women in rural areas rarely if ever report that they have stopped breast-feeding because of lack of milk.[125] Some women may be rationalizing their desire to switch to formula. It might also be that stress and anxiety in the urban environment contribute to the failure of the natural system.[126] For example, urban women often lack the multigenerational female support system to help teach them about breast-feeding. Also, by definition, the urban environment means an emphasis on work that is physically and emotionally separated from home life; breast-feeding, or any kind of child care, is sequestered from the rest of urban daily life, unlike the environments of hunters and gatherers, nomadic herders, and horticulturists. In fact, the urban and Western styles of caretaking make breast-feeding particularly challenging; it is therefore not surprising that mothers in these environments give up.

About the time I finished writing this chapter, I met a woman who is an engineer for a large corporation. Having recently returned to work after a three-month maternity leave, she had just gone on an out-of-town trip, her first overnight experience away from her son. She was committed to breast-feeding and so, instead of carrying a portable computer on the plane, she had hauled a small suitcase of equipment that included a breast pump (which elicited some embarrassed comments from airport security, but they let her go through without having to demonstrate that it wasn't a bomb), so that she could milk her breasts and keep them producing while she was away. How different her life would be if she could simply bring her baby on the plane and into the boardroom, as a San woman would carry her infant on her gathering route. But Western culture has distinctly separated woman as the worker from woman as the mother. The workplace, at times, is conducted in such a way that it seems to deny that we are mammals.

The point is that ever since humans could construct feeding vessels out of clay or gourds, ever since milk-secreting animals were domesticated and available for milking, mothers have sought ways to stop or supplement breast-feeding. And yet, mothers instinctively know that their milk is best for their babies. We were designed that way millions of years ago, and mammals evolved that way even before there were primates. Humans evolved in such a way that babies were sustained on continuous feeding with a substance relatively low in fat and protein, a system that requires constant access to the mother. But today, in industrialized countries, we have become a cache species, expecting to feed at intervals and be able to place the baby at some distance from its mother.[127]

Some might say that disconnecting ourselves from the dictates of biology is progress—that this is exactly the direction humans might go in. Bottle-feeding and early weaning free women from the intensive demands of parenting and allow fathers to share in the burden of child care. What is the trade-off for this choice? Yes, there is independence, but there is also "insufficient-milk syndrome," higher rates of SIDS, increased numbers of medical problems and fatalities, and a lot of crying. Surely we can come up with a biologically sounder way to combine the lifestyles we live, or are compelled to accommodate to, with the biological needs of an infant. Maybe if breasts were perceived less as sexual objects and more as nutritional devices; if fashion followed suit and gave nursing women clothes designed to slip a baby's head inside; if the sight of women breast-feeding in public became more common and therefore not as shocking; if sanitary wet-nursing became more acceptable; or if babies were allowed into the workplace—maybe then we could better interface biology and culture for this issue.

CHAPTER SEVEN

UNPACKING
THE CARETAKING
PACKAGE

"Ask me anything about the Ache, I love to talk about the Ache!" Anthropologist Magdalena Hurtado and I were standing at the hors d'oeuvres table after a long day of talks, each of us sipping a glass of wine. It was the end of a two-day workshop on ethnopediatrics funded by the Social Science Research Council, and my brain was spinning from all I had heard over the past few days.[1] Childhood asthma, infant crying, ethnic labeling, the squeeze of the current health care system on pediatric practice. I had taken thirty-two pages of notes, used up the ink in a new pen, and both sets of batteries for my tape recorder were dead. But I remembered the one question I was dying to ask Hurtado. Earlier that day, she had mentioned that the year she and her husband Kim Hill arrived at their study site in the forest of Paraguay with their infant daughter in tow, the Ache greeted her in a whole new way. They took her aside and in friendly and intimate but no-nonsense terms told her all the things she was doing wrong as a mother. I asked her exactly what they had said.

"This older woman sat with me and told me that I *must* sleep with my daughter. They were horrified that I had a basket with me for her to sleep in, and this older woman told me that I must sleep with my baby," explained Hurtado. They did not, thank goodness, expect her to sleep sitting up as nursing Ache mothers do. "I found it so funny," Hurtado continued, laughing at the shift in typical Ache behavior, "that the Ache, who never tell people what to do, were so open about telling me how I should treat my baby." She had been going to this site for years, ever the observer. But now that she had come as a mother, it was time for them to take her under their wing and tell her how to do it "right." Even more odd, here was a group of forest hunter-gatherers, people living in what Westerners would call basic conditions, giving instructions to a highly educated woman from a technologically sophisticated culture. Parenting, it seems, is the great leveler.

No matter the cultural difference, no matter the possible language barriers, every mother and father, every aunt, uncle, grandmother, and grandfather, has an idea about what is "correct" parenting, and everyone feels it is his or her duty to correct the obviously "wrong" ways of other parents. But the two days of that workshop highlighted for me the fact that infant care is one of the most variable, and also most fragile, of human endeavors. Unlike the parenting of most animals, which has a circumscribed timetable, human parenting is a lifelong job. Bringing up our babies may be the most important, most involved job on earth. But unfortunately, babies do not come with written instructions or an operator's manual. As a result, there are all kinds of paths to take in accomplishing that job; parenting is necessary but there are no fixed rules. More significant, since we humans are big-brained sentient beings, we make conscious decisions about how we want our parenting duties to be constructed. Every day, every parent makes major and minor, conscious and unconscious decisions about how to interact with their children. We may be pushed by the traditions of culture, or the approval or disapproval of family members, but in the end, all parents decide for themselves how to treat their children.

CONTRASTS AND OPTIONS

Consider the prominent Western caretaking package. Infants sleep in their own beds, are expected to sleep through the night as soon as possible and to feed in intervals; and once they are fed and changed, a delayed response by caretakers to crying and fretting is acceptable. Babies are pushed in strollers or carried in backpacks and are often set upright in stable seats to view the social action. Such parenting supposedly helps to foster independence and quickly put the baby on the right path toward self-reliance. Parents in much of the industrialized West are told that babies need to be controlled and trained, set on a fixed schedule, and given a structure. The message underlying such advice is that following these rules will free the parents from being manipulated by their babies, who, after all, seem never to be satisfied, as any number of exhausted parents attest. Compared to other styles described in this book, the one just outlined might fairly be called "distanced." Think about this caretaking package in comparison to the way !Kung San parents raise their children. !Kung San babies are continuously held, sleep in contact with others, and feed continuously. Every peep receives a response, 92 percent within ten seconds, and every cry is answered with the breast. From the Western perspective, such caretaking might be labeled "indulgent." An even more striking comparison is the way Efé pygmies of the Ituri forest of Zaire raise their children.[2] Their parenting style fits neither the "indulgent" category nor the "distanced" model. From the moment of birth, Efé infants are passed among a number of group members, starting with the group of midwives attending the birth. Other lactating women nurse the infant for the first few days until the mother's milk comes in. Once the mother is mobile and back at work in the forest, babies are carried to the work site but child care is shared among various members of the work party. All women respond to the fussiness of babies, including placing the baby at the breast even if it is not her child.

At three weeks of age, infants spend 39 percent of their time in physical contact with group members other than the mother, and by eighteen weeks the contact with other adults increases to 60 percent. Also, Efé infants are passed around at a rate that would terrify Western or !Kung San parents; at three weeks they are handed off from one person to another roughly four times an hour, and by eight weeks the number of people who hold the baby each hour doubles to eight. Observers calculate that Efé infants are cared for by about fourteen different people, and some infants have as many as twenty-four different people interacting with them on a regular basis. Like San parents, Efé group members respond within ten seconds to infant fussing; but the difference is that the responder could be the mother or any of a variety of group members, and the nipple offered might well not be the mother's. The Efé caretaking package, as anthropologist Edward Tronick explains, is one that meets the infants' needs in much the same way as the continuous care of the !Kung San—babies are always carried, receive quick responses to fussing, and are fed continuously. The only difference is that Efé infants experience a variety of reactions from a variety of adults. Such caretaking might be called "multiple caretaking." It is a style, as might be expected, that nicely fits the way of life of a highly social interactive band in which communal connections are the basis of their subsistence pattern and the foundation upon which their social system operates. Early on, Efé infants experience and presumably learn all about these interpersonal connections; they quickly learn social skills by navigating a series of coordinated and miscoordinated interactions while being held and fed and cared for by several adults. Whereas a child brought up in a mono-bonded situation, such as the Western or San approach, experiences most of its interactions from one or two adults—thereby placing excessive demands for interaction on one or two people—the child from a more multi-bonded situation such as the Efé will presumably be more socially adept at interactions with a multiple of others, and will probably be less demanding in general.[3]

More significant, the Efé caretaking package proves a point—there are a variety of caretaking styles that humans practice which meet the needs of the infant and also reflect, and reinforce, the social or economic needs of the community and culture. "Distanced" Westerners and "indulgent" !Kung San might be placed on two opposite ends of a caretaking package continuum; and there are any number of styles that fall in between, with resulting trade-offs and compromises. Parenting styles, then, fit on a flexible continuum from one end to the other, and all parents and all communities find ways to both meet the needs of infants and carry on their lives. Tamang women in Nepal feed their babies continuously at night but interval feed during the day when they are out working the rice terraces. Gusii mothers do not take their babies into the garden plots where they work but they do keep a close eye on the baby sitter who is in charge of the infant, and mothers come in from the garden when the baby is truly unhappy. Western mothers who work away from home still phone the baby sitter periodically to see how things are going. This kind of flexibility and continuum across the species can in fact be easily documented. In a survey of 186 societies, comparing the parental style of hunter-gatherer societies with those of other nonindustrial societies and with the United States, researchers found that parental care across cultures forms a continuum for almost any measure of care one wishes to explore.[4] For example, infants are carried most of the time in nonindustrial societies, 56 percent of the time in less traditional societies, and 25 percent of the time in the United States. Babies in most cultures most often sleep in the same bed with parents, but they also sometimes sleep in a bed right next to the mother, or in the same room but some distance away.

There is no "perfect" way to care for babies, only trade-offs in which parents weigh the needs of infants against the constraints of daily life. Babies are clearly adaptable, at least within the parameters of their most basic organic needs. As long as the entwined infant–adult dyad is being attended to, babies are content. But an examination of the basic elements of caretaking, including a culture's fundamental ideology, reveals some surprising perspectives that can alter both parenting strategies and the way parents think about their behavior and their culture.

The Relative Concept of "Normal"

Everything we do during the day is molded by who we are within a particular social milieu. What feels "normal" is also molded by the same forces. Sitting at my desk typing seems "normal" to me, throwing a spear at a monkey seems normal to a forest hunter, digging for hours in a garden plot seems normal to an East African. Most of these differences in the construct of "normal" are exotica, exciting contrasts among peoples, but they can also have a profound impact on human life. And nowhere is this more crucial than in how individuals conceive of "normal" parental care. The very construct of "normal" is integral to a cross-cultural and evolutionary view of babyhood.

What is "normal" is directly tied to an understanding of how each culture views life, and the quality of life. Discussions of abortion, genetic testing, or the right-to-die, for example, are so fundamental and so controversial because they touch on our very life values. The most difficult concept to digest is that not all cultures, and not all people, place the same value on life or what the quality of life should be like. More significant, other cultures feel their views on life are just as valid, just as good, just as normal, as ours. One driving force of Western culture, for example, is that everyone expects a happy life and good health. But clearly that is not what we all get. As a result, there is a wide gap between expectations and reality, and much effort—and money—is spent trying to achieve that expected perfection. Other cultures do not necessarily have this drive toward perfect health over a perfect lifespan, and so their life course may be radically different from ours. The point is that the whole concept of what is normal, what is expected, is a product of culture as well.

The notion that "normal" might have more than one face is critical for examining patterns of child care because it intersects at every level. As the world becomes more multicultural, we will be faced with other concepts of normality at every turn. Imagine the Cambodian woman who immigrates to Los Angeles and is arrested when she breast-feeds in public. Knowing that breast-feeding in public is normal in Cambodia would make this situation less fraught with conflict. I recently read a letter to the editor of a newspaper that expressed indignation that women in the refugee camps in Zaire were carrying infants. How dare they have children, the writer commented, when they are refugees and without permanent homes and resources. What the writer did not understand was that in Hutu culture, offspring are considered an asset, not a deficit; knowing that might make the situation a bit more understandable.

A more flexible construct of normality also has practical applications. As all parents in Western culture know, there is a "normal growth curve" against which all infants are compared when they are brought in for visits to the pediatrician. This standard is used to evaluate babies' growth, and if the baby falls drastically below the curve, pediatricians recommend intervention. But pediatrician Glen Flores, who codirects the Pediatric Latino Clinic at the Boston University School of Medicine, points out that comparing Latino babies to that "normal" curve is a mistake. That initial and now widely accepted curve was developed based on a group of white bottle-fed babies from Yellow Spring, Ohio, during the 1950s.[5] This information is important not only because white babies are born heavier, but bottle-fed infants also grow faster and fatter than breast-fed infants, regardless of their ethnicity. In this particular case, Latino babies in America are also born smaller and therefore follow a slower growth-rate curve.[6] The curve, then, in reality is "normal" only for other white bottle-fed infants. Using that curve to evaluate Latino babies may cause pediatricians to intervene in unnecessary and inappropriate ways. And how disturbing it must be for Latino parents to be shown that curve and made to feel that their baby is not healthy. What is needed, points out Flores, is more data on birth weights, growth curves and such from various ethnic populations—that is, a widening of the concept of the normal growth curve.

Standards and expected norms are also tied up with individual parental belief systems about health and disease that are rooted in ethnicity and race. Puerto Ricans categorize diseases into hot and cold and act accordingly;[7] some white Americans believe that many diseases, such as colds and flu, are the product of a weak will; some tribal peoples believe that diseases can be caused by curses laid on by others. All of these beliefs not only influence when and if parents bring their babies in for care, they also influence whether or not parents will complete treatment. Knowing the parameters of individual and cultural concepts of normality—that is, of health and well-being—is important for clinical practice, public health, and foreign aid.

This is not just a parental issue, it is also a larger social issue. In a way, norms actually govern the health care system. We now have drugs that offset hyperactivity, therapy to dampen behavioral disorders, and special tutors to help the learning-disabled. But who decides when these interventions are necessary? And how can anyone make these decisions given that we do not even have normal values for most of these so-called pathologies? We cannot yet characterize these disorders because no one really knows the range of normality in these areas. Labeling these patterns of behavior as "disorders" is a cultural construction based on the assumption that everyone should have a perfect life in which we all act, learn, and behave in some idealized way. The point is that these so-called disorders take on new meaning when a wider net of normality is cast across childhood behaviors.[8] Since clinicians are concerned with normality, and their job is to return a child to a normal state when parents bring them in with complaints, the very concept of normal becomes a major issue.

Pediatrician Ronald Barr uses the example of a crying complaint to illustrate this point. When a parent brings in a baby and says she is crying "too much," what, Barr asks himself, does "too much" mean? On what is the parent basing this judgment? And as a pediatrician, how does Barr decide what "too much" is? If this mother was a !Kung San, crying for ten minutes might be "too much," but for a Canadian the "too much" line might be crossed after an hour. Also, different parents have different tolerance levels. Barr has found that some parents say their babies cry too much even though they don't fit the Wessel definition of colic, whereas other babies clearly cry that much but their parents don't complain. Individual parental tolerance levels, then, also become part of the diagnostic tool that pediatricians must rely on, and there is wide variability in what each parent thinks is normal.

The same analysis can be applied to issues of sleep. As Jim McKenna has pointed out, standards for infant sleep have been established on solitary-sleeping, bottle-fed babies. We now know that bottle-fed babies sleep long and hard because their food contains more fat, and that babies fed on long-interval schedules soon learn not to wake at night because there is little possibility of food being offered. And yet for most of human history, babies have been breast-fed and have slept next to their mothers, which means, McKenna's work has shown, they sleep much lighter and wake up often. Which pattern is normal for babies, long sleep or waking often and feeding? In the evolutionary and cross-cultural view, light sleep is normal and a deep six hours is pathological. Aware only of the all-night sleeping condition that is currently ingrained in Western culture, and therefore expected, parents might believe that something is wrong if the baby doesn't sleep through the night. But with a broader view of normal infant sleep, and other infant behaviors, these worried parents might be assured that their baby is just fine.

Narrow standards of normality for crying and sleeping frequently send parents to the pediatrician's office with complaints. Taking a world-wide and more historical view suggests that normality in these matters might be more variable, broader, and open to redefinition. It would surely be of practical value for a parent to hear that although a sleepless, crying two-month-old might be annoying, his behavior is perfectly normal for an infant.

The previous chapters have shown that standards of normality (that is, what is expected) guide so much of parenting that no one notices how odd they are until they are highlighted against another culture. One of the more charming research reports on cultural norms was conducted by

Rebecca New in which she interviewed Italian and American mothers.[9] The American mothers were typically the most worried about sleep and crying. They knew exactly where the babies had spent the night, how much sleep they had gotten, and how many times the mother had to get out of bed to comfort the crying baby. For the Italian mothers, questions about sleep were unanswerable—they just didn't keep track. The Italian mothers had no idea how long the babies slept because their babies slept with them, and mothers weren't keeping close track of their own sleeping hours; sleep was not an issue and the questions about sleep appeared quite odd to them. But the Italian mothers were very concerned with what their babies ate. Early on, Italian mothers begin feeding pasta and other foods and they assume that breast-feeding alone is not enough to build a healthy, happy child. These Italian mothers knew exactly how much their babies had eaten and when (usually with the family), and could answer any questions about the babies' diet. The American mothers were clearly less interested in the issue of food except as a device to keep the babies from crying. Food was such an issue for the Italians, and they were so sure of their strategy, that when the researcher pointed out that the baby was uncomfortable and crying with a big pasta spoon shoved in its mouth, one mother responded, "He'll get used to it."

While some of these parenting styles are harmless, and often amusing, others are more critical. When, for example, does a pediatrician intervene in complaints of sleep or crying? And in terms of foreign aid, how do relief workers figure out what the norm might be for a culture and thus more easily implement healthful interventions according to those norms? Must African babies be put on bottle formula because they do not match the Western growth curve? Or should American newborns who stay awake at night be put in car seats and driven around until they nod off? The unpacking and examining of accepted norms is perhaps one of the most fruitful areas of enlightenment that ethnopediatrics has to offer us.

Evolution's Role

Obtaining a more broadly informed view of parenting means examining parenting styles not just cross-culturally but through evolutionary history as well. Underneath the cultural twists that skew our behavior lies a natural biology, a human nature, that evolved a certain way for good biological reasons. Organic beings are, of course, subject to natural selection, and the path of evolution is not a perfect path. Contrary to popular belief, evolution does not select away all the defects and save only the perfect models. Instead, natural selection navigates a trade-off between cost and benefit; it deals with existing constraints and checks out the options, and then ends up with a compromise. Every species, every organism, is a compromise. As anthropologist Carol Worthman puts it, "Biological systems are Rube Goldberg systems. They don't always work perfectly but they work well enough." Apply that evolutionary framework to the evolved parent–infant dyad, and the same kind of Rube Goldberg solution appears. The human baby has a big head and has to be born too soon, so it is more dependent than the babies of other mammals. As a result, all kinds of mechanisms kick in to attach parents and infant in a physiological and emotional dyad. It's a patched-together sort of system, with strange bells and odd little whistles, and it often breaks down; but for the most part, it does work and babies grow up healthy.

The evolutionary perspective can be both comforting *and* disquieting. The best thing that evolution gives us is the flexibility to deal with all the various pathways to the same end result—a healthy, successful offspring that will grow to reproductive age and pass on more genes. "If evolution was going to design an adaptive organism," says Ronald Barr, "it would design one with multiple pathways."

On the other hand, we learn that human infants are evolutionarily— that is, biologically over generations—designed to be part of an intimate physical dyad with an adult. Cross-cultural studies, observations of nonhuman primates, and historical fact all combine to paint a portrait of a human infant entwined with a parent. It might be discomforting to realize that in some cultures, this evolutionarily designed package has been somewhat disassembled. What will be the long-term effect? Evolution has designed primates as flexible beings in order to be able to adapt culturally to the various trade-offs that come with parenting.

Taking into account the evolutionary view of parenting can only help one gain a sense of perspective. Imagine this scene: An infant is crying and a father moves immediately to pick it up and comfort it. Instead of feeling manipulated by the cry, the father may realize that the baby cried because there was some sort of mismatch in its world, and so the infant was crying out to the other part of its dyad for response. This realization might dampen a negative or distancing response from the parent. In the end, this is good for all concerned.

The Pediatrics of Ethnopediatrics

In most societies around the world, child care is a learned skill, and learning takes place all day, every day, because every community has babies. Growing up in Venezuela, Magdalena Hurtado explained to me, she was surrounded by babies, and knowing how to parent was never an issue for her. But now she worries about her two daughters who, as Americans, rarely see infants at all. How will they learn how to care for babies? How odd it would be to tell Ache or !Kung San women that in this country, we learn our parenting skills from books and from doctors (mostly male). In modern Western culture, it is not their mothers or grandmothers or sisters to whom parents turn for counsel. They turn instead to the pediatrician, an expert in pathology who is trained in detecting organic diseases but who is now being asked about what is "normal" behavior. The several pediatricians I spoke to have all mentioned that the vast majority of complaints they deal with in their practice are behavioral: complaints about sleep, feeding, and crying. Excessive crying, for example, is an organic problem only 5 percent of the time at most, and yet pediatricians are mandated to spend the short time they have with a patient ruling out all organic possibilities. Only later, when the organic is eliminated, can they move into the more murky area of behavior and caretaking style. The pediatrician must at some point remove the hat of medical investigator and put on a new hat of behaviorist or developmental psychologist. Are they trained for this switch? More important, is it asking too much for the pediatrician who has been trained in the medical—that is, organic—model of pathology to also be responsible for nonorganic syndromes and disorders? No matter the correct answer to this question, the situation at present in Western culture is that pediatricians hold the key role in dealing with infants and parents. As such, pediatricians are the ones who could benefit most from a cross-cultural and evolutionary view of infants and parents—the ethnopediatric view.

As pediatrician Ronald Barr explains, one of the frustrations of any medical practice is the unexplained variance that a physician must deal with when diagnosing a patient, recommending a treatment, and then tracking the outcome.[10] First of all, there is variance in why a mother or father brings a baby into the office at all. Again, parents have individual tolerances for infant behavior—what is excessive crying to one might be simply natural and expected to another. Second, there is variance in the personal styles that parents have in caring for infants, and there is no way, short of following that parent around minute by minute, that the physician can fully gain a picture of that infant's lifestyle. Third, physicians constantly deal with the variance in patient compliance; they might recommend a particular course of treatment, but there is no way they can enforce compliance. All parents have a belief system within which they both practice care and implement intervention as recommended by doctors. And people are notorious for going to the doctor for advice but not following it to the letter. And so when the physician tries to measure the effect of a treatment, the issue of unexplained variance raises its ugly head again. In a sense, the pediatrician is working with several gray areas—complaint, treatment, and outcome—in which human behavior, with all its individual twists and turns, makes medical practice difficult. And this is where an ethnopediatric approach might have an added value.

Ethnopediatrics, as these scientists and pediatricians conceive of it, is designed to address many of these areas of unexplained variance. It takes into account parental belief systems, how culture influences parental decisions, even the very idea that infant behavior might or might not be a problem—that is, the question of what is normal. Ronald Barr uses the example of a complaint that the baby cries too much to explain how a pediatrician, a developmental pediatrician, and an ethnopediatrician might approach this problem. The pediatrician would first try to rule out all organic possibilities—allergies, gastrointestinal blockages, and the like. Then the pediatrician might recommend treatment, such as a change in infant formula or medications, that would relieve the symptoms. The developmental pediatrician, a person schooled not only in organic disease but also in the path of child development, would also first rule out organic causes, and then tackle the behavioral sphere. He or she might bring up the normal crying curve and explain to parents that the crying peak will soon be over and tell them not to worry. The developmental pediatrician might also query the parents about their state of mind and what they expect from this baby, and from parenting; the goal would not necessarily be to treat the symptoms but to restore the parent–infant dyad to a functional and pleasant interaction for both parties. The ethnopediatrician would take this one step further by explaining *why* crying is there in the first place—as a signal of infant distress over something, not necessarily food, and that it evolved to get some kind of response from an adult. The ethnopediatrician might also explain that cross-cultural work has shown wide variation in caretaking across cultures, and that although the parent has been led to believe there is only one way to care for an infant, there are actually a variety of ways to do so on a day-to-day basis. The ethnopediatrician might also explain the concept of trade-offs—that it is perfectly reasonable to let the baby cry when the parents are occupied with something else, but that every choice has consequences and every parent has to weigh the trade-offs when making parenting decisions. More important, the ethnopediatrician might suggest alterations in the caretaking package that might change the amount and duration of crying, such as carrying the baby more of the time, or responding more quickly to its fussing.

The added value of the ethnopediatrician is one of information, and information can be the most important prescription of all because it often provides simple reassurance. The baby's crying is not pathological—all infants around the world do this at two months. Waking up several times a night is not strange—this is what babies are designed to do. Constantly demanding interaction and attention is not the sign of a hyperactive infant—this is what babies need as social animals. And if you, as a parent, feel the urge to sleep with your baby or breast-feed her until she is two, that's okay, because for millions of years people have been doing exactly that.

NEW-AGE PARENTS AND
OLD-AGE BABIES

Most humans no longer live in small nomadic kin-based bands with overlapping generations of family members. Although kinship and close social relationships are still important to our social structure, the settled agricultural-based life seems to be the general ecology in which most humans now live. Our babies have passed with us from the ancestral "environment of evolutionary adaptedness" into the present settled ways; and across the globe, this shift in economic base is currently changing the overall lifeways of the remaining forest- or savanna-dwelling hunters and gatherers. We are not yet a global culture nor a global society, but cultures do seem to be seeping into one another. But no matter this melding of societies and culture, humans still express a wide variety of parenting styles. In all cases, these caretaking packages reflect local subsistence bases, economies, and cultural ideologies. The package also evolves from individual experience, tolerance levels, and expectations; tradition and style do not develop in a vacuum—they have personal, historical, and cultural roots and influences. Parenting is further complicated by the fact that the way we bring up children involves so many people—parents, the community, and the babies themselves.

Parenting is a veritable circus of interacting egos and needs, biological constraints and evolutionary expectations. As in all things in life, parenting too is a series of trade-offs; there is no perfect way, only a series of options, a bundle of possible pathways, that pilot adults through the hazardous job of bringing up babies. And it is indeed so much trouble that one may wonder why people have children at all. But as Jim McKenna once glibly pointed out to me when I commented on the excessive investment infants require, "Evolution never promised us a rose garden." Our nature is to pass on our genes and so we must pay the price that infants extract. Parenting is, in fact, supposed to be a lot of work and a major drain on the adult organism because that's the way the human animal is designed. If we, as parents, accept this fundamental truth—that having a baby and bringing it into adulthood is a major constraint on life, on resources, on our physical and emotional selves, and a big job not for the squeamish—we are then essentially in line with and accepting of our evolutionary heritage.

Intersecting with this fundamental truth is the escape hatch of culture that lets us try all sorts of ways to manage this job. Culture and tradition are part of our flexibility, and we can, therefore, change the dictates of culture because we *are* culture. This is why cultures not only evolve, they can also be forced to change, can be revolutionized. In that sense, if we all agree that a closely entwined relationship between an infant and at least one caretaker is a good idea, then we can "borrow back"[11] those elements that we feel are most useful and germane to the modern parenting situation and *decide* to parent with this or that element. No one expects any mother to live in a grass hut and hunt and gather with a baby on her back. But it is reasonable to suggest that sleeping with a baby is good and will not make him a dependent screamer. We might not want to feed a baby continuously as the San do, but a mother can certainly decide to decrease the interval between feeds, or feed out of schedule if she feels like it. And there is no shame in deciding to "wear" a baby rather than cache it in a playpen. Culture should not be a dictator but a facilitator.

And every parent has the option of sorting through and either accepting or rejecting cultural baggage. For example, parents in the technologically sophisticated West can make personal decisions about the gear that manufacturers thrust upon us in an attempt to make life easier. It is a simple matter of evaluating those devices in light of an evolutionarily and cross-culturally enlightened view of babies that gives us the option of rejecting these so-called innovations if we want to. We might decide that the use of a playpen when there are people around to hold the baby is not the best choice, or that using a car seat to contain a baby in the living room is not the way to make the baby spend its day. We might choose to turn the walkie-talkie in the opposite direction and let the solitary-sleeping baby be immersed in family noises rather than sequestering it away from its social group.[12]

The human infant is not just a bundle of reflexes that develops into a sentient adult. Babies have been, and continue to be, molded by evolution to make it through the birth canal, to express their needs by crying and fidgeting once outside, and to engage in the world around them. As pediatrician T. Berry Brazelton puts it, "It constantly surprises me how early an infant picks up cues from his environment that lead him to 'want' to become part of it."[13] This is how the baby enters the world, but it is not necessarily how the world sees the baby. Because humans are such slowly developing organisms, there are plenty of opportunities, and plenty of time, for mismatches and misunderstandings to appear between babies whose internal needs expect certain things, and parents who are simply trying to get on with life. It really is the proverbial two-edge sword—evolution has given humans this wide arena in which to operate but we sometimes don't have a clue about how to most efficiently meet our needs. We are supposed to have sex, conceive infants containing our genes, and assure they make it to reproductive age—this is the master plan of nature. But there's a lot of slack in the system, a lot of room to maneuver, and there are a lot of ways to mess up. "Evolution has provided us with an arena in which caregiving *can* be learned," explains anthropologist Jim McKenna, "but it doesn't say *what* is to be learned, and so we learn all sorts of crazy things about babies." Nowhere is the slippery slope between what nature might compel and what actually happens more apparent than in the arena of infant care.

Accepting that babies are sometimes a burden, and then trying to parent in a style that does not interrupt the natural parent–infant dyad but does make life a little easier, is the challenge we all face. Most often, this means trusting the parental instinct—that is, common sense, which also evolved as a guide. And babies, too, help out with their reaching out, their goofy smiles, and their crying and fussing to let us know if we are on the right track.

Focusing on parents and babies in my own culture for these past many months, I have gained great respect for parents who put so much energy and care into navigating the trade-offs of parenting. I have also been sometimes amused at their efforts. Last summer, for example, I kept track of the various infant-carrying devices that I came across— during the summer months, babies in my area are trotted out in all manner of contraptions that highlight the best and the worst that technology has to offer. The results of my nonscientific survey suggest that most American parents prefer the stroller, both as baby carrier and shopping cart. The second runner-up is the baby backpack with smaller infants on the front or older babies on the back; mimicking the !Kung San *kaross*, the Indonesian sling, or the Quecha manta pouch, these more technologically advanced canvas versions seem to ride quite easily on adults and make babies happy. Although the baby backpack worked well for most, some models could use improvement, like the flag-sized bolt of billowing cloth that seemed to overwhelm the devoted father who was trying to hold the sides together while searching for the baby lying somewhere deep inside. And even more hilarious was the contraption of metal bars, canvas straps, and mesh awning, a tentlike structure so hi-tech and complicated that the baby could only peer out of one tiny corner because the scaffolding got in the way. These parents are all trying their best to carry, not cache, their babies, but somehow technology has brought them more than they asked for. Over the summer I waved at many babies perusing the crowd from their perch atop Mom or Dad, and some even waved back by kicking their arms and legs or giving me a big smile.

Riding down the street on my bike one day early in the autumn, still keeping an eye on infant-carrying devices, I passed a man walking along with a three-year-old boy sitting upright in a hip sling, a simple matter of plaid cloth and a big plastic buckle. Surprised to see such a simple device among all those I had seen over the previous few months, I stopped and asked where he had bought the sling, and we chatted for a while. Not knowing who I was, he admitted, embarrassed, that he and his wife always carried this boy: "He just always wanted to be carried from the moment he was born, even after he could walk." The father apologized, as if it were a psychological defect, a pathology. With his arm resting lightly on his father's shoulder, the boy also looked at me, not the least bit embarrassed, simply happy to be where he was. "Yes, of course he wants to be carried, that's how he's designed," I answered, offering him reassurance from a perfect stranger that he was doing a great job. To me, they looked like people from another culture where no one is ashamed about maintaining the parent–infant bond, where independence is not an issue, not a goal. To carry a child that size must surely be hard work, but the parents had responded to the child's needs and their own intuition that this was okay. Even though carrying a toddler all the time is unacceptable in this culture, and though surely these parents must put up with an endless stream of comments from others, even strangers, the little boy looked perfectly content to me.

Jumping back on my bike, I pedaled away and thought once again about how many decisions there are that parents can and must make, so many subtle ways to interact with children that affect both the welfare of the baby and the tenor of family life. And as I took a quick glance backward, the father shifted the boy to his other hip, smiled at his son, and continued his slow and dedicated voyage through parenthood.

NOTES

INTRODUCTION

1. Clutton-Brock, 1991.
2. LeVine, Dixon et al., 1994.

CHAPTER ONE: THE EVOLUTION OF BABIES

1. Martin, 1990.
2. Martin, 1990.
3. Dienske, 1986.
4. Martin, 1990.
5. Martin, 1990.
6. Whittenberger, 1981.
7. Tague and Lovejoy, 1986; Trevathan, 1987. Scientists use the word "platypelloid" to describe this shape.
8. Berge et al., 1984; Tague and Lovejoy, 1986; Lovejoy, 1988.
9. Rodman and McHenry, 1980; Isbell and Young, 1996.
10. Leutenegger, 1972.
11. Berge et al., 1984.
12. Tague and Lovejoy, 1986.
13. There is currently a controversy regarding the path of Australopithecine birth. Leutenegger claims the passage was easy, much like an ape's (Leutenegger, 1972; Leutenegger, 1982); McHenry feels the process was much like modern birth (Mc-

Henry, 1986); and Tague and Lovejoy propose it was unlike any known primate (Tague and Lovejoy, 1986; Lovejoy, 1988). For an excellent review of this controversy see Rosenberg (1992).

14. Fleagle, 1988.

15. Leutenegger, 1972; Jordon, 1976.

16. Leutenegger, 1982.

17. Rosenberg, 1992; Rosenberg and Trevathan, 1995/96.

18. Resent research shows that other primates also do a twist. Melissa Stoller of the University of Chicago X-rayed squirrel monkeys and baboons giving birth and has shown that some infant monkeys do indeed rotate during birth. Their rotation, however, does not seem to follow the constraints of the inner pelvic architecture (Culotta, 1995).

19. Trevathan, 1987; Rosenberg, 1992.

20. Hammerschmidt and Ansorge, 1989.

21. Trevathan, 1987.

22. Trevathan, 1987. See also Barash, 1979; Rosenberg, 1992.

23. Jolly, 1986.

24. Lorenz, 1935.

25. Trevathan, 1987.

26. Lamb and Hwang, 1982.

27. For a review of maternal responses in rats, mice, and rabbits see Insel, 1990; Rosenblatt, 1990.

28. Klopfer, 1971.

29. Klopfer, 1971; Trevathan, 1987.

30. Trevathan, 1987.

31. Harlow and Harlow, 1965.

32. For an interesting discussion of the history of Bowlby's concept of bonding see Chisolm, 1996.

33. Bowlby, 1969.

34. The environment of evolutionary adaptation is defined today as 1.5 million years ago when the first *Homo* species evolved from the Australopithecines. The concept is used frequently today by a group of evolutionary psychologists who are investigating why we humans act the way we do. They believe that much of our behavior can be explained by relating it to evolutionary behavioral adaptations during the Plio-Pleistocene when the human genus first appeared (Barkow et al., 1992; Wright, 1994).

35. Klaus and Kennell, 1976.

36. (Kennell et al., 1975; Klaus and Kennell, 1976; Hales et al., 1977). Differences were also found among Guatemalan mothers. Mothers with early contact engaged in more eye contact, more soothing behaviors, and more contact during pediatric exams.

37. Lamb, 1982; Lamb and Hwang, 1982; Goldberg, 1983; Trevathan, 1987.

38. Klaus and Kennell, 1976; Klaus and Kennell, 1976; Lamb and Hwang, 1982.

39. Trevathan, 1987.

40. Lamb and Hwang, 1982; Warren and Shortle, 1990.

41. Lamb and Hwang, 1982.

42. Smith, 1986.

43. Holman and Goy, 1979.

44. Lamb and Hwang, 1982.

45. Scheper-Hughes, 1985; Scheper-Hughes, 1992.

46. Tronick et al., 1992.

47. Lamb, 1982.

48. In a study comparing birth and mothering practices of Hispanic and non-Hispanic women in Texas, anthropologist Wenda Trevathan questioned the women about when and how often they went out after giving birth. She was unable to compare data from the two groups because the Hispanic women went out, but they could not understand the category of "going out without the baby." Only the non-Hispanic women thought of leaving their babies with someone else as normal behavior (Trevathan, 1987).

49. *New Book of World Rankings*, 3rd Edition, 1991.

50. Trevathan, 1987.

51. Fleming, 1990.

52. Bleichfield and Moely, 1984.

53. Feldman and Nash, 1978.

54. Fleming, 1990; Warren and Shortle, 1990.

55. Insel, 1990; Insel and Shapiro, 1992.

56. Kimball, 1979.

57. Porter et al., 1983; Fleming, 1990.

58. Formby, 1967.

59. Sagi, 1981.

60. Fleming, 1990.

61. Male care of infants is seen mostly in primates, carnivores, and perissodactyls, and is usually associated with obligate monogamy, whereby males are assured they are the true biological fathers of the infants they care for (Clutton-Brock, 1991).

62. Taub, 1984; Clutton-Brock, 1991.

63. Alexander, 1990.

64. Recent work by Ryne Palombit on gibbons and siamangs has shown that some of what we used to assume were monogamous mating pairs and nuclear families are really a mix and match of individuals living together. Also, Palombit has shown that those that are couples are not necessarily exclusively monogamous (Palombit, 1994 a, b).

65. Wilson Goldizen, 1987.
66. Taub, 1984.
67. Yogman, 1982; Lamb, 1987.
68. Whiting and Whiting, 1975; West and Konner, 1976; Yogman, 1990.
69. Lipkin and Lamb, 1982; Yogman, 1990.
70. Lipkin and Lamb, 1982.
71. Yogman, 1990.
72. Yogman, 1990.
73. Greenberg and Morris, 1974.
74. Parke, 1979; Yogman, 1984; Yogman, 1990.
75. Frodi et al., 1978.
76. Zazlow, reported in Yogman, 1984.
77. Kotelchuck, 1976; Lamb, 1976.
78. Yogman, 1982; Yogman, 1984.
79. Greenberg and Morris, 1974.
80. Daly and Wilson, 1982.
81. Diamond, 1992; Buss, 1994.
82. Lamb, 1976.
83. Yogman, 1990.
84. Coe et al., 1985.
85. Rice, 1977.
86. White and Labarba, 1976.
87. Mehler et al., 1990.
88. DeCasper and Fifer, 1980.
89. Fernald, 1992; Fernald, 1992; Kuhl et al., 1997.
90. Condon and Sander, 1974.
91. Fernald, 1992.
92. Pinker, 1994.
93. Brazelton, 1969.
94. Brazelton et al., 1974.
95. Tronick, 1980.
96. Brazelton et al., 1975; Tronick et al., 1978; Cohn and Tronick, 1983.
97. Tronick, 1980.
98. Yogman et al., 1983.
99. Brazelton et al., 1975, p. 148.
100. For fathers see Greenberg and Morris, 1974.
101. Brazelton, 1982.
102. Wisenfeld, Malatesta et al., 1985.
103. Greenberg and Morris, 1974.

Chapter Two: The Anthropology of Parenting

1. Harkness and Super, 1996.
2. Bohannan and Glazer, 1973.
3. This concept, called "cultural relativism," is the earlier version of today's "multiculturalism" movement.
4. Culture was considered "superorganic," that is, above instinct, and therefore not "animal."
5. It might be that by pushing the role of culture in forming personality and behavior, these early anthropologists went too far. They dismissed the influence of biology on human behavior, and even now many cultural anthropologists still refuse to accept that humans have any connection with other primates or other animals. They see humans as separate from all animals, special because we have culture.
6. Mead, 1930/1975.
7. Mead, 1930/1975; Mead, 1956.
8. This idea is back in fashion, and there is some evidence from primate research that so-called inborn personality types can be changed by social learning. Frans de Waal and colleagues placed rhesus, macaque, and stumptail macaque youngsters together for five months. The stumptails were older than and thus dominant over the rhesus monkeys, and de Waal hypothesized that the rhesus would learn the stumptail's more peaceable ways of reconciliation after aggressive interactions, and they did. The "sociable" rhesus youngsters continued to be like the stumptails even when they were finally separated from their "good examples" (de Waal and Johanowicz, 1993). De Waal suggests that if it is possible for a rhesus monkey to learn better methods of sociality, the same sort of social teaching should be easily accomplished with human children (de Waal, 1996).
9. Benedict, 1938.
10. Mead, 1956.
11. Benedict, 1938; LeVine et al., 1994; Harkness and Super, 1996.
12. LeVine et al., 1994.
13. Whiting, 1963; Whiting and Whiting, 1975.
14. Whiting, 1963.
15. Barry et al., 1959; LeVine et al., 1994.
16. Draper and Cashdan, 1988.
17. LeVine, 1974; Bornstein, 1991.
18. Whiting and Child, 1953; Bornstein, 1991; Harkness and Super, 1996.
19. Bornstein, 1991.
20. Harkness and Super, 1980.

21. Bronfenbrenner, 1979; Harkness and Super, 1994.
22. Harkness, 1992; Harkness and Super, 1994.
23. My favorite description of childhood and what it means to grow up is by Annie Dillard in *An American Childhood,* 1987, Harper and Row.
24. LeVine, 1988; Goodnow and Collins, 1990; LeVine, Dixon et al., 1994.
25. Harkness and Super, 1992.
26. Harkness and Super, 1992.
27. Harkness and Super, 1992.
28. Harkness and Super, 1992.
29. LeVine, 1974; LeVine, 1988.
30. LeVine, 1988.
31. Howrigan, 1988.
32. Harkness, 1992.
33. Pinker, 1994, p. 40.
34. Harkness and Super, 1996.
35. Barr and Worthman, 1995; Worthman, 1995a, b.
36. LeVine, 1974.
37. Myers, 1995.
38. Wilson, 1975; Barkow et al., 1992.
39. Vygotsky, 1978.
40. Rogoff and Morelli, 1989.
41. Rogoff and Morelli, 1989.
42. Gajdusik, 1963, p. 554.
43. Worthman has written several symposium papers and grant applications (Worthman, 1995a, b), but the roots of her thinking about ethnopediatrics as a separate science can be seen in her writing (e.g., Worthman, 1993).
44. World Bank, 1993.
45. Hahn, 1995.
46. Scheper-Hughes, 1992.
47. Rohde, 1984.
48. Harkness, 1992.
49. Richman et al., 1988.
50. Goodnow et al., 1984.
51. Hess et al., 1980.
52. Rogoff and Morelli, 1989.

CHAPTER THREE: OTHER PARENTS, OTHER WAYS

1. Dugger, 1996.
2. Sculpin and DeCorse, 1992; Crapo, 1995.
3. Harkness and Super, 1996.
4. McGrew 1992; Small, 1993; Wrangham et al., 1994.
5. Eldridge, 1995.
6. Cavalli-Sforza, 1994.
7. There are several recent collections of studies that provide an array of research on child development and parenting across cultures. For a more extensive view than the one presented here, read Field et al., 1981; Munroe et al., 1981; Wagner and Stevenson, 1982; Bornstein, 1991; Harkness and Super, 1996, among others.
8. Barkow et al., 1992.
9. The !Kung San were first studied by Laurence and Lorna Marshall in the 1950s. In the 1960s Irven DeVore and Richard Lee began work with a different group of San, work that eventually included a number of researchers and a number of projects. My description here relies on the work of Lee, Shostak, and Konner (Lee, 1979; Shostak, 1981; Lee, 1984).
10. "Bushman" is a derogatory colonial term and San or !Kung San is the preferred term. San is the Khoi (Hottentot) term for aboriginal people.
11. Lee, 1984, p. ix.
12. DeVore and Konner, 1974.
13. Konner, 1972.
14. This fact is important to scenarios of hominid evolution. Lovejoy (1981) maintains that the hominid social system is based on monogamy, with females staying at camp with children while males hunt. Clearly, as the San prove, mothers stay home only some of the time and babies leave camp when mothers do.
15. Konner, 1972.
16. Konner, 1976; Konner, 1977.
17. Barr and Elias, 1988.
18. Konner, 1972.
19. Zelazo et al., 1972; Konner, 1973.
20. Konner, 1977.
21. Konner, 1977. Another study shows that Kikuyu babies in East Africa do better on both motor and cognitive skills than do Western babies. In fact, it may not be that African babies do "better," but that Western babies are delayed in their development. Researchers speculate that the higher abilities of these Kikuyu infants are due to a

social component because these babies interact physically and socially with several adults, not just mothers (Leiderman et al., 1973).

22. Konner, 1977.
23. Draper and Cashdan, 1988.
24. The account here is based on the excellent volume by Kim Hill and Magdalena Hurtado (1996).
25. Hill and Hurtado, 1996, p. 235.
26. Hill and Hurtado, 1996, p. xii.
27. Hill and Hurtado, 1996, p. 250.
28. Kaplan and Dove, 1987; Hill and Hurtado, 1996.
29. Kaplan and Dove, 1987.
30. Kaplan and Dove, 1987.
31. Hill and Hurtado, 1996, p. 222.
32. Kim Hill, personal communication.
33. The LeVines have worked in this area for 40 years and their publication record is extensive. The summary here is based mostly on their most recent book, *Child Care and Culture: Lessons from Africa* (LeVine et al., 1994) and their first reports (1973, 1974, 1988). See also Dixon et al., 1981.
34. LeVine, 1994.
35. Explanations of Japanese culture, especially the work culture, are many. This book is not the place to cover these references in depth, but I did want to present a generalized and brief picture of Japanese culture that would underscore its parenting practices. For my comparative approach to Japanese parenting, I have relied on the excellent explanation by my esteemed colleague at Cornell, Robert J. Smith (1983). Smith is an internationally respected ethnographer of Japan, and his volume on Japanese society was invaluable to my thinking about Japanese parenting.
36. Smith, 1983.
37. Smith, 1983, p. 124.
38. Shwalb et al., 1996.
39. Trevathan and McKenna, 1994; Wolf et al., 1996.
40. Bornstein, 1989; Shwalb et al., 1996.
41. Shwalb et al., 1996.
42. Caudill and Weinstein, 1969.
43. Smith, 1983.
44. Bornstein et al., 1991.
45. Otaki et al., 1986.
46. Shand and Kosawa, 1985.
47. Hess et al., 1980.
48. Shwalb et al., 1996.
49. The research on Japan above is a case in point. In almost all the studies, Japanese

parents and children were described in comparison to Caucasian middle-class Americans.

50. See any of the work by Sara Harkness, references on Japan, or any cross-cultural studies mentioned above. Also see Whiting and Child, 1953.

51. Richman et al., 1988; Dunn and Brown, 1991. The goal of independence is not necessarily a product of industrialization, as Japan and other first-world cultures show. In Sweden as well, concern for the collective is a major goal of parents (Welles-Nyström, 1996).

52. Fisher and Fisher, 1963.

53. LeVine et al., 1994.

54. LeVine et al., 1994.

55. Fisher and Fisher, 1963; Goodnow et al., 1984.

56. Harkness et al., 1996.

57. Richman et al., 1988.

58. Fisher and Fisher, 1963.

59. Richman et al., 1988; New and Richman, 1996; also see next chapter.

60. New and Richman, 1996.

61. Richman et al., 1988.

62. Caudill and Weinstein, 1969; Hess et al., 1980; LeVine et al., 1994.

63. LeVine et al., 1994.

64. Fernald, 1992.

65. Tronick, 1997.

66. LeVine, 1988.

67. LeVine, 1974.

CHAPTER FOUR: A REASONABLE SLEEP

1. Small, 1992.

2. McKenna, Toman et al., 1993.

3. Thevenin, 1987; Jackson, 1989; McKenna, 1993.

4. Whiting, 1964.

5. Barry and Paxson, 1971; Konner and Super, 1987.

6. Schachter et al., 1989.

7. Burton and Whiting, 1961; Morelli et al., 1992.

8. McKenna, 1993.

9. Morelli et al., 1992.

10. Morelli et al., 1992, p. 609.

11. Farooqi et al., 1991; Gantley et al., 1993.

12. Schachter et al., 1989.

13. Lozoff et al., 1984.

14. Lozoff et al., 1984; Mandansky and Edlebrock, 1990.

15. Abbott, 1992.

16. Main, 1982.

17. Abbott, 1992.

18. Sloane, 1978, cited in Abbott, 1992.

19. Shweder et al., 1995.

20. Elias et al., 1986.

21. Caudill and Plath, 1966; Wolf et al., 1996.

22. Caudill and Plath, 1966. According to Caudill and Path, the Japanese take great pleasure in eating, bathing, and sleeping as social rather than solitary activities. See also Shweder et al., 1995.

23. Harkness et al., 1995.

24. Ferber, 1985.

25. Harkness et al., 1995.

26. Lozoff et al., 1984.

27. Parmalee et al., 1964.

28. Harkness et al., 1995.

29. Rybczynski, 1986, p. 26.

30. Norvenius, 1993.

31. Norvenius, 1993; Trevathan and McKenna, 1994.

32. McKenna, 1993; Trevathan and McKenna, 1994.

33. McKenna, 1993; Trevathan and McKenna, 1994.

34. Trevathan and McKenna, 1994.

35. Stoppard, 1995, p. 120.

36. Leach, 1976.

37. J. J. McKenna, personal communication.

38. Coe et al., 1985.

39. McKenna, 1995; Mosko et al., 1997.

40. Mosko et al., 1997.

41. Mosko et al., 1997.

42. Richard et al., 1997.

43. Mosko et al., 1997.

44. Anderson, 1991.

45. Ludington-Hoe et al., 1991.

46. McKenna, 1996.

47. Anders et al., 1980.

48. The SIDS diagnosis has been used a little too easily to account for any infant deaths. One study that thoroughly investigated infant death scenes reported that almost all the infant deaths over a one-year period could be attributed to "accident"

or something better described as bad child care. SIDS was named on the death certificate even though, for example, the infant had been placed next to a heater with toxic gases blowing in its face, or when a baby had been left unattended for six hours, or crushed by an obese mother. And in five out of twenty-six so-called SIDS cases, the infants were part of multiple births, making infanticide or neglect a real possibility. In other words, authorities, and societies, need to be more careful about what they call SIDS (Bass et al., 1986).

49. McKenna, 1996, and the Sudden Infant Death Syndrome Alliance.

50. Davies, 1985; Lee et al., 1989; McKenna, 1996.

51. Grether et al., 1990.

52. Balarajan et al., 1989.

53. McKenna et al., 1994; McKenna, 1995; McKenna, 1996.

54. Kahn, Groswasser et al., 1993.

55. Cunningham, 1976; Konner and Super, 1987; McKenna et al., 1997; also see Chapter Five.

56. Gantley et al., 1993.

57. Mitchell and Scragg, 1993.

58. Klonoff-Cohen and Edelstein, 1995.

59. Trevathan and McKenna, 1994.

60. McKenna, Toman et al., 1993; McKenna, 1995.

CHAPTER FIVE: CRYBABY

1. Barr et al., 1996.

2. Brazelton et al., 1974; Brazelton, 1982.

3. Barr et al., 1991, p. 601.

4. Newman, 1985.

5. Frodi, 1985.

6. Wolff, 1965.

7. Lester, 1985.

8. Lester, 1985.

9. Wolff, 1965.

10. Barr, 1995.

11. Barr, 1990.

12. Rebelsky and Black, 1972.

13. Brazelton, 1962; Barr, 1990; Lee, 1994; Barr et al., 1996.

14. Wolff, 1965.

15. Leiberman, 1985; Lester, 1985; Pinker, 1994.

16. Fernald, 1992; Fernald, 1992.

17. Barr, 1997.
18. Wolff, 1965.
19. Brazelton, 1962.
20. Brazelton, 1962, p. 579.
21. Forsyth, 1989.
22. Barr et al., 1992.
23. Barr, 1997.
24. Poole, 1991.
25. Barr, 1993; Barr, 1997.
26. Barr, 1997.
27. Forsyth, 1989.
28. Forsyth et al., 1985; Forsyth, 1989.
29. Barr et al., 1992.
30. Barr, 1993.
31. Barr, 1997.
32. Brazelton, 1962.
33. Birns et al., 1966.
34. Birns et al., 1966.
35. Harlow and Harlow, 1965.
36. Bell and Ainsworth, 1972.
37. Hunziker and Barr, 1986.
38. Barr et al., 1991. In another proactive study that compared increased carrying and increased parental responsiveness to infant cries, there was no difference in total crying relative to advice given to mothers (St. James-Roberts et al., 1995). However, this study tells us little about caretaking and parenting because it dichotomized responsiveness and carrying as if they were opposite types of parenting, although they are two connected parts of a total package.
39. Barr and Elias, 1988.
40. Murray, 1979; Barr, 1997.
41. Barr, 1990; Barr et al., 1991.
42. Brazelton et al., 1969.
43. Lee, 1994.
44. Bell and Ainsworth, 1972.
45. Barkow et al., 1992.
46. Papousek and Papousel, 1990.
47. Barr, 1997.
48. Barr, 1997.
49. Barr, 1990.
50. Barr, 1997.
51. Zeanah et al., 1985.

52. Stagner and Solley, 1970; Myers, 1995.
53. Goldsmith and Campos, 1982.
54. Lewis, 1989.
55. Kagan et al., 1992.
56. Goldsmith, A. H. et al., 1987.
57. Goldsmith, A. H. et al., 1987.
58. Keener, Zeanah et al., 1988.
59. Zeanah, Keener et al., 1985.
60. Kagan and Snidman, 1991.
61. Kagan, 1989; Kagan and Snidman, 1991a, b.
62. Kagan et al., 1992.
63. Benjamin, Li et al., 1996.
64. Clarke et al., 1988; Clarke and Boinski, 1995; Wilson and Clark, 1996.
65. Kagan and Snidman, 1991a, b.
66. Hsu et al., 1981.
67. Freeman and Freeman, 1969.
68. Freeman, 1971; Lester and Brazelton, 1982.
69. Glick, 1975.
70. de Vries, 1984; de Vries, 1987.
71. Thoman et al., 1983.
72. Gianino and Tronick, 1988; Tronick, 1989.
73. Tronick, 1989.
74. Tronick, 1989.
75. Brazelton et al., 1974; Blehar et al., 1977; Symons and Moran, 1987; Tronick, 1989.
76. Tronick and Cohn, 1989.
77. See also Wiesenfeld and Malatesta, 1983.
78. Miller et al., 1993.
79. Miller et al., 1993.
80. Tronick et al., 1978; Cohn and Tronick, 1983.
81. Field, 1977.
82. Cohn and Tronick, 1982; Cohn and Tronick, 1983.
83. Ainsworth and Bell, 1969.
84. Lozoff and Brittenham, 1979.

CHAPTER SIX: FOOD FOR THOUGHT

1. Righard and Alade, 1990.
2. Jelliffe and Jelliffe, 1978.

3. Pond, 1977; Jelliffe and Jelliffe, 1978.

4. Pond, 1977; Hayssen, 1995.

5. Hayssen, 1995.

6. Blackburn et al., 1989.

7. Jelliffe and Jelliffe, 1978; Blackburn et al., 1989.

8. Blackburn et al., 1989.

9. Blackburn et al., 1989.

10. Pond, 1977.

11. Pond, 1977.

12. Konner, 1977; Konner and Worthman, 1980.

13. Konner and Worthman, 1980.

14. See also Chapter Three for a description of forest hunter-gatherers.

15. Gussler and Briesemeister, 1980; Stuart-Macadam, 1995.

16. Dettwyler, 1995.

17. Dettwyler, 1995.

18. Harvey and Clutton-Brock, 1985; Dettwyler, 1995.

19. Ford, 1964.

20. Stuart-Macadam, 1995a, b.

21. Fogel et al., 1989.

22. Fildes, 1986.

23. Tuross and Fogel, 1994.

24. Stuart-Macadam, 1995a, b.

25. Knight and Peaker, 1982.

26. Wood, 1994.

27. Wood, 1994.

28. Cernoch and Porter, 1985.

29. Lawrence, 1994.

30. Stuart-Macadam, 1995a, b.

31. Jelliffe and Jelliffe, 1978; Lawrence, 1994; Baumslag and Michels, 1995.

32. Two good books explain the lactation process in detail. See Jelliffe and Jelliffe, 1978, and Lawrence, 1994. See also Wood, 1994.

33. Short, 1984.

34. Wood, 1994.

35. Quandt, 1995.

36. Baumslag and Michels, 1995.

37. Woodridge, 1995.

38. Baumslag and Michels, 1995; Woodridge, 1995.

39. Woodridge, 1995.

40. Jelliffe and Jelliffe, 1978.

41. Jelliffe and Jelliffe, 1978; Baumslag and Michels, 1995.

42. Jelliffe and Jelliffe, 1978.
43. Woodridge, 1995. Diane Wiessinger points out that women today in Western culture have grown up watching bottle-feeding, which sets the baby face up, away from the body, in a loose position. Breast-feeding, in contrast, requires that the baby be angled into the breast, tucked close, and that the breast be offered like a sandwich, compressed horizontally relative to the baby's mouth. In essence, Wiessinger says, breast-feeding asks the baby to suck on a breast while bottle-feeding asks the baby to suck on a nipple, and these are different mechanisms.
44. Cant, 1981; Gallup, 1982; Mascia-Lees et al., 1986; Caro, 1987; Low et al., 1987; Anderson, 1988; Caro and Sellen, 1990; Small, 1995.
45. Dettwyler, 1995.
46. Prentice and Prentice, 1988.
47. Prentice and Whitehead, 1987.
48. Khin et al., 1980.
49. Shaul, 1962.
50. Baumslag and Michels, 1995.
51. Baumslag and Michels, 1995.
52. Clutton-Brock, 1991.
53. Cunningham, 1995.
54. Baumslag and Michels, 1995.
55. Cunningham, 1995.
56. McClelland, 1982; Short, 1984.
57. Newman, 1995.
58. Lawrence, 1994.
59. Sheard and Walker, 1988; Newman, 1995.
60. Stuart-Macadam, 1995a, b.
61. Several books and articles have excellent reviews of this frightening situation: Short, 1984; Baumslag and Michels, 1995; Stuart-Macadam and Dettwyler, 1995.
62. Ford et al., 1993.
63. Cunningham, 1995.
64. McKenna et al., 1997.
65. McKenna and Bernshaw, 1995.
66. Cunningham, 1995.
67. Stuart-Macadam, 1995a, b.
68. Insel, 1990.
69. Morrow-Tlucak et al., 1988.
70. Morely et al., 1988; Baumslag and Michels, 1995.
71. Quandt, 1995.
72. Stuart-Macadam, 1995a, b.
73. Post, 1982; Baumslag and Michels, 1995; Micozzi, 1995.

74. Short, 1987.
75. Wood, 1994; Quandt, 1995.
76. Ellison, 1995.
77. Wood, 1994.
78. Short, 1987; Lawrence, 1994.
79. Howie and McNeilly, 1982.
80. Lawrence, 1994.
81. For example, Deivoye et al., 1977; Bonte and van Balen, 1969; Jenkins and Heywood, 1985.
82. Konner and Worthman, 1980.
83. Short, 1984.
84. Wood et al., 1985; Wood, 1994.
85. Short, 1984.
86. Ellison, 1995.
87. Short, 1987, p. 210.
88. Blaffer Hrdy, 1995.
89. Hull and Simpson, 1985.
90. Levine, 1988; Panter-Brick, 1991; Panter-Brick, 1992.
91. LeVine et al., 1994.
92. Creyton, 1992.
93. Baumslag and Michels, 1995.
94. Drewett et al., 1993.
95. Vitzthum, 1989.
96. Baumslag and Michels, 1995.
97. Newton, 1995.
98. Ryan et al., 1991.
99. Gabriel et al., 1986.
100. Gabriel et al., 1986.
101. Fildes, 1986; Stuart-Macadam, 1995a, b.
102. For an excellent and detailed account of the history of artificial feeding see Baumslag and Michels, 1995, or Fildes, 1995.
103. Short, 1987.
104. Blaffer Hrdy, 1995; Stuart-Macadam, 1995a, b.
105. Maher, 1992; Blaffer Hrdy, 1995.
106. Blaffer Hrdy, 1995.
107. Stuart-Macadam, 1995a, b.
108. Baumslag and Michels, 1995; Stuart-Macadam, 1995.
109. Baumslag and Michels, 1995.
110. Baumslag and Michels, 1995.
111. Quandt, 1995.

112. The story of the politics of breast-feeding can be found in Van Esterick, 1989; Baumslag and Michels, 1995; Van Esterick, 1995.
113. Cunningham, 1974; Cunningham et al., 1991; Cunningham, 1995.
114. Baumslag and Michels, 1995.
115. Short, 1984; Baumslag and Michels, 1995; Stuart-Macadam and Dettwyler, 1995.
116. Baumslag and Michels, 1995.
117. Shand, 1981; Baumslag and Michels, 1995.
118. Baumslag and Michels, 1995.
119. Forsyth et al., 1985; Forsyth, 1989.
120. Gussler and Briesemeister, 1980.
121. Baumslag and Michels, 1995.
122. Jelliffe and Jelliffe, 1978.
123. DeCarvalho et al., 1983.
124. Gussler and Briesemeister, 1980; Khin et al., 1980.
125. Gussler and Briesemeister, 1980.
126. Gussler and Briesemeister, 1980.
127. Gussler and Briesemeister, 1980.

Chapter Seven: Unpacking the Caretaking Package

1. Most of this chapter grows from that two-day workshop on ethnopediatrics. I want to thank Frank Kessel, Ronald Barr, and Carol Worthman for inviting me to the workshop, and the participants for some of the most exciting and provocative discussions I have ever heard. The ideas and commentary in this chapter are here only because of what I experienced that weekend, and attribution must be given to this group of pediatricians and social scientists: Ronald Barr, W. Thomas Boyce, James Chisolm, Suzanne Dixon, Glen Flores, Jacqueline Goodnow, Ana Magdalena Hurtado, James McKenna, Marty Stein, Edward Tronick, and Carol Worthman.
2. Tronick et al., 1985; Tronick et al., 1987; Morelli and Tronick, 1991.
3. Tronick et al., 1987; LeVine, 1990; LeVine et al., 1994.
4. Lozoff and Brittenham, 1979.
5. Binns et al., 1996.
6. Other studies have shown the "normal" curve to be not easily applicable to non-white populations. For example, Hmong babies in the United States are born heavier but by eight months of age their weight gain is similar to that of white infants. Hmong babies at birth are also the same length as those in the "normal" curve, but

after one year, their stature levels off below that of the curve (Gjerdingen et al., 1996).

7. Harwood, 1971.

8. Barr, 1993.

9. New and Richman, 1996.

10. I thank Ronald Barr for this lucid explanation of the unexplained variance in medical practice.

11. A phrase borrowed sideways from Jim McKenna.

12. Trevathan and McKenna, 1994.

13. Brazelton, 1969, p. 33.

REFERENCE LIST

Abbott, S. (1992). Holding on and pushing away: Comparative perspectives on an eastern Kentucky child-rearing practice. 20:33–65.

Ainsworth, M. D. S., and S. M. Bell (1969). Some contemporary patterns of mother–infant interactions in the feeding situation. In *Early Infancy*, A. Ambrose, ed. New York: Academic Press. 133–163.

Alexander, R. D. (1990). How did humans evolve? *University of Michigan Special Publications* 1:1–38.

Anders, T. F., M. A. Carskadon, and W. C. Dement (1980). Sleep and sleepiness in children and adolescents. *Pediatric Clinics of North America* 27:29–43.

Anderson, G. C. (1991). Current knowledge about skin-to-skin (kangaroo) care for preterm infants. *Journal of Perinatology* 11:216–226.

Anderson, J. L. (1988). Breasts, hips, and buttocks revisited. *Ethology and Sociobiology* 9:319–324.

Balarajan, R., V. Soni Raleigh, and B. Botting (1989). Sudden Infant Death Syndrome and postnatal mortality in immigrant England and Wales. *British Medical Journal* 298:716–720.

Barash, D. (1979). *The Whisperings Within.* London: Penguin Books.

Barkow, J. H., L. Cosmides, and J. Tooby (1992). *The Adapted Mind: Evolutionary Psychology and the Generation of Culture.* Oxford: Oxford University Press.

Barr, R. G. (1990). The early crying paradox. *Human Nature* 1:355–389.

Barr, R. G. (1990). The normal crying curve: What do we really know? *Developmental Medicine and Child Neurology* 32:356–362.

Barr, R. G. (1993). Normality: A clinically useless concept. The case of infant crying and colic. *Developmental and Behavioral Pediatrics* 14:264–270.

Barr, R. G. (1995). The enigma of infant crying: The emergence of defining dimensions. *Early Development and Parenting* 4:225–232.

Barr, R. G. (1997). Infant crying and colic: An interpretation in evolutionary perspective. In *Evolutionary Medicine,* W. Trevathan, E. O. Smith, and J. J. McKenna, eds. Oxford: Oxford University Press.

Barr, R. G., and M. F. Elias (1988). Nursing interval and maternal responsivity: Effect on early infant crying. *Pediatrics* 81:529–536.

Barr, R. G., and C. Worthman (1995). *Ethnopediatrics: A contribution to the science and practice of developmental–behavioral pediatrics?* Philadelphia: The Society for Behavioral Pediatrics.

Barr, R. G., S. Chen, B. Hopkins, and T. Westra (1996). Crying patterns in pre-term infants. *Developmental Medicine and Child Neurology* 38:345–355.

Barr, R. G., M. Konner, R. Bakeman, and L. Adamson (1991). Crying in !Kung San infants: A test of the cultural specificity hypothesis. *Developmental Medicine and Child Neurology* 33:601–610.

Barr, R. G., S. J. McMullen, H. Spiess, D. G. Ledrio, J. Yaremko, R. Barfield, T. E. Francoeur, and U. A. Hunziker (1991). Carrying as colic "therapy": A randomized controlled trial. *Pediatrics* 87:623–629.

Barr, R. G., A. Rotman, J. Yaremko, D. Ledue, and T. E. Francoeur (1992). The crying of infants with colic: A controlled empirical description. *Pediatrics* 90:14–21.

Barry, H., and L. M. Paxson (1971). Infancy and early childhood: Cross-cultural codes 2. *Ethnology* 10:466–508.

Barry, H., I. L. Child, and M. K. Bacon (1959). Relation of child training to subsistence economy. *American Anthropologist* 61:51–63.

Bass, M., R. E. Kravath, and L. Glass (1986). Death-scene investigation in sudden infant death. *New England Journal of Medicine* 315:100–105.

Baumslag, N., and D. L. Michels (1995). *Milk, Money, and Madness: The Culture and Politics of Breastfeeding.* Westport: Bergin and Garvey.

Bell, S. M., and D. S. Ainsworth (1972). Infant crying and maternal responsiveness. *Child Development* 43:1171–1190.

Benedict, R. (1938). Continuities and discontinuities in cultural conditioning. *Psychiatry* 1:161–167.

Benjamin, J., L. Li, C. Patterson, B. D. Greenberg, D. L. Murphy, and D. H. Hamer (1996). Population and familial association between the D4 dopamine receptor gene and measures of novelty seeking. *Nature Genetics* 12:81–84.

Berge, C., R. Orban-Segebarth, and P. Schmid (1984). Obstetrical interpretation of the Australopithecine pelvic cavity. *Journal of Human Evolution* 13:573–587.

Binns, H. J., Y. D. Senturia, S. LeBailly, M. Donovan, and K. Kaufer Christoffel (1996). Growth of Chicago-area infants, 1985–1987. *Archives of Pediatric and Adolescent Medicine* 130:842–849.

Birns, B., M. Blank, and W. H. Brigder (1966). The effectiveness of various soothing techniques on human neonates. *Psychosomatic Medicine* 28:316–322.

Blackburn, D. G., V. Hayssen, and C. J. Murphy (1989). The origins of lactation and the evolution of milk: A review with a new hypothesis. *Mammal Review* 19:1–26.

Blaffer Hrdy, S. (1995). Liquid Assets: A brief history of wet nursing. *Natural History* 104:40.

Blehar, M., A. Lieberman, and M. Ainsworth (1977). Early face-to-face interaction and its relation to later mother–infant attachment. *Child Development* 48:182–194.

Bleichfield, B., and B. E. Moely (1984). Psychophysiological responses to an infant cry: Comparison of groups of women in different phases of the maternal cycle. 20:1082–1091.

Bohannan, P., and M. Glazer (1973). *High Points in Anthropology.* New York: Alfred A. Knopf.

Bonte, M., and J. van Balen (1969). Prolonged lactation and family spacing in Rwanda. *Journal of Biosocial Science* 1:97–100.

Bornstein, M. H. (1991). Approaches to parenting in culture. In *Cultural Approaches to Parenting,* pp. 3–19, M. H. Bornstein, ed. Hillsdale, N.J.: Lawrence Erlbaum.

Bornstein, M. H. (1989). Cross-cultural developmental comparisons: The care of Japanese and American infants and mothers' activities and interactions. What we know, what we need to know, and why we need to know. *Developmental Review* 9:171–204.

Bornstein, M. H. (1991). *Cultural Approaches to Parenting.* Hillsdale, N.J.: Lawrence Erlbaum.

Bornstein, M. H., J. Tal, and C. Tamis-LeMonda (1991). Parenting in crosscultural perspective: The United States, France, and Japan. In *Cultural Approaches to Parenting,* pp. 69–90, M. H. Bornstein, ed. Hillsdale, N.J.: Lawrence Erlbaum.

Bowlby, J. (1969). *Attachment and Loss.* London: Hogarth Press.

Brazelton, T. B. (1962). Crying in infancy. *Pediatrics* 29:579–588.

Brazelton, T. B. (1969). *Infants and Mothers: Differences in Development.* New York: Delacorte Press.

Brazelton, T. B. (1982). Joint regulation of neonatal–parent behavior. In *Social Interchange in Infancy: Affect, Cognition, and Communication,* pp. 7–22, E. Z. Tronick, ed. Baltimore: University Park Press.

Brazelton, T. B., B. Koslowski, and M. Main (1974). The origins of reciprocity: The early mother–infant interaction. In *The Effect of the Infant on Its Caregiver*, pp. 49–76, M. Lewis and L. A. Rosenblum, eds. New York: John Wiley.

Brazelton, T. B., J. S. Robey, and G. A. Collier (1969). Infant development in the Zincanteco Indians of Southern Mexico. *Pediatrics* 44:277–290.

Brazelton, T. B., E. Tronick, L. Adamson, H. Als, and S. Wise (1975). Early mother–infant reciprocity. *Ciba Foundation Symposium* 33:137–154.

Bronfenbrenner, U. (1979). *The Ecology of Human Development.* Cambridge: Harvard University Press.

Burton, R., and J. Whiting (1961). The absent father and cross-sex identity. *Merrill-Palmer Quarterly* 7:85–95.

Buss, D. M. (1994). *The Evolution of Desire.* New York: Basic Books.

Cant, J. G. H. (1981). Hypothesis for the evolution of human breasts and buttocks. *American Naturalist* 117:199–204.

Caro, T. M. (1987). Human breasts: Unsupported hypotheses reviewed. *Human Evolution* 2:271–282.

Caro, T. M., and D. W. Sellen (1990). The reproductive advantages of fat in women. *Ethology and Sociobiology* 11:51–66.

Caudill, W., and D. W. Plath (1966). Who sleeps by whom? Parent–child involvement in urban Japanese families. *Psychiatry* 29:344–366.

Caudill, W., and H. Weinstein (1969). Maternal care and infant behavior in Japan and America. *Psychiatry* 32:12–43.

Cavalli-Sforza, L. (1994). *The History and Geography of Human Genes.* Princeton: Princeton University Press.

Cernoch, J. M., and R. H. Porter (1985). Recognition of maternal axillary odors by infants. *Child Development* 56:1593–1598.

Chisolm, J. S. (1996). The evolutionary ecology of attachment organization. *Human Nature* 7:1–38.

Clarke, A. S., and S. Boinski (1995). Temperament in nonhuman primates. *American Journal of Primatology* 37:103–125.

Clarke, A. S., W. A. Mason, and G. P. Moberg (1988). Differential behavioral and adrenocortical responses to stress among macaque species. *American Journal of Primatology* 14:37–52.

Clutton-Brock, T. H. (1991). *The Evolution of Parental Care.* Princeton: Princeton University Press.

Coe, C. L., S. G. Wiener, L. T. Rosenberg, and S. Levine (1985). Endocrine and immune response to separation and maternal loss in nonhuman primates. In *The Psychobiology of Attachment and Separation*, pp. 163–199, M. Reite and T. Fields, eds. New York: Academic Press.

Cohn, J. F., and E. Z. Tronick (1982). Communicative rules and the sequential structure of infant behavior during normal and depressed interactions. In *Social Interchange in Infancy: Affect, Cognition and Communication*, pp. 59–77, E. Z. Tronick, ed. Baltimore: University Park Press.

Cohn, J. F., and E. Z. Tronick (1983). Three-month-old infants' reactions to simulated maternal depression. *Child Development* 54:185–193.

Condon, W. S., and L. W. Sander (1974). Neonate movement is synchronized with adult speech: Interaction participation and language acquisition. *Science* 183:99–101.

Crapo, R. H. (1995). *Cultural Anthropology: Understanding Ourselves and Others.* Madison, Wis.: Brown and Benchmark.

Creyton, M. (1992). Breast-feeding and *baraka* in Northern Tunisia. In *The Anthropology of Breast-Feeding*, pp. 37–58, V. Maher, ed. Oxford: Berg.

Culotta, E. (1995). Birth tale gets a new twist. *Science* 268:365.

Cunningham, A. S. (1976). Infant feeding and SIDS. *Pediatrics* 58:467–468.

Cunningham, A. S. (1974). Morbidity in breastfeeding and artificial feeding II. *Pediatrics* 95:685–689.

Cunningham, A. S. (1995). Breastfeeding: Adaptive behavior for child health and longevity. In *Breastfeeding: Biocultural Perspectives*, pp. 243–264, P. Stuart-Macadam and K. A. Dettwyler, eds. New York: Aldine de Gruyter.

Cunningham, A. S., D. B. Jelliffe, and E. F. P. Jelliffe (1991). Breast-feeding and health in the 1980s: A global epidemiological review. *Pediatrics* 118:659–666.

Daly, M., and M. I. Wilson (1982). Whom are newborn babies said to resemble? *Ethology and Sociobiology* 3:69–78.

Davies, D. P. (1985). Cot death in Hong Kong: A rare problem? *The Lancet* II:1346–1348.

DeCarvalho, M., S. Robertson, A. Friedman, and M. Klaus (1983). Effect of frequent breast-feeding on early milk production and infant weight gain. *Pediatrics* 72:307–316.

DeCasper, A. J., and W. P. Fifer (1980). Of human bonding: Newborns prefer their mothers' voices. *Science* 208:1174–1176.

Deivoye, P., P. Damaegd, J. Delogne-Desnoech, and C. Robyn (1977). The influence of the frequency of nursing and previous lactation experience on serum prolactin in lactating mothers. *Journal of Biosocial Science* 9:447–451.

Dettwyler, K. A. (1995). Beauty and the breast: The cultural context of breastfeeding in the United States. In *Breastfeeding: Biocultural Perspectives*, pp. 167–215, P. Stuart-Macadam and K. A. Dettwyler, eds. New York: Aldine de Gruyter.

Dettwyler, K. A. (1995). A time to wean: The hominid blueprint for the natural age of weaning in modern human populations. In *Breastfeeding: Biocultural Perspectives*, pp. 39–73, P. Stuart-Macadam and K. A. Dettwyler, eds. New York: Aldine de Gruyter.

DeVore, I., and M. J. Konner (1974). Infancy in hunter-gatherer life: An ethological perspective. In *Ethology and Psychiatry*, pp. 113–141, N. F. White, ed. Toronto: University of Toronto Press.

de Vries, M. W. (1984). Temperament and infant mortality among the Masai of East Africa. *American Journal of Psychiatry* 141:1189–1194.

de Vries, M. W. (1987). Cry babies, cultures, and catastrophe: Infant temperament among the Masai. In *Child Survival*, pp. 165–185, N. Sheper-Hughes, ed. Dordrecht: D. Reidel Publishing Co.

de Waal, F. (1996). *Good Natured: The Origins of Right and Wrong in Humans and Other Animals*. Cambridge: Harvard University Press.

de Waal, F., and D. L. Johanowicz (1993). Modification of reconciliation behavior through social experience: An experiment with two macaque species. *Child Development* 64:897–908.

Diamond, J. (1992). *The Third Chimpanzee*. New York: HarperCollins.

Dienske, H. (1986). A comparative approach to the question of why human infants develop so slowly. In *Primate Ontogeny, Cognition, and Social Behavior*, pp. 147–154, J. G. Else and P. C. Lee, eds. Cambridge: University of Cambridge Press.

Dixon, S., E. Tronick, C. Keefer, and T. B. Brazelton (1981). Mother–infant interaction among the Gusii of Kenya. In *Culture and Early Interactions*, pp. 149–168, T. Filed, A. M. Sostek, P. Vietze, and P. H. Leiderman, eds. Hillsdale, N.J.: Lawrence Erlbaum.

Draper, P., and E. Cashdan (1988). Technological change and child behavior among the !Kung. *Ethnology* 27:339–365.

Drewett, R., A. Amataycihul, L. Wongsawasdu, A. Mangklabruks, S. Ruckpaopurt, C. Ruangyuttikarn, D. Baum, S. Imog, D. Kackson, and M. Woolridge (1993). Nursing frequency and the energy intake from breast milk and supplementary foods in a rural Thai population: A longitudinal study. *Journal of Clinical Nutrition* 47:880–891.

Dugger, C. W. (1996). A cultural reluctance to spare the rod. *The New York Times*.

Dunn, J., and J. Brown (1991). Becoming American or English? Talking about the social world in England and the United States. In *Cultural Approaches to Parenting*, pp. 155–172, M. H. Bornstein, ed. Hillsdale, N.J.: Lawrence Erlbaum.

Eldridge, N. (1995). *Dominion*. New York: Henry Holt and Company.

Elias, M. F., N. A. Nicholson, C. Bora, and J. Johnston (1986). Sleep/wake patterns of breast-fed infants in the first two years of life. *Pediatrics* 77:322–329.

Ellison, P. T. (1995). Breastfeeding, fertility, and maternal condition. In *Breastfeeding: Biocultural Perspectives*, pp. 305–345, P. Stuart-Macadam and K. A. Dettwyler, eds. New York: Aldine de Gruyter.

Farooqi, S., I. J. Perry, and D. G. Beevers (1991). Ethnic differences in sleeping position and risk of cot death. *The Lancet* 338:1455.

Feldman, S. S., and S. C. Nash (1978). Interest in babies during young adulthood. *Child Development* 49:617–622.

Ferber, R. (1985). *Your Child's Sleep Problems*. New York: Simon and Schuster.

Fernald, A. (1992). Human maternal vocalizations to infants as biologically relevant signals: An evolutionary perspective. In *The Adapted Mind: Evolutionary Psychology and the Generation of Culture*, pp. 391–428, J. Barkow, L. Cosmides, and J. Tooby, eds. Oxford: Oxford University Press.

Fernald, A. (1992). Meaningful melodies in mothers' speech to infants. In *Nonverbal Vocal Communication: Comparative and Developmental Approaches*, pp. 262–282, H. Papousek, U. Jurgens, and M. Papouske, eds. Cambridge: Cambridge University Press.

Field, T. M. (1977). Effect of early separation, interaction deficits, and experimental manipulations on infant–mother face-to-face interaction. *Child Development* 48:763–771.

Field, T., A. M. Sosteck, P. Vietze, and P. H. Leiderman (1981). *Culture and Early Interaction*. Hillsdale, N.J.: Lawrence Erlbaum.

Fildes, V. A. (1986). *Breasts, Bottles and Babies*. Edinburgh, Edinburgh University Press.

Fildes, V. A. (1995). The culture and biology of breastfeeding: An historical review of western Europe. *Breastfeeding: Biocultural Perspectives*, pp. 101–126, P. Stuart-Macadam and K. A. Dettwyler, eds. New York: Aldine de Gruyter.

Fisher, J. L., and A. Fisher (1963). The New Englanders of Orchard Town, U.S.A. In *Six Cultures: Studies of Child Rearing*, pp. 873–1010, B. Whiting, ed. New York: John Wiley and Sons.

Fleagle, J. G. (1988). *Primate Adaptation and Evolution*. New York: Academic Press.

Fleming, A. S. (1990). Hormonal and experiential correlates of maternal responsiveness in human mothers. In *Mammalian Parenting*, pp. 184–208, N. A. Krasnegor and R. S. Bridges, eds. Oxford: Oxford University Press.

Fogel, M., N. Tuross, and D. Owsley (1989). Nitrogen isotope tracers of human lactation in modern and archaeological populations. *Annual Report of the Director, Geophysical Laboratory* 2150:111–117.

Ford, C. S. (1964). *A Comparative Study of Human Reproduction.* New Haven: Yale University Publications in Anthropology.

Ford, R. P. K., B. J. Taylor, E. A. Mitchell, S. A. Enright, A. W. Stewart, D. M. O. Becroft, R. Scragg, I. B. Hassalb, I. M. J. Barry, E. M. Allen, and A. P. Roberts (1993). Breastfeeding and the risk of Sudden Infant Death Syndrome. *International Journal of Epidemiology* 22:885–890.

Formby, D. (1967). Maternal recognition of infant's cry. *Developmental Medicine and Child Neurology* 9:293–298.

Forsyth, B. W. C. (1989). Colic and the effect of changing formulas: A double-blind multiple cross-over study. *Journal of Pediatric Research* 115:521–526.

Forsyth, B. W. C., P. C. McCarty, and J. M. Leventhal (1985). Problems of early infancy, formula change, and mothers' beliefs about their infants. *Pediatrics* 106:1012–1017.

Freeman, D. G. (1971). Genetic influences on development of behavior. In *Normal and Abnormal Development and Behavior,* pp. 208–229, J. J. Werff Ten Bosch, ed. Leiden: Leiden University Press.

Freeman, D. G., and N. Freeman (1969). Behavioral differences between Chinese-American and European-American newborns. *Nature* 224:1127.

Frodi, A. (1985). When empathy fails. *Infant Crying: Theoretical and Research Perspectives,* pp. 263–277, B. M. Lester and C. F. Zachariah Boukydis, eds. New York: Plenum Press.

Frodi, A. M., M. E. Lamb, L. A. Leavitt, and W. Donovan (1978). Fathers' and mothers' responses to infant smiles and cries. *Infant Behavior and Development* 1:187–198.

Gabriel, A., K. R. Gabriel, and R. A. Lawrence (1986). Cultural values and biomedical knowledge. *Social Science and Medicine* 23:501–509.

Gajdusik, D. C. (1963). Ethnopediatrics as a study of cybernetics of human development. *American Journal of Diseases of Children* 105:554–559.

Gallup, G. G. (1982). Permanent breast enlargement in human females: A sociobiological analysis. *Journal of Human Evolution* 11:597–601.

Gantley, M., D. P. Davies, and A. Murcote (1993). Sudden infant death syndrome: Links with infant care practices. *British Medical Journal* 306:16–20.

Gianino, A., and E. Z. Tronick (1988). The mutual regulation mode: The infant's self and interactive regulation and coping and defensive capacities. In *Stress and Coping Across Development,* pp. 47–68, T. M. Field, P. M. McCabe, and N. Schneiderman, eds. Hillsdale, N.J.: Lawrence Erlbaum.

Gjerdingen, D. K., M. Ireland, and K. M. Chaloner (1996). Growth among Hmong children. *Archives of Pediatric and Adolescent Medicine* 150:1295–1298.

Glick, J. (1975). Cognitive development in cross-cultural perspective. In *Review* of *Child Development Research*, pp. 595–654, F. Horowitz, ed. Chicago: University of Chicago Press.

Goldberg, S. (1983). Parent–infant bonding: Another look. *Child Development* 54:1355–1382.

Goldsmith, H. H., and J. J. Campos (1982). Toward a theory of infant temperament. *The Development of Attachment and Affiliation Systems*, pp. 161–193, R. Emde and R. Harmon, eds. New York: Plenum Press.

Goldsmith, H. H., B. A. H. Buss, R. Plomin, M. K. Rothbart, A. Thomas, S. Chess, R. A. Hinde, and R. B. McCall (1987). Roundtable: What is temperament? Four approaches. *Child Development* 58:505–529.

Goodnow, J. J., and W. A. Collins (1990). *Development According to Parents: The Nature, Sources, and Consequences of Parents' Ideas*. Hillsdale, N.J.: Lawrence Erlbaum.

Goodnow, J. J., J. Cashmore, S. Cotton, and R. Knight (1984). Mothers' developmental timetables in two cultural groups. *International Journal of Psychology* 19:193–205.

Greenberg, M., and N. Morris (1974). Engrossment: The newborn's impact upon the father. *American Journal of Orthopsychiatry* 44:520–531.

Grether, J. K., J. Schulman, and L. A. Croen (1990). Sudden Infant Death Syndrome among Asians in California. *Journal of Pediatrics* 116:525–528.

Gussler, J. D., and L. H. Briesemeister (1980). The insufficient milk syndrome: A biocultural explanation. *Medical Anthropology* 4:145–174.

Hahn, R. A. (1995). *Sickness and Healing*. New Haven: Yale University Press.

Hales, D. J., B. Lozoff, R. Sosa, and J. H. Kennell (1977). Defining the limits of the maternal sensitive period. *Developmental Medicine and Child Neurology* 19:454–461.

Hammerschmidt, K., and V. Ansorge (1989). Birth of a Barbary macaque (*Macaca sylvanus*): Acoustic and behavioral features. *Folia Primatologica* 52:78–87.

Harkness, S. (1992). Cross-cultural research in child development: A sample of the state of the art. *Developmental Psychology* 28:622–625.

Harkness, S., and C. M. Super (1980). Child development theory in anthropological perspective. In *Anthropological Perspectives on Child Development*, pp. 1–6, C. M. Super and S. Harkness, eds. San Francisco: Jossey-Bass.

Harkness, S., and C. M. Super (1992). Parental ethnotheories in action. In *Parental Belief Systems: The Psychological Consequences for Children*, pp. 373–391, I. E. Sigel, A. V. McGillicuddy-DeLisi, and J. J. Goodnow, eds. Hillsdale, N.J.: Lawrence Erlbaum.

Harkness, S., and C. M. Super (1994). The developmental niche: A theoretical framework for analyzing the household production of health. *Social Science Medicine* 38:217–226.

Harkness, S., and C. M. Super (1996). Culture and parenting. In *Handbook of Parenting*, pp. 211–243, M. H. Bornstein, ed. Hillsdale, N.J.: Lawrence Erlbaum.

Harkness, S., and C. M. Super (1996). Introduction. *Parents' Cultural Belief Systems: Their Origins, Expressions, and Consequences*, pp. 1–23, S. Harkness and C. M. Super, eds. New York: Guilford Press.

Harkness, S., and C. M. Super (1996). *Parents' Cultural Belief Systems: Their Origins, Expressions, and Consequences*. New York: Guilford Press.

Harkness, S., and C. M. Super (1998). From parents' cultural belief systems to behavior: Implications for the development of early intervention programs. In *Early Education and Culture: Culture-Sensitive Strategies for Empowering Parents and Children* (in press), L. Eldering and P. Leseman, eds. New York: Garland Press.

Harkness, S., C. M. Super, C. H. Keefer, N. van Tijin, and E. van der Vlugt (1995). *Cultural Influences on Sleep Patterns in Infancy and Early Childhood*. Atlanta: American Association for the Advancement of Science.

Harkness, S. M., C. M. Super, C. H. Keefer, C. S. Raghavan, and E. K. Campbell (1996). Ask the doctor: The negotiation of cultural models in American parent–pediatrician discourse. In *Parents' Cultural Belief Systems*, pp. 289–310, S. Harkness and C. M. Super, eds. New York: Guilford Press.

Harlow, H. F., and M. K. Harlow (1965). The affectional systems. In *Behavior of Nonhuman Primates*, pp. 287–334, A. M. Schrier, H. F. Harlow, and F. Stollnitz, eds. New York: Academic Press.

Harvey, P. H., and T. H. Clutton-Brock (1985). Life history variation in primates. *Evolution* 39:559–581.

Harwood, A. (1971). The hot-cold theory of disease: Implications for the treatment of Puerto Rican patients. *Journal of the American Medical Association* 216:1153–1158.

Hayssen, V. (1995). Milk: It does a baby good. *Natural History* 104:36.

Hess, R. D., K. Kashigawi, H. Azuma, G. R. Price, and W. P. Dickson (1980). Maternal expectations for mastering of developmental tasks in Japan and the United States. *International Journal of Psychology* 15:259–271.

Hill, K., and A. M. Hurtado (1996). *Ache Life History: The Ecology and Demography of a Foraging People*. New York: Aldine de Gruyter.

Holman, S. D., and R. W. Goy (1979). Behavioral and mammary responses of adult female rhesus to strange infants. *Hormones and Behavior* 12:243–252.

Howie, P. W., and A. S. McNeilly (1982). Effect of breast-feeding patterns on human birth intervals. *Journal of Reproduction and Fertility* 65:545–557.

Howrigan, G. A. (1988). Fertility, infant feeding, and change in the Yucatán. *Parental Behavior in Diverse Societies*, pp. 37–50, R. A. LeVine, P. M. Miller, and M. Maxwell West, eds. San Francisco: Jossey-Bass.

Hsu, C., W. Soong, J. W. Stigley, H. C. Leang, and C. Leang (1981). The temperamental characteristics of Chinese babies. *Child Development* 52:1337–1341.

Hull, V., and M. Simpson (1985). *Breastfeeding and Child Health and Child Spacing: Cross-cultural Perspectives*. London: Croom Helm.

Hunziker, U. A., and R. G. Barr (1986). Increased carrying reduces infant crying: A randomized controlled trial. *Pediatrics* 77:641–648.

Insel, T. R. (1990). Oxytocin and maternal behavior. In *Mammalian Parenting*, pp. 260–280, N. A. Krasnegor and R. S. Bridges, eds. Oxford: Oxford University Press.

Insel, T. R., and L. E. Shapiro (1992). Oxytocin receptor distribution reflects social organization in monogamous and polygamous voles. *Proceedings of the National Academy of Sciences* 89:5981–5985.

Isbell, L. A., and T. P. Young (1996). The evolution of bipedalism in hominids and reduced group size in chimpanzees: Alternative responses to decreased resource availability. In *Journal of Human Evolution* 30:389–397.

Jackson, D. (1989). *Three in a Bed*. London: Bloomsbury.

Jelliffe, D. B., and E. F. Jelliffe (1978). *Human Milk in the Modern World*. Oxford: Oxford University Press.

Jenkins, C. L., and P. F. Heywood (1985). Ethnopediatrics and fertility among the Amele of lowland Papua New Guinea. In *Breastfeeding and Child Health and Child Spacing: Cross-cultural Perspectives*, pp. 11–34, V. Hull and M. Simpson, eds. London: Croom Helm.

Jolly, A. (1986). *The Evolution of Primate Behavior*. New York: Macmillan.

Jordon, H. V. F. (1976). Newborn:adult brain ratios in hominid evolution. *American Journal of Physical Anthropology* 44:271–278.

Kagan, J. (1989). Temperamental contribution to social behavior. *American Psychologist* 44:668–674.

Kagan, J., and N. Snidman (1991a). Infant predictors of inhibited and uninhibited profiles. *Psychological Science* 2:40–44.

Kagan, J., and N. Snidman (1991b). Temperamental factors in human development. *American Psychologist* 46:856–862.

Kagan, J., N. Snidman, and D. M. Arcus (1992). Initial reactions to unfamiliarity. *Current Directions in Psychological Science* 1:171–174.

Kahn, A., J. Groswasser, M. Sottiaux, E. Ribuffat, P. Franco, and M. Dramaix (1993). Prone or supine body position and sleep characteristics in infants. *Pediatrics* 91:1112–1115.

Kaplan, H., and H. Dove (1987). Infant development among the Ache of Paraguay. *Developmental Psychology* 23:190–198.

Keener, M. A., C. H. Zeanah, and T. F. Anders (1988). Infant temperament, sleep organization and negative parental intervention. *Pediatrics* 81:762–771.

Kennell, J. H., M. A. Trause, and M. H. Klaus (1975). Evidence for a sensitive period in the human mother. *Ciba Foundation Symposium* 33:87–95.

Khin, M.-N., T.-O. Tin, T. Kywl, and N.-H. Nwl (1980). Study on lactation performance of Burmese mothers. *American Journal of Clinical Nutrition* 33:2665–2668.

Kimball, C. D. (1979). Do endorphin residues of beta lipotropin in hormones reinforce reproductive functions? *American Journal of Obstetrics and Gynecology* 134:127–132.

Klaus, M. H., and J. H. Kennell (1976). Human maternal and paternal behavior. In *Maternal–Infant Bonding*, pp. 38–48, M. H. Klaus and J. H. Kennell, eds. St. Louis: C. V. Mosby Co.

Klaus, M. H., and J. H. Kennell (1976). Maternal–infant bonding. In *Maternal-Infant Bonding*, pp. 1–15, M. H. Klaus and J. H. Kennell, eds. St. Louis: C. V. Mosby Co.

Klonoff-Cohen, H., and S. L. Edelstein (1995). Bed sharing and the sudden infant death syndrome. *British Medical Journal* 311:1269–1272.

Klopfer, P. H. (1971). Mother love: What turns it on? *American Scientist* 59:404–407.

Knight, C. H., and M. Peaker (1982). Development of the mammary gland. *Journal of Reproduction and Fertility* 65:521–536.

Konner, M., and C. Worthman (1980). Nursing frequency, gonadal function, and birth spacing among !Kung hunter-gatherers. *Science* 207:788–791.

Konner, M. J. (1972). Aspects of developmental ethology of a foraging people. In *Ethological Studies of Child Behavior*, pp. 285–304, N. Blurton Jones, ed. Cambridge: Cambridge University Press.

Konner, M. J. (1973). Newborn walking: Additional data. *Science* 179:307.

Konner, M. J. (1976). Maternal care, infant behavior and development among the !Kung. In *Kalahari Hunter-Gatherers: Studies of the !Kung San and their Neighbors*, pp. 218–245, R. B. Lee and I. DeVore, eds. Cambridge: Harvard University Press.

Konner, M. J. (1977). Infancy among the Kalahari Desert San. In *Culture and Infancy: Variations in the Human Experience*, pp. 287–327, P. H. Leiderman, S. R. Tulin, and A. Rosenfeld, eds. New York: Academic Press.

Konner, M. J., and C. M. Super (1987). Sudden infant death syndrome: An anthropological hypothesis. In *The Role of Culture in Developmental Disorders*, pp. 95–108, C. M. Super, ed. New York: Academic Press.

Kotelchuck, M. (1976). The infant's relationship to the father: Experimental evidence. In *The Role of the Father in Child Development*, pp. 329–344, M. E. Lamb, ed. New York: John Wiley.

Kuhl, P. K., J. E. Andrushi, I. A. Chestovick, L. A. Chestovick, E. V. Kozheonikova, V. L. Ryskina, E. I. Stolyarova, U. Sundberg, and F. Lacerda (1997). Cross-language analysis of phonetic units in languages addressed to infants. *Science* 277:684–686.

Lamb, M. E. (1976). The role of the father: An overview. In *The Role of the Father in Child Development*, pp. 1–63, M. E. Lamb, ed. New York: John Wiley.

Lamb, M. E. (1982). Early contact and maternal–infant bonding: One decade later. *Pediatrics* 70:763–768.

Lamb, M. E. (1987). *The Father's Role: Cross-Cultural Perspectives*. Hillsdale, N.J.: Lawrence Erlbaum.

Lamb, M. E., and C. P. Hwang (1982). Maternal attachment and mother–neonate bonding: A critical review. In *Advances in Developmental Psychology*, pp. 1–39, M. E. Lamb and A. L. Brown, eds. Hillsdale, N.J.: Erlbaum.

Lawrence, R. A. (1994). *Breastfeeding: A Guide to the Medical Profession*. St. Louis: Mosby.

Leach, P. (1976). *Babyhood.* New York: Knopf.

Lee, K. (1994). The crying patterns of Korean infants and related factors. *Developmental Medicine and Child Neurology* 36:601–607.

Lee, N. N. Y., Y. F. Chan, D. P. Davis, E. Lau, and D. C. P. Yip (1989). Sudden Infant Death Syndrome in Hong Kong: Confirmation of low incidence. *British Medical Journal* 298:721.

Lee, R. B. (1979). *The !Kung San: Men, Women, and Work in a Foraging Society.* Cambridge: Cambridge University Press.

Lee, R. B. (1984). *The Dobe !Kung.* New York: Holt, Rinehart, and Winston.

Leiberman, P. (1985). The physiology of cry and speech in relation to linguistic behavior. In *Infant Crying: Theoretical and Research Perspectives*, pp. 29–57, B. M. Lester and C. F. Zachariah Boukydis, eds. New York, Plenum Press.

Leiderman, P. H., B. Babu, J. Kagia, H. Kraemer, and G. F. Leiderman (1973). African infant precocity and some social influences during the first year. *Nature* 242:247–249.

Lester, B. M. (1985). Introduction: There's more to crying than meets the ear. In *Infant Crying: Theoretical and Research Perspectives*, pp. 1–27, B. M. Lester and C. F. Zachariah Boukydis, eds. New York: Plenum Press.

Lester, B. M., and T. B. Brazelton (1982). Cross-cultural assessment of neonatal behavior. In *Cultural Perspectives on Child Development*, pp. 20–53, D. A. Wagner and H. W. Stevenson, eds. San Francisco: W. H. Freeman.

Leutenegger, W. (1972). Newborn size and pelvic dimensions of Australopithecus. *Nature* 240:568–569.

Leutenegger, W. (1982). Encephalization and obstetrics in primates with particular reference to human evolution. In *Primate Brain Evolution: Methods and Concepts*, pp. 85–95, E. Armstrong and D. Falk, eds. New York, Plenum Press.

Levine, N. E. (1988). Women's work and infant feeding: A case from rural Nepal. *Ethnology* 27:231–251.

LeVine, R. A. (1973). *Culture, Behavior and Personality.* Chicago: Aldine.

LeVine, R. A. (1974). Parental goals: A cross-cultural view. *Teachers College Record* 76:226–239.

LeVine, R. A. (1988). Human parental care: Universal goals, cultural strategies, individual behavior. In *Parental Behavior in Diverse Societies*, pp. 3–12, R. A. LeVine, P. M. Miller, and M. Maxwell West, eds. San Francisco: Jossey-Bass.

LeVine, R. A. (1990). A cross-cultural perspective on parenting. In *Parenting in a Multicultural Society*, pp. 17–26, M. Fantini and R. Cardenas, eds. New York: Longman.

LeVine, R. A., S. Dixon, S. LeVine, A. Richman, P. H. Leiderman, C. Keefer, and T. B. Brazelton (1994). *Child Care and Culture: Lessons from Africa.* Cambridge: Cambridge University Press.

Lewis, M. (1989). Culture and biology: The role of temperament. In *Challenges to Developmental Paradigms*, pp. 203–223, P. R. Zelazo and R. G. Barr, eds. Hillsdale, N.J.: Erlbaum.

Lipkin, M., and G. S. Lamb (1982). The couvade syndrome: An epidemiological study. *Annals of Internal Medicine* 96:509–511.

Lorenz, K. (1935). *Der Kumpan in der Umwelt des Vogels. Journal of Ornithology* 83:137–213.

Lovejoy, O. C. (1981). The origin of man. *Science* 211:341–350.

Lovejoy, O. C. (1988). The evolution of human walking. *Scientific American* November:118–125.

Low, B. S., R. D. Alexander, and K. M. Noonan (1987). Human hips, breasts and buttocks: Is fat deceptive? *Ethology and Sociobiology* 8:249–257.

Lozoff, B., and G. Brittenham (1979). Infant care: Cache or carry. *Pediatrics* 95:478–483.

Lozoff, B., A. W. Wolf, and N. S. Davis (1984). Cosleeping in urban families with young children in the United States. *Pediatrics* 74:171–182.

Ludington-Hoe, S. M., A. J. Hadeed, and G. C. Anderson (1991). Physiological responses to skin-to-skin contact in hospitalized premature infants. *Journal of Perinatology* 11:19–24.

Maher, V. (1992). Breast-feeding in cross-cultural perspective: Paradoxes and proposals. In *The Anthropology of Breast-Feeding: Natural Law or Social Construct*, pp. 1–36, V. Maher, ed. Oxford: Berg.

Main, G. (1982). *Tobacco Country: Life in Early Maryland, 1650–1720*. Princeton: Princeton University Press.

Mandansky, D., and C. Edlebrock (1990). Cosleeping in a community sample of 2- and 3-year-old children. *Pediatrics* 86:197–203.

Martin, R. D. (1990). *Primate Origins and Evolution: A Phylogenetic Reconstruction*. Princeton: Princeton University Press.

Mascia-Lees, F. F., J. H. Relethford, and T. Sorger (1986). Evolutionary perspectives on permanent breast enlargement in human females. *American Anthropologist* 88:423–428.

McClelland, D. B. L. (1982). Antibodies in milk. *Journal of Reproduction and Fertility* 65:537–543.

McGrew, W. (1992). *Chimpanzee Material Culture*. Cambridge: Cambridge University Press.

McHenry, H. M. (1986). The first bipeds: A comparison of the *A. afarensis* and *A. africanus* postcranium and implications for the evolution of bipedalism. *Journal of Human Evolution* 15:177–191.

McKenna, J. J. (1993). Co-sleeping. In *Encyclopedia of Sleep and Dreaming*, pp. 143–148, M. A. Carskadon, ed. New York: Macmillan.

McKenna, J. J. (1995). The potential benefits of infant–parent co-sleeping in relation to SIDS prevention: Overview and critique of epidemiological bedsharing studies. In *Sudden Infant Death Syndrome: New Trends in the Nineties*, pp. 256–265, T. O. Rognum, ed. Oslo: Scandinavian University Press.

McKenna, J. J. (1996). Sudden Infant Death Syndrome in cross-cultural perspective: Is infant–parent cosleeping proactive? *Annual Review of Anthropology* 25:201–216.

McKenna, J., and N. J. Bernshaw (1995). Breastfeeding and infant–parent cosleeping as practical strategies: Are they protective against SIDS? In *Breastfeeding: Biocultural Perspectives*, pp. 265–303, P. Stuart-Macadam and K. A. Dettwyler, eds. New York: Aldine de Gruyter.

McKenna, J. J., S. S. Mosko, and C. Richard (1997). Bedsharing promotes breast-feeding in Latino mother–infant pairs. *Pediatrics* 100:214–219.

McKenna, J. J., S. S. Mosko, C. Richard, S. Drummond, L. Hunt, M. B. Cetel, and J. Arpaia (1994). Experimental studies of infant–parent co-sleeping: Mutual physiological and behavioral influences and their relevance to SIDS (Sudden Infant Death Syndrome). *Early Human Development* 38:187–201.

McKenna, J. J., E. B. Toman, T. F. Anders, A. Sadeh, V. L. Schechtman, and S. F. Gotzbach (1993). Infant–parent co-sleeping in an evolutionary perspective: Implications for understanding infant sleep development and the Sudden Infant Death Syndrome. *Sleep* 16:263–282.

Mead, M. (1930/1975). *Growing Up in New Guinea*. New York: William Morrow.

Mead, M. (1956). *New Lives for Old*. New York: William Morrow.

Mehler, J., P. Jusczyk, G. Lambertz, N. Halsted, J. Bertoncini, and C. Amiel-Tison (1990). A precursor of language acquisition in young infants. *Cognition* 29:143–178.

Micozzi, M. S. (1995). Breast cancer, reproductive biology, and breastfeeding. In *Breastfeeding: Biocultural Perspectives*, pp. 347–384, P. Stuart-Macadam, and K. A. Dettwyler, eds. New York: Aldine de Gruyter.

Miller, A. R., R. G. Barr, and W. O. Eaton (1993). Crying and motor behavior of six-week-old infants and postpartum maternal mood. *Pediatrics* 92:551–558.

Mitchell, E. A., and R. Scragg (1993). Are infants sharing a bed with another person at increased risk of sudden infant death syndrome? *Sleep* 16:387–389.

Morelli, G., B. Rogoff, D. Oppenheim, and D. Goldsmith (1992). Cultural variation in infants' sleeping arrangements: Questions of independence. *Developmental Psychology* 28:604–613.

Morelli, G. A., and E. Z. Tronick (1991). Parenting and child development in the Efé foragers and Lese farmers of Zaire. *Cultural Approaches to Parenting*, pp. 91–113, M. Bornstein. ed. Hillsdale, N.J.: Lawrence Erlbaum.

Morely, R., T. J. Cole, R. Powell, and A. Lucas (1988). Mothers' choice to provide breast milk and developmental outcome. *Archives of the Diseases of Childhood* 63:1382–1385.

Morrow-Tlucak, M., R. H. Haude, and C. B. Ernhart (1988). Breastfeeding and cognitive development in the first 2 years of life. *Social Science and Medicine* 26:635–639.

Mosko, S., C. Richard, J. J. McKenna, and S. Drummond (1996). Infant sleep architecture during bedsharing and possible implications for SIDS. *Sleep* 19:677–684.

Mosko, S. S., C. A. Richard, C. A. McKenna, S. Drummond, and D. Mukai (1997). Co2 environment of the cosleeping infant: The parent's contribution. *American Journal of Physical Anthropology* 103:315–328.

Munroe, R. H., R. L. Munroe, and B. B. Whiting (1981). *Handbook of Cross-Cultural Development*. New York: Garland Press.

Murray, A. D. (1979). Infant crying as an elicitation of parental behavior: An examination of two models. *Psychological Bulletin* 86:191–215.

Myers, D. G. (1995). *Psychology*. New York: Worth.

New, R. S., and A. L. Richman (1996). Maternal beliefs and infant care practices in Italy and the United States. In *Parents' Cultural Belief Systems*, pp. 385–404, S. Harkness and C. M. Super, eds. New York: Guilford Press.

Newman, J. (1995). How breast milk protects newborns. *Scientific American* December:76–79.

Newman, J. D. (1985). The infant cry of primates: An evolutionary perspective. In *Infant Crying: Theoretical and Research Perspectives*, pp. 307–323, B. M. Lester and C. F. Zachariah Boukydis, eds. New York: Plenum Press.

Newton, E. (1995). Forward. In *Breastfeeding: Biocultural Perspectives*, pp. ix–xi, P. Stuart-Macadam and K. A. Dettwyler, eds. New York: Aldine de Gruyter.

Norvenius, S. G. (1993). Some medico-historic remarks on SIDS. *Acta Paediatric Supplement* 389:3–9.

Otaki, M., M. E. Durret, P. Richards, L. Nyquist, and J. W. Pennebaker (1986). Maternal and infant behavior in Japan and America: A partial replication. *Journal of Cross-Cultural Psychology* 17:251–268.

Palombit, R. A. (1994a). Dynamic pair bonds in hylobatids: Implications regarding monogamous social systems. *Behaviour* 128:65–101.

Palombit, R. A. (1994b). Extra-pair copulations in a monogamous ape. *Animal Behaviour* 47:721–723.

Panter-Brick, C. (1991). Lactation, birth spacing and maternal workloads among two castes in rural Nepal. *Journal of Biosocial Science* 23:137–154.

Panter-Brick, C. (1992). Working mothers in rural Nepal. In *The Anthropology of Breast-Feeding*, pp. 133–150, V. Maher, ed. Soford: Berg.

Papousek, M., and H. Papousel (1990). Excessive infant crying and intuitive parental care: Buffering support and its failure in parent–infant interaction. *Early Child Development and Care* 65:117–126.

Parke, R. (1979). Perspectives on father–infant interaction. In *Handbook of Infancy*, pp. 549–590, J. D. Osofsky, ed. New York: John Wiley.

Parmalee, A. H., W. H. Wenner, and H. R. Schultz (1964). Infant sleep patterns: From birth to 16 weeks of age. *Journal of Pediatrics* 65:576–582.

Pinker, S. (1994). *The Language Instinct*. New York: William Morrow and Co.

Pond, C. M. (1977). The significance of lactation in the evolution of mammals. *Evolution* 31:177–199.

Poole, S. R. (1991). The infant with acute, unexplained, excessive crying. *Pediatrics* 88:450–455.

Porter, R. H., J. M. Cernock, and F. J. McLaughlin (1983). Maternal recognition of neonates through olfactory cues. *Physiology and Behavior* 30:151–154.

Post, R. H. (1982). Breast cancer, lactation and genetics. *Social Biology* 29:357–386.

Prentice, A. M., and A. Prentice (1988). Energy costs of lactation. *Annual Review of Nutrition* 8:63–79.

Prentice, A. M., and R. G. Whitehead (1987). The energetics of human reproduction. *Symposium of the Zoological Society of London* 57:275–304.

Quandt, S. A. (1995). Sociocultural aspects of the lactation process. In *Breastfeeding: Biocultural Perspectives*, pp. 127–143, P. Stuart-Macadam and K. A. Dettwyler, eds. New York: Aldine de Gruyter.

Rebelsky, F., and R. Black (1972). Crying in infancy. *Journal of Genetic Psychology* 121:49–57.

Rice, R. D. (1977). Neurophysiological development in premature infants following stimulation. *Developmental Psychology* 13:69–76.

Richard, C., S. Mosko, and J. J. McKenna (1996). Sleeping position, orientation and proximity in bedsharing infants and mothers. *Sleep* 19:677–684.

Richman, A. I., P. M. Miller, and M. Johnson Solomon (1988). The socialization of infants in suburban Boston. *Parental Behavior in Diverse Societies*, pp. 65–74, R. A. LeVine, P. A. Miller, and M. M. West, eds. San Francisco: Jossey-Bass.

Righard, L., and M. O. Alade (1990). Effect of delivery room routines on success of first breast-feed. *The Lancet* 336:1105–1107.

Rodman, P. S., and H. M. McHenry (1980). Bioenergetics and the origin of hominid bipedalism. *American Journal of Physical Anthropology* 52:103–106.

Rogoff, B., and G. Morelli (1989). Perspectives on children's development from cultural psychology. *American Psychologist* 44:343–348.

Rohde, J. E. (1984). Oral rehydration therapy. In *The State of the World's Children, 1984*, pp. 72–77, J. P. Grant, ed. New York: Oxford University Press.

Rosenberg, K. R. (1992). The evolution of modern human birth. *Yearbook of Physical Anthropology* 35:89–124.

Rosenberg, K., and W. Trevathan (1995/1996). Bipedalism and human birth: The obstetrical dilemma revisited. *Evolutionary Anthropology* 4:161–168.

Rosenblatt, J. S. (1990). Landmarks in the physiological study of maternal behavior with special reference to the rat. In *Mammalian Parenting*, pp. 40–60, N. A. Krasnegor and R. S. Bridges, eds. Oxford: Oxford University Press.

Ryan, A. S., D. Rush, F. W. Krilger, and G. E. Lewandowski (1991). Recent declines in breast-feeding in the United States, 1984–1989. *Pediatrics* 88:719–727.

Rybczynski, W. (1986). *Home: A Short History of an Idea*. New York: Penguin.

Sagi, A. (1981). Mother's and non-mother's identification of infant cries. *Infant Behavior and Development* 4:37–40.

St. James-Roberts, I., J. Hurry, J. Bower, and R. G. Barr (1995). Supplementary carrys compared with advice to increase responsive parenting as intervention. *Pediatrics* 95:381–388.

Schachter, F. F., M. L. Fuches, P. Bijur, and R. K. Stone (1989). Cosleeping and sleep problems in Hispanic-American urban young children. *Pediatrics* 84:522–530.

Scheper-Hughes, N. (1985). Culture, scarcity, and maternal thinking: Maternal detachment and infant survival in a Brazilian shantytown. *Ethos* 13:291–317.

Scheper-Hughes, N. (1992). *Death Without Weeping*. Berkeley: University of California Press.

Sculpin, R., and C. R. DeCorse (1992). *Anthropology, a Global Perspective*. Englewood Cliffs, N.J.: Prentice Hall.

Shand, N. (1981). The reciprocal impact of breast-feeding and culture on maternal behavior and infant development. *Journal of Biosocial Science* 13:1–17.

Shand, N., and Y. Kosawa (1985). Japanese and American behavior types at three months: Infant and infant–mother dyads. *Infant Behavior and Development* 8:225–240.

Shaul, B. (1962). The composition of milk in wild animals. *International Zoological Yearbook* 4:333–342.

Sheard, N. F., and W. A. Walker (1988). The role of breast milk in the development of the gastrointestinal tract. *Nutrition Reviews* 46:1–8.

Short, R. V. (1984). Breast feeding. *Scientific American* 250:35–41.

Short, R. V. (1987). The biological basis for the contraceptive effects of breast feeding. *International Journal of Gynaecology and Obstetrics Supplement* 25:207–217.

Shostak, M. (1981). *Nisa: The Life and Words of a !Kung Woman*. Cambridge: Harvard University Press.

Shwalb, D. W., B. J. Shwalb, and J. Shoji (1996). Japanese mothers' ideas about infants and temperament. In *Parents' Cultural Belief Systems: Their Origins, Expressions, and Consequences*, pp. 169–191, S. Harkness and C. M. Super, eds. New York: Guilford Press.

Shweder, R. A., L. A. Jensen, and W. M. Goldstein (1995). Who sleeps by whom revisited: A method for extracting the moral goods implicit in practice. In *Cultural Practices as Contexts for Development*, pp. 21–39, J. J. Goodnow, P. J. Miller, and F. Kessel, eds. San Francisco: Jossey-Bass.

Sloane, V. M. (1978). *Common Folks*. Pepper Passes, Ky.: Alice Lloyd College.

Small, M. F. (1992). A reasonable sleep. *Discover* 13:83–88.

Small, M. F. (1993). Closing the gap. *Wildlife Conservation* 96:16–23.

Small, M. F. (1995). *What's Love Got to Do With It? The Evolution of Human Mating*. New York: Anchor Books.

Smith, R. J. (1983). *Japanese Society: Tradition, Self, and the Social Order*. Cambridge: Cambridge University Press.

Smith, S. (1986). Infant cross-fostering in captive rhesus monkeys *(Macaca mulatta)*. *American Journal of Primatology* 11:229–237.

Stagner, R., and C. M. Solley (1970). *Basic Psychology*. New York: McGraw-Hill.

Stoppard, M. (1995). *Complete Baby and Childcare*. London: Dorling Kindersley.

Stuart-Macadam, P. (1995a). Biocultural perspectives on breastfeeding. *Breastfeeding: Biocultural Perspectives*, pp. 1–37, P. Stuart-Macadam and K. A. Dettwyler, eds. New York: Aldine de Gruyter.

Stuart-Macadam, P. (1995b). Breastfeeding in prehistory. *Breastfeeding: Biocultural Perspectives*, pp. 75–99, P. Stuart-Macadam and K. A. Dettwyler, eds. New York: Aldine de Gruyter.

Stuart-Macadam, P., and K. A. Dettwyler (1995). *Breastfeeding: Biocultural Perspectives*. New York: Aldine de Gruyter.

Symons, D. K., and G. Moran (1987). The behavioral dynamics of mutual responsiveness in early face-to-face mother–infant interactions. *Child Development* 58:1488–1495.

Tague, R. G., and O. C. Lovejoy (1986). The obstetric pelvis of AL 288-1 (Lucy). *Journal of Human Evolution* 15:237–255.

Taub, D. M. (1984). *Primate Paternalism*. New York: Van Nostrand Reinhold.

Thevenin, T. (1987). *The Family Bed: An Age-Old Concept in Childrearing*. New York: Avery.

Thoman, E. B., C. Acebo, and P. T. Bicher (1983). Infant crying and stability in the mother–infant relationship: A systems analysis. *Child Development* 54:653–659.

Trevathan, W. R. (1987). *Human Birth: An Evolutionary Perspective*. New York: Aldine de Gruyter.

Trevathan, W. R., and J. J. McKenna (1994). Evolutionary environments of human birth and infancy: Insights to apply to contemporary life. *Children's Environments* 11:88–104.

Tronick, E., A. Hudelise, L. Adamson, S. Wise, and T. B. Brazelton (1978). The infant's response to entrapment between contradictory messages in face-to-face interaction. *Journal of the American Academy of Child Psychology* 17:1–13.

Tronick, E. Z. (1989). Emotions and emotional communication in infants. *American Psychologist* 44:112–119.

Tronick, E. Z. (1997). Doctor's orders. *Natural History Magazine* 106:46.

Tronick, E. Z. (1980). The primacy of social skills in infancy. In *Exceptional Infant: Psychosocial Risks in Infant–Environment Transactions*, pp. 144–160, D. B. Sawin, R. C. Hawkins, L. O. Walker, and J. H. Penticoff, eds. New York: Brummer/Mazel.

Tronick, E. Z., and J. F. Cohn (1989). Infant–mother face-to-face interaction:

Age and gender differences in coordination and the occurrence of miscoordination. *Child Development* 60:85–92.

Tronick, E. Z., G. A. Morelli, and P. K. Ivey (1992). The Efé forager infant and toddler's pattern of social relationships. *Developmental Psychology* 28:568–577.

Tronick, E. Z., G. A. Morelli, and S. Winn (1987). Multiple caretaking of Efé (pygmy) infants. *American Anthropologist* 89:96–106.

Tronick, E. Z., S. Winn, and G. A. Morelli (1985). Multiple caretaking in the context of human evolution: Why don't the Efé know the Western prescription for child care? In *The Psychobiology of Attachment and Separation*, pp. 293–322, M. Reite and T. Field, eds. New York: Academic Press.

Tuross, N., and M. Fogel (1994). Stable isotope analysis and subsistence pattern of the Sully Site. In *Skeletal Biology in the Great Plains: Migration, Warfare, Health and Subsistence*, pp. 283–289, D. W. Owsley and R. L. Jantz, eds. Washington, D.C.: Smithsonian Press.

Van Esterick, P. (1989). *Beyond the Breast-Bottle Controversy.* New Brunswick, Rutgers University Press.

Van Esterick, P. (1995). The politics of breastfeeding: An advocacy perspective. *Breastfeeding: Biocultural Perspectives*, pp. 145–165, P. Stuart-Macadam and K. A. Dettwyler, eds. New York: Aldine de Gruyter.

Vitzthum, V. J. (1989). Nursing behavior and its relation to duration of postpartum amenorrhea in an Andean community. *Journal of Biosocial Science* 21:145–160.

Vygotsky, L. S. (1978). *Mind in Society: The Development of Higher Psychological Processes.* Cambridge: Harvard University Press.

Wagner, D., and H. W. Stevenson (1982). *Cultural Perspectives on Child Development.* San Francisco: W. H. Freeman.

Warren, M. P., and B. Shortle (1990). Endocrine correlates of human parenting: A clinical perspective. In *Mammalian Parenting*, pp. 209–226, N. A. Krasnegor and R. S. Bridges, eds. Oxford: Oxford University Press.

Welles-Nyström, B. (1996). Scenes from a marriage: Equality, ideology in Swedish family policy, maternal ethnotheories, and practice. In *Parents' Cultural Belief Systems*, pp. 192–214, S. Harkness and C. M. Super, eds. New York: Guilford Press.

West, M. M., and M. J. Konner (1976). The role of the father: An anthropological perspective. *The Role of the Father in Child Development*, pp. 185–216, M. E. Lamb, ed. New York: Wiley.

White, J. L., and R. C. Labarba (1976). The effects of tactile and kinesthetic stimulation on neonatal development in the premature infant. *Developmental Psychobiology* 9:569–577.

Whiting, B. (1963). *Six Cultures: Studies of Child Rearing.* New York: John Wiley.

Whiting, B., and J. Whiting (1975). *Children of Six Cultures.* Cambridge: Cambridge University Press.

Whiting, J. W. (1964). Effects of climate on certain cultural practices. In *Explorations in Cultural Anthropology,* pp. 511–544, W. H. Goodenough, ed. New York: McGraw-Hill.

Whiting, J. W., and I. L. Child (1953). *Child Training and Personality: A Cross-Cultural Study.* New Haven: Yale University Press.

Whittenberger, J. F. (1981). *Animal Social Behavior.* Boston: Duxbury Press.

Wiesenfeld, A. R., and C. Z. Malatesta (1983). Assessing caregiver sensitivity to infants. In *Symbiosis in Parent-Offspring Interaction,* pp. 173–188, L. A. Rosenblum and H. Molty, eds. New York: Plenum Press.

Wiesenfeld, A. R., C. Z. Malatesta, C. Whitman, C. Granrose, and R. Vili (1985). Psychophysiological responses of breast- and bottle-feeding mothers to their infants' signals. *Psychophysiology* 22:79–86.

Wilson, D. S., and A. B. Clark (1996). The shy and the bold. *Natural History* 105:26–28.

Wilson, E. O. (1975). *Sociobiology: The New Synthesis.* Cambridge: Harvard University Press.

Wilson Goldizen, A. (1987). Tamarins and marmosets: Communal care of offspring. In *Primate Societies,* pp. 34–43, B. B. Smuts, D. L. Cheney, R. M. Seyfarth, R. Wrangham, and T. T. Strusaker, eds. Chicago: University of Chicago Press.

Wolf, A. W., B. Lozoff, S. Latz, and R. Paludette (1996). Parental theories in the management of young children's sleep in Japan, Italy, and the United States. In *Parents' Cultural Belief Systems,* pp. 364–384, S. Harkness and C. M. Super, eds. New York: Guilford Press.

Wolff, P. H. (1965). The natural history of crying and other vocalizations in early infancy. *Determinants of Infant Behavior,* pp. 81–109, B. M. Foss, ed. London: Methuen.

Wood, J. W. (1994). *Dynamics of Human Reproduction.* New York: Aldine de Gruyter.

Wood, J. W., D. Lai, P. L. Johnson, K. L. Campbell, and I. A. Maslar (1985). Lactation and birth spacing in highland New Guinea. *Journal of Biosocial Science Supplement* 9:159–173.

Woodridge, M. W. (1995). Baby-controlled breast feeding; Biocultural implications. In *Breastfeeding: Biocultural Perspectives,* pp. 217–242, P. Stuart-Macadam and K. A. Dettwyler, eds. New York: Aldine de Gruyter.

World Bank (1993). *World Development Report 1993: Investing in Health.* Washington, D.C.: Oxford University Press.

Worthman, C. (1993). Bio-cultural interactions in human development. In *Juvenile Primates: Life History, Development and Behavior*, pp. 339–358, M. Pereira and L. Fairbanks, eds. New York: Oxford University Press.

Worthman, C. (1995a). Ethnopediatrics: An outline. *Items (SSRC)* 49:6–10.

Worthman, C. (1995b). *Ethnopediatrics: Cultural Factors in Child Survival and Growth.* Atlanta: American Association for the Advancement of Science.

Wrangham, R. W., W. C. McGrew, F. M. B. de Waal, and P. G. Heltney (1994). *Chimpanzee Cultures.* Cambridge: Harvard University Press.

Wright, R. (1994). *The Moral Animal.* New York: Pantheon Books.

Yogman, M. W. (1982). Development of the father–infant relationship. In *Theory and Research in Behavioral Pediatrics*, pp. 221–279, H. E. Fitzpatrick, B. M. Lester, and M. W. Yogman, eds. New York: Plenum Press.

Yogman, M. W. (1984). The father's role with preterm and fullterm infants. In *Frontiers of Infant Psychiatry*, pp. 361–374, J. D. Call, E. Galenson, and R. L. Tyson, eds. New York: Basic Books.

Yogman, M. W. (1990). Male parental behavior in human and nonhuman primates. In *Mammalian Parenting*, pp. 461–481, N. A. Krasnegor and R. S. Bridges, eds. Oxford: Oxford University Press.

Yogman, M. W., B. M. Lester, and J. Hoffman (1983). Behavioral and cardiac rhythmicity during mother-father-stranger infant social interaction. *Pediatric Research* 17:872–876.

Zeanah, C. H., M. Keener, L. Stewart, and T. F. Anders (1985). Prenatal perceptions and infant personality: A preliminary investigation. *Journal of the American Academy of Child Psychiatry* 24:204–210.

Zelazo, P. R., N. A. Zelazo, and S. Kolb (1972). "Walking" in the newborn. *Science* 176:314–315.

ACKNOWLEDGMENTS

During the process of writing this book, I was surrounded by researchers who were incredibly kind and forthcoming. I thank Ronald Barr, W. Thomas Boyce, James Chisolm, Suzanne Dixon, Glen Flores, Jacqueline Goodnow, Sara Harkness, Ana Magdalena Hurtado, Robert LeVine, James McKenna, Marty Stein, Charles Super, Edward Tronick, and Carol Worthman. Several of these researchers were also gracious enough to spend time with me and talk at length about their work. I thank especially Ronald Barr, Sara Harkness, Robert Le-Vine, James McKenna, Edward Tronick, and Carol Worthman. From the beginning, Carol Worthman has encouraged me to write about ethnopediatrics for the popular audience. Her support has been invaluable.

Jim McKenna merits special thanks. Jim was the first person to turn me on to this fascinating work. He has also put up with two lengthy interviews and shared all his writing with me. But most of all, Jim's boundless enthusiasm for the subject and his ability to articulate artfully all sides of the story have been an inspiration.

Ronald Barr, Sara Harkness, Kim Hill, Jim McKenna, and Carol Worthman read portions of the manuscript to check for accuracy. I am sure this is not the book they would have written, and I thank them for letting me interpret their work in my own way.

Other scientists and researchers were also kind enough to talk with me about baby stuff—human, nonhuman, ancient, and current: Stephen Emlen, Mark Flinn, Sarah Blaffer Hrdy, and Karen Rosenberg. I also am grateful to lactation consultant Diane Wiessinger who spent so many hours with me discussing breast-feeding in the modern context.

A hug and a free book to my "writer friends" who provided the best support and encouragement anyone could ask for: Paul Cody (because we are still drifting with giants), Anne Gibbons, Jim Gould, Marguerite Holloway, Mike May, James Shreeve, and especially Steve Mirsky.

Also thanks to my pals and family members who kept asking, "Are you done with that book yet?" and then letting me go on and on and on, and actually listening and responding: Krysia Small Bruck, Dan Burgevin, Leslie Burgevin, Dede Hatch, Ann Jereb, Jon Reis, Andrea Small Perkins, Becky Rolfs, Charles Small, Chuck Small, Marysia Small, Carol Terrizzi, Tom Terrizzi, and Ute van den Bergh. I also gained an intimate perspective on childrearing in my own culture by listening to my friends tell me how it feels to struggle with, and also enjoy, parenting. I thank especially Adam and Peggy Arcadi, Krysia Small Bruck, Paul Cody and Liz Holmes, Ann and Don Jereb, Nancy Magruder, Ryne and Kristen Palombit, and Carol and Tom Terrizzi.

And, of course, thanks to my partner Tim Merrick. As Tim and I navigate trade-offs in parenting our daughter, Francesca, it is from this wonderful father that I am truly learning what an entwined adult–infant relationship is all about.

My agent Anne Sibbald at Janklow and Nesbit was as excited about this book as I was, and her advice and guidance was, and continues to be, extremely important during all phases of this and other books.

Roger Scholl at Anchor Books joined me on this journey into ethnopediatrics. Roger's ideas about structure, his attention to voice, his detailed editing, and his ability to make suggestions in a kind but straightforward way—suggestions that always turn out to be right, I might add—have had a major and extremely positive impact on this book. I also want to give a special thanks to Roger's daughter, Rebecca Scholl. Rebecca was born just when the proposal for this book arrived on his desk. I later learned that Roger read the proposal to Kate, his wife, and baby Rebecca on their first quiet evening at home. Although I know Roger would have been interested in this book anyway, reading the proposal while holding his newborn daughter surely brought home, in the most personal of ways, how important are the issues in this book. And so I thank Rebecca for great timing.

Dede Hatch provided many of the photographs for the book, including the evocative cover. I thank Dede for not only her technical skill, but also for her creative ideas which are, once again, so perfect.

Parts of this work have been published in other forms in various magazines. Most recently, I guest-edited a piece for *Natural History* on parenting in cross-cultural and biological perspective (October, 1997). I want to thank the editor-in-chief of *Natural History*, Bruce Stutz, for having the wisdom to accept my query and then let me run with it, Rebecca Finnell for working with me on the development of the piece, and Vittorio Maestro for guiding it through publication. An earlier version on ethnopediatrics appeared in *New Scientist* in 1995, and I thank David Concar for recognizing a good story. Jim McKenna and I worked together on a piece for *Scientific American*, and I thank editor-in-chief John Renne for allowing me to use some of that material here. Also, I wrote a piece in 1992 on Jim McKenna for *Discover*, and I thank Paul Hoffman for allowing me to use that as well. Mike May at *American Scientist* asked me to write about how I feel about this book for their "Macroscope" column (November/December, 1997), and I thank Mike for giving me the opportunity to express how this book has so deeply affected who I am.

I am also indebted to the anthropologists who have gathered ethnographic data on parenting in other cultures, because rereading those comparative ethnographies over the past few years has been a life-changing experience. I have since spent many hours thinking about parenting in my own culture, and contemplating how the American style of caretaking makes for a particular kind of society. Nothing in my training as an anthropologist, nothing in my years as a working anthropologist, has altered my view of my own culture as much as the past two years of working on this book. I have been at times startled by, and also sometimes ashamed of, my own culture. But most important, many aspects of daily life in America now make sense.

And finally, I thank all the babies, in all cultures, who have been watched by anthropologists, tested by psychologists, weighed, examined, and photographed. The tiniest and most vulnerable of our kind are owed my greatest thanks.

MEREDITH F. SMALL
Ithaca, N.Y.
September 1997

INDEX

ABOUT THE AUTHOR

Meredith F. Small is a professor of anthropology at Cornell University. She is the author of *Female Choices: Sexual Behavior of Female Primates* (Cornell University Press) and *What's Love Got to Do With It? The Evolution of Human Mating* (Anchor Books).